Better Behaviour through Home–School Relations

How can we create effective partnerships between home, school and the community?

How can the relationships and communication between families and school be strengthened?

How can families help schools to improve behaviour in their children, both at home and at school?

Using a tried and tested framework that has been successfully implemented throughout a wide range of very different schools and settings, Family Values is a scheme that engages and empowers families to work in close collaboration with schools and organisations, and results in long-term improvements in behaviour, communication, pupil achievement and relationships. The Family Values Scheme has been proven to:

- help pupils to be more academically diligent;
- help schools to assume a calmer, more peaceful ambience;
- forge better pupil–teacher relationships;
- improve pupil and teacher well-being;
- help parents to be more engaged with the school;
- improve children's literacy, behaviour and attendance;
- provide head teachers and their staff with an effective whole-school strategy.

The authors' award-winning Family Values Scheme is underpinned by sound theoretical principles, and they show here how it has been successfully put into practice through case studies in real school settings. The book explores how the scheme promotes social, emotional and family system theories, and, in linking effectively to SEAL (social and emotional aspects of learning), the scheme compliments existing personal and social education programmes in all schools.

Showing schools and organisations how to create effective partnerships with families and the community in a fun, exciting and sustainable way, *Better Behaviour through Home–School Relations* will be of huge benefit to all school staff, as well as local authorities, support groups, parents, charities and services.

Gill Ellis is the head teacher of a large primary school in South Wales.

Nicola S. Morgan is a qualified teacher and behaviour management consultant.

Ken Reid (OBE) is presently the adviser to the Welsh government on behaviour and attendance. He was formerly Deputy Vice Chancellor and Research Professor at Swansea Metropolitan University. He is also the national president of SEBDA.

Better Behaviour through Home–School Relations

Using values-based education to promote positive learning

Gill Ellis, Nicola S. Morgan and Ken Reid

Routledge
Taylor & Francis Group
LONDON AND NEW YORK

First published 2013
by Routledge
2 Park Square, Milton Park, Abingdon, Oxon OX14 4RN

Simultaneously published in the USA and Canada
by Routledge
711 Third Avenue, New York, NY 10017

Routledge is an imprint of the Taylor & Francis Group, an informa business

© 2013 Gill Ellis, Nicola S. Morgan and Ken Reid

The right of Gill Ellis, Nicola S. Morgan and Ken Reid to be identified as authors of this work has been asserted by them in accordance with sections 77 and 78 of the Copyright, Designs and Patents Act 1988.

All rights reserved. No part of this book may be reprinted or reproduced or utilised in any form or by any electronic, mechanical, or other means, now known or hereafter invented, including photocopying and recording, or in any information storage or retrieval system, without permission in writing from the publishers.

Trademark notice: Product or corporate names may be trademarks or registered trademarks, and are used only for identification and explanation without intent to infringe.

British Library Cataloguing in Publication Data
A catalogue record for this book is available from the British Library

Library of Congress Cataloging in Publication Data
Ellis, Gill.
  Better behaviour through home–school relations: using values-based education to promote positive learning/authored by Gill Ellis, Nicola S. Morgan and Ken Reid.
  p. cm.
  Includes bibliographical references and index.
  1. Home and school. 2. School discipline. 3. Classroom management.
  I. Morgan, Nicola S. II. Reid, Ken. III. Title.
  LC225.E445 2013
  371.19'2 – dc23   2012030599

ISBN: 978-0-415-50416-4 (hbk)
ISBN: 978-0-415-50417-1 (pbk)
ISBN: 978-0-203-12854-1 (ebk)

Typeset in Galliard
by Florence Production Ltd, Stoodleigh, Devon, UK

Printed and bound in Great Britain by
TJ International Ltd, Padstow, Cornwall

To my husband Stuart, my children Catherine, Michael and Charlotte, and my adorable grandson Oliver George who brightens up our day!
—Gill Ellis

To my family, who I love very much: my mum Virginia, dad Alvin, brother Gareth, sister-in-law Clare and our six four-legged friends.
—Nicola S. Morgan

To my three grown-ups: Becky, Nick and Jo, and to Gill and Nic for all their enthusiasm and hard work.
—Ken Reid

Contents

Preface ix
Acknowledgements xiii

1 Introduction: what is a family? 1
2 The family unit: benefits of family involvement 4
3 One-parent families, schools and raising achievement 14
4 Engaging with parents 30
5 Values-based education: values, morals, ethics 52
6 How the Family Values Scheme works: key principles 68
7 How the Family Values Scheme operates in practice 84
8 Establishing the Family Values Scheme: the Coed Eva story 103
9 Case studies 124
10 The head teacher's perspective 135
11 Log files 143
12 Courage 177
13 Even more evaluation 197
14 Conclusion 206

References 209
Index 219

Preface

This book is about the development and potential use of the Family Values Scheme (FVS) by head teachers and schools as part of their interaction with their children's parents and their extended families. Good communication between the home and school is an essential prerequisite of effective schooling. However, unfortunately, it is not always something that is done well. Why?

First, because not all teachers and head teachers are naturally able and competent at making effective home–school communications and, truthfully, some staff probably dislike this aspect of their work more than anything else. Indeed, it is also probably fair to say that a significant proportion of parents also do not enjoy liaising with their children's class teachers and head teachers and other staff within their children's schools. For some parents, this is often due to their own poor experiences while at school, perhaps due to their own underachievement or learning difficulties, poor attendance or bad behaviour, or it may be caused by their own low self-esteem or shyness.

Second, because modern-day life within some families is exceedingly complicated and, unlike 40 or 50 years ago, there is no longer any such thing as a generic or standardised common experience for today's children within their everyday family experiences. So much has changed in recent years. Why? Around half of today's children who start school at age 3 or 4 will no longer live in the same home together with their natural father and mother by the time they leave school, mainly because of the high rate of divorce and separation. For many children in such places as the UK and the US, and in some other parts of the world, their childhood experiences will comprise of a range of changing home life experiences due to such complexities as cohabitation arrangements, frequent house and/or area moves, and periods of time living as a single-parent family. Increasingly, some children live in families without a consistent male role model or in situations where they only see their father at weekends or on an occasional basis. These societal changes have made it more difficult for teachers and head teachers to communicate effectively with both parents and their families, and, in a high percentage of cases, some schools increasingly have little or limited contact with fathers.

Third, because of changing economic circumstances, most women now work, especially after they start their families and the children reach school age. Hence, more families than ever before rely upon childcare arrangements, and fewer and fewer are able to call upon extended family members such as grandparents for support, often because they live in different parts of the country.

For all these reasons, governments around the world are becoming equally concerned about the diminishing influence of the family in supporting their children's education through, for example, providing reading and homework support and in providing good role models over such issues as behaviour, regular school attendance, the appropriate use of the Internet, the prevention of victimisation and bullying, healthy eating, punctuality and having an appropriate dress sense, to name but a few. Therefore, governments are beginning to react by re-stressing the importance of parents and families in the everyday life and learning of their children and, in some cases, by introducing such events as parenting classes either for all or for those who are perceived in some way/s to be failing their children. For instance, it has been a concern for many years how many parents condone their children's non-attendance from school or truancy.

Fourth, research and reports are recognising increasingly the importance of much earlier intervention (Allen, 2010). Moreover, the crucial importance of how parents and teachers influence and shape the everyday lives and behaviour of their children critically recurs in the evidence from empirical research (Walberg, 1984; Ebbut and Elliott, 1985; Covey, 1989; Astone and McLanahan, 1991; Browne and Rife, 1991; Fruchter *et al.*, 1992; Reid, 1985, 1999; Epstein, 2001; Desforges *et al.*, 2005; SEAL, 2005, 2006, 2007; Buchanan *et al.*, 2008; Common Assessment Framework, 2009; Gingerbread, 2012). In fact, some parents and carers are not naturally good communicators or even people to whom it is easy to relate (White-Clark and Decker, 1996; Webster-Stratton, 1999), which does not make the everyday tasks of teachers or other caring professionals any easier (Reid and Morgan, 2012). Therefore, with increasing familial breakdown, disaffection (Reid, 1986, 2012a) and even disintegration (Patterson *et al.*, 1993; Allen, 2010), politicians, policymakers, teachers, caring professionals and parents have become concerned increasingly with better ways to support parents, children and pupils' schooling and learning; more especially those from deprived economic and socio-economic backgrounds (Mosley and Thompson, 1995; National Center for Education Statistics, 1997; Jenkins and Keating, 1998; Humphrey *et al.*, 2008; Hawkes, 2009; National College for School Leadership, 2010).

It was partly for all these reasons that Gill and Nicola started to formulate their interest in family values and began to take an avid interest in the ideas of such luminaries as Dr Neil Hawkes and Professor Terry Lovat. After Gill was appointed to her second headship of a large primary school (following the merger of two previous schools) with over 500 pupils in a very deprived area, she began to reflect on how she could turn around her children's educational opportunities. Although starting a theoretically new school from scratch in a deprived community, she inherited a situation in which 37 primary pupils had been 'excluded' during her first year and where a high percentage of pupils were on free school meals, and had special or additional learning needs, behavioural, psychological or attendance problems, and numeracy and literacy deficits. Gill teamed up with Nicola, a behaviour consultant and former teacher, and the two of them started to plan to change and turn around the fortunes of the school, greatly facilitated by the willingness and enthusiasm of a caring staff. Gradually, through their reading and attendance at in-service training events and their developing interest in values-based education, they developed their own Family Values Scheme (FVS). This book partly tells the story of this journey and how it has unfolded and spread to date.

In order to validate their experience and concepts, they approached me for help shortly after I had completed the National Behaviour and Attendance Review (NBAR) for the Welsh government in 2008, partly because of my previous research background (Reid, 1980, 1985, 1986, 1987, 1989a, 1989b, 1999, 2000, 2002a, 2002b 2012a, 2012b, 2012c; Bernbaum *et al.*, 1982, 1983; Hopkins and Reid, 1985, 2012; Reid *et al.*, 1987). They each began undertaking an advanced research degree under my supervision evaluating their work. They also formed a website and training company, which can be accessed at www.behaviour stop.co.uk. Since then, they have published a series of books. These include: *Behaviour Management Ideas for the Classroom* (Morgan, 2009), *A Kit Bag for Promoting Positive Behaviour in the Classroom* (Morgan and Ellis, 2011), *The 5-Step Behaviour Programme: A Whole-School Approach to Behaviour Management* (Morgan and Ellis, 2009), and *The Good Choice Teddy Approach* (Morgan and Ellis, 2012).

Subsequently, Nicola and I have written a book on primary school behavioural management for primary teachers: *Tackling Behaviour in the Primary School: A Practical Handbook for Teachers* (Reid and Morgan, 2012).This is probably the first text to be written on implementing and improving children's behaviour in the context of the Children Act 2004 (HMSO, 2004) and related and subsequent legislation.

Since then, Gill, Nicola and myself have combined for this follow-up book on the Family Values Scheme. In this book we have pieced together the pioneering work of Gill and Nicola in the development of their Family Values Scheme by placing it in a national, international, theoretical and practical context, and combined their everyday practical experience on utilising the FVS with my research, supervisory and editing skills (Reid, 2012b).

Therefore, the text of this book covers such issues as: the family unit in context; how to engage families; the concepts involved in values-based education; and the Family Values Scheme (FVS) – how it works, is established and benefits schools, children, parents and extended families alike. In order to make the text more interesting and meaningful, we provide a range of embryonic case studies in order to show how the FVS was developed initially and is subsequently growing and being utilised around the country in response to need. We very much hope these case studies will help to make our book a more enjoyable read.

We also provide information on the log files and their usage in Chapter 11. In Chapter 12, in order to give you a flavour of the practical materials covered in the value 'courage', we enclose a sample pack – one of the 22 values, with other packs prepared on other key issues for use during implementation and evaluation, and on some core aspects of schools' work such as literacy, behaviour and attendance. Chapter 13 provides even more detail on the use of the scheme in schools in Herefordshire. The final chapter is the conclusion.

Should you be interested further, you will be able to find supplementary information at www.behaviourstop.co.uk.

Professor Ken Reid
Summer 2012

Acknowledgements

Gill, Nicola and Ken would like to thank a number of people in relation to the contents and production of this book. These include all the staff, parents, children and extended family members involved in the Family Values Scheme. We are particularly grateful for the helpful comments and support received from Dr Neil Hawkes on Chapter 5 and would like to express our appreciation to him.

Gill would especially like to thank all the staff at Coed Eva Primary School, including all the members of the senior leadership team and the governing body, for their dedication to the school and for the help and support she has received since she was appointed head teacher at the school.

We would also like to thank all the editorial help received from the team at Routledge and for the superb way in which they have helped to produce this book.

Chapter 1
Introduction
What is a family?

This book is about the background to the development and implementation of the Family Values Scheme (FVS) and places the scheme into a proper philosophical and research context. The FVS was conceived in south Wales and builds on the previous pioneering work of Dr Neil Hawkes and Professor Terry Lovat in Australia in this field.

The basic idea behind the scheme is to improve the quality of communication, care and interaction between the home and a child's school. The ability of schools to interact well with parents and carers is a considerable skill and not one that is always undertaken particularly effectively, not least because some parents are more amenable towards head teachers and teachers than others (Dalziel and Henthorne, 2005). This is often disproportionately important for schools located in deprived catchment areas, including those with a high percentage of pupils on free school meals, designated as having special or additional learning needs, behavioural or attendance problems or located in areas with a wide range of diversity or economic needs. Various governments around the world have therefore been considering how best to involve parents in a more meaningful way in their children's schooling (Walker, 2008; Bywater and Utting, 2012; Hutchins and Gardner, 2012).

In order to present the background to our creation of the FVS, we will subdivide this book into a number of distinct chapters. In the first three chapters, we will consider some of the research evidence related to the family unit and recent changes within its constitution, such as the escalation in the number of one-parent families and the role of fathers and children within these units, as well as the role of parents and families in their interaction with their children's schools and in helping their children to achieve and learn successfully fully supported by their families. Thereafter, in Chapter 5, we will outline some of the main issues and ideas behind values-based education, which influenced our thinking about the planning and implementation of the FVS. In Chapters 6 and 7, we outline how the FVS operates before further considering values in other educational settings. The remaining chapters are devoted to presenting information about how the FVS operates in a practical setting, which includes some detailed case studies, as well as providing some evidence of recent evaluation.

What is a family?

As long ago as 1975, Edith Schaeffer posed an interesting question: What is a family? Today, definitions of a family vary from country to country, culture to culture and person to person. We all know instinctively what a family is and what it means. But, in everyday life, it means different things to different people, especially for children. At one level, a family is about those people who are closest to you such as your mother, father, husband/wife, partner, children, brothers and sisters, grandparents, aunts, uncles, nieces and so forth. You may be part of a large or small family, an extended family or a 'broken' one. With members of your family, you share your home, belongings and happiest and saddest moments. These moments might include celebrating Christmas or Eid, Easter, births, marriages and successes at school or university, as well as sad events such as deaths, funerals, illnesses, failures and break-ups. Your role in all these events will probably depend upon such factors as your age, gender, maturity and seniority within your particular family unit.

This is what families are all about: unity and diversity; form and freedom; togetherness and individuality; cooperation, unity and unexpected challenges.

Most people generally accept that it is best for any child to be brought up within loving and caring family relationships where they can be nurtured, treasured and allowed to grow and develop slowly, normally and happily. This wonderful age-old model of the traditional family unit has, however, started to change significantly within the last 50 years as more and more families split up and marriages or relationships break down. A lot of children in our schools today are having to learn to adjust periodically or on a day-to-day basis to changing family life and home circumstances.

Most adults remember their childhood days well and happily. Some, however, much less fortunate, do so with much less warmth. So much depends upon your own personal experiences. What is clear is that children need their parents and families to feel safe and happy, to interact with, to develop friendships and, later, to mature and develop into first teenagers and then adults before probably starting their own families and family units.

Schaeffer (1975) considered a family unit to be:

1. a shelter in the eye of a storm;
2. a learning centre to formulate, interact with and understand human relationships;
3. the birthplace of creativity;
4. an ecologically balanced environment;
5. a perpetual backdrop to the acquisition of values such as truth and honesty;
6. an economic unit;
7. a museum of memories;
8. a revolving door with hinges and a lock;
9. your own time machine; and
10. a provider of checks and balances such as hope and realism.

The truth, of course, is that a family is all of these things and much more.

This is precisely why the relationship between a child, his or her family and the school is so important. It is also why, when things go wrong, that we need to find a way of changing and improving the situation, and this is precisely what this book and our FVS is all about.

We hear a lot in the media about the breakdown of traditional families and traditional family values, almost on a daily basis. Whatever our personal perspectives, no one can truly measure with complete accuracy the family life of 50, 100 or 200 years ago and compare it with today's family unit. What we can do is to try to begin to understand the child within his or her family unit and its relationship with his or her schooling and learning. This is what this book and the FVS is all about.

Therefore, in the next two introductory chapters, we will set the scene for the rest of the book. In particular, we will consider:

1. benefits of family involvement;
2. recent changes to family life;
3. recent research into family life;
4. the impact of parent involvement and what works;
5. providing services to parents;
6. changing family patterns and one-parent families;
7. stigma;
8. children in a single-parent family;
9. fathers;
10. fathers and single-parent families;
11. parents and schools including barriers to achievement;
12. schools and one-parent families;
13. engaging parents in raising achievement;
14. parents and literacy; and
15. some 'tips' for parents.

Issues 1–5 are covered in Chapter 2, while the remainder will be discussed in Chapter 3.

Chapter 2

The family unit
Benefits of family involvement

The benefits of involving parents in school life are well documented. Bastiani (2003), for example, lists a number of significant and lasting benefits. These include:

1. an increased parental participation in, and support for, the life and work of the school;
2. a greater willingness for parents and school to share information and tackle misunderstandings and problems at an early stage;
3. improved levels of achievement, parents' active encouragement and support for children's learning to produce tangible academic benefits that last throughout a child's school career; and
4. more positive pupil attitudes and behaviour.

However, Desforges and Abouchaar (2003), in their meta-study analysis, found that parent–child conversations in the home were more valuable, particularly in terms of enhancing children's school achievement, than parents' involvement in school activities. This finding suggests that schools should encourage parents to talk to their children about school activities at home, and this issue is at the heart of the FVS, as well as providing a structure for the discourse and related activities to take place.

So, how do schools currently involve parents in school life? Chamberlain et al. (2006) reported on the annual survey of trends in school life and, in particular, how schools involved parents in school life. The major methods, cited in order, were:

1. by producing school newsletters;
2. by gathering parents' views as part of school self-evaluation;
3. by encouraging parents to contact and/or visit the school;
4. by holding special events for parents (e.g. information/discussion evenings);
5. through the school website;
6. by being involved with an active parent–teacher association (PTA);

7 by parents becoming involved in out-of-school learning activities (Reid, 2002b);
8 by parent involvement in the classroom;
9 by providing educational opportunities for parents (e.g. ICT or numeracy classes); and
10 through a range of other miscellaneous activities.

The Chamberlain *et al.* (2006) study showed that, on average, more parents became involved with their children's schools at the primary than secondary stage. For example, 23 per cent more parents were engaged with a PTA at their children's primary (83 per cent) than secondary (60 per cent) stage. Other ways of involving parents included the use of focus groups, parental forums, online communication (e.g. email), the creation of virtual learning environments (VLEs), family learning or parent–child workshops, and parent governors.

There were also differences between the organisation of parental communication/activities between primary and secondary schools and in different kinds of geographical and socio-economic locations. For example, in primary schools, those with the highest free school meal (FSM) eligibility were less likely than other primary schools to make use of an active PTA or a website to involve parents in school life. Conversely, they were more likely to involve parents in such educational opportunities as ICT, literacy or numeracy classes for parents as a school strategy. By contrast, the highest-attaining primary schools were less likely to involve parents in the use of educational opportunities and, perhaps surprisingly, often involved parents less in school life.

Head teachers considered that the most effective ways of involving parents in school life at the primary phase were through school visits, encouraging open parental contact and holding special events for parents. At the secondary stage, the gathering of parental views either through the use of questionnaires or as part of ongoing self-evaluations were valued more highly, although, in general, similar processes between both phases were normally used (Lewis *et al.*, 2007).

Changes to family life

According to recent evidence, the family unit and life inside the family unit has undergone major changes over the last 50 to 60 years. In the 1950s, fewer than 2 per cent of parents ever divorced and the extended family unit consisted of major contributions from grandparents and other relatives. Often, members of extended families lived in the same village, town or local community. Since then, major demographic changes have taken place. With the growth and development of transport systems, technology, housing and significant improvements in employment conditions, wages, health, social services, educational opportunities, equality and diversity, family life within the era of the computer, mobile phone and laptop has undergone considerable movement.

One of these significant changes has been a fast and increasing breakdown in traditional and religious values. For example, two reports from the Centre for Social Justice (2011, 2012) have found that, in the UK, nine out of ten couples now live together out of wedlock. Forty-six per cent of children are born to unmarried mothers. Forty-eight per cent of children experience their family breaking up before they are 16 (a rise of 8 per cent in only 10 years). In some parts of the country (e.g. London), this figure reaches around 55 per cent of all children. The same studies also show that a child growing up in a one-parent family is 75 per cent more likely to fail at school. The reports express concern about the growing state of fatherlessness, family dysfunction and parental separation and divorce, and their impact upon younger and older children alike.

In the 1950s, it was relatively unusual for mothers, especially those with young children, to work. According to the OECD (2012), within the UK, 67 per cent of mothers are employed after their children begin school at age 3 or 4 (close to the international average for developed nations of 66 per cent). The OECD currently keeps track of family life statistics, gathering 63 indicators under four different headings:

1. the structure of families;
2. the labour market position of families;
3. public policies for families and children; and
4. child outcomes.

Explicitly, one such measure is family well-being, which falls within the OECD Better Life Index. This shows that families in Denmark supposedly enjoy the best quality of life through their work-life balance. The two other Scandinavian countries, Sweden and Norway, are in the top seven, while the US is currently in 23rd position.

Recent research into family life

Research into family life and the family unit is gathering pace (Cowan and Cowan, 2008; Jordan, 2008; Walker, 2008; Layard and Dunn, 2009; Daly, 2011; Bywater and Utting, 2012; Hutchins and Gardner, 2012). In a summary on the current state of family life following a major conference, Hooper and Clulow (2008) indicated that the key points in our existing knowledge are as follows:

1. Research consistently demonstrates that it is the quality of family relationships, rather than the forms they take, that is significantly related to child outcomes. This suggests that improving the quality of relationships provides a proper focus for parenting support.
2. For both intact and separated families, the quality of the relationship between parents affects their individual capacities as parents and the emotional security of their children. Reticence about supporting co-parenting relationships

detracts from the value of parenting support proposals currently being espoused by some governments, including the UK government.
3   Involving fathers can improve the life of children. A key to engaging fathers as parents is to improve the quality of co-parenting relationships.
4   Other family members such as step-parents and grandparents may act as co-parents to a child's biological parents, contributing to the emotional and economic security of the environment in which they are brought up. Parenting support needs to take account of the wide network of family relationships that contributes directly and indirectly to the well-being of children.
5   The pace of change in the twenty-first century presents all parents with challenges for which their own childhood will only have partially prepared them (e.g. cyber bullying). Effective parenting support means making information and services available to all parents and not just to those that may be having problems.
6   Existing institutions within communities can provide a non-stigmatised base from which parenting support can be provided. Extending the role of schools makes sense in terms of increasing parenting education opportunities for adults and learning opportunities for children. There are also important health dimensions in bringing up children.

The impact of parent involvement

The work of Desforges and Abouchaar

The meta-analysis study undertaken by Desforges and Abouchaar (2003) on the impact of parent involvement, parental support and family education on pupil achievement and adjustment provides us with a great deal of definitive information, which we will now present and consider. Their key findings suggest:

1   Parent involvement takes many forms, including good parenting in the home. This includes the provision of a secure and stable environment, intellectual stimulation, parent–child discussion, sound models of constructive social and educational values and high aspirations relating to personal fulfilment and good citizenship, contact with schools to share information, participation in school events, participation in the work of the school, and participation in school governance.
2   The extent and form of parent involvement is strongly influenced by family social class, maternal level of education, material deprivation, maternal psychosocial health and single parent status, and, to a lesser degree, family ethnicity.
3   The extent of parent involvement diminishes as the child gets older and is strongly influenced at all ages by the child characteristically taking a very active mediating role.

4 Parent involvement is strongly and positively influenced by the child's level of attainment; interestingly, the higher the level of attainment, the more parents get involved.
5 The most important finding from their meta-analysis review was that parent involvement in the form of 'at-home' good parenting has a significant and positive effect on children's achievement and adjustment even after all other factors shaping attainment have been taken out of the equation. In the primary age range, the impact caused by different levels of parent involvement is much greater than differences associated with variations in the quality of schools. The scale of the impact is evident across all social classes and all ethnic groups.
6 Other forms of parent involvement do not appear to contribute to the scale of the impact of 'at-home' parenting.
7 Differences between parents in their levels of involvement are associated with social class, poverty, health, and also parental perception of their roles and their levels of confidence in fulfilling them. Some parents are put off by feeling put down by schools and teachers, particularly those who had bad experiences themselves at school (cf. Dalziel and Henthorne, 2005).
8 Research affords a clear model of how parent involvement operates. Essentially, parents have a strong influence upon their children indirectly by helping to shape their levels of self-esteem and self-confidence, especially as a learner and through setting high goals and high aspirations.

Desforges and Abouchaar (2003) also found that schools used a wide range of interventions to promote parent involvement, which ranged from parent training programmes through to initiatives to enhance home–school links and on to programmes of family and community education. Their evaluations showed that there is an increased perceived need and demand for such support. High levels of creativity and commitment are evident among providers and high levels of appreciation are recorded by clients.

One of the problems from our point of view was that Desforges and Abouchaar also found that the evaluations of such interventions were so weak that there few definitive clues. They concluded that the existing knowledge base was sufficient to understand how spontaneous parent involvement works in promoting achievement. However, current interventions, while promising, have yet to deliver convincingly the achievement bonus that might be expected. Therefore, in our own thinking and planning, we had to take account of these findings. As there were not many previous and satisfactory good practice evaluations, we decided to develop our own methodology and processes for the implementation of the FVS. We did so, however, on the basis of our own experiences of undertaking field work in related areas over a 35-year period (e.g. Reid, 1989a, 1989b, 2012a, 2012b).

We were particularly heartened by the conclusion by Desforges and Abouchaar (2003: 3) that:

> The achievement of working class pupils could be significantly enhanced if we systematically apply all that is known about parental involvement. A programme of parental involvement development initiatives taking the form of multi-dimensional intervention programmes, targeted on selected post code areas and steered by a design process is implicated.

The NFER report (C4EO)

The report for the National Foundation for Educational Research (NFER) by Waldman *et al.* (2008) also reached some significant and important conclusions. They found that, with regard to the effectiveness of family-based support of early learning in improving children's outcomes, the following aspects were paramount:

1 Family support encompasses a wide range of interventions aimed at promoting parent involvement. Such diversity in provision is beneficial to provide multiple entry routes for families that meet their different needs (Desforges and Abouchaar, 2003).
2 There is an association between high-quality pre-school provision and children's learning at home with improvement in children's outcomes (Sylva *et al.*, 2004, 2008; Melhuish *et al.*, 2006).
3 Success factors include multidimensional interventions and delivery modes that address more than one facet of children's lives and meet the needs of a wide range of users (Harvard Family Research Project, 2006).
4 Timing is an issue. As a general rule, the earlier the intervention at pre-school age, the better. There is strong evidence for the benefits of targeting interventions on socio-economically disadvantaged groups (Moran *et al.*, 2004).
5 Caution should be exercised when considering the transferability of specific strategies or interventions to different contexts and countries (Penn *et al.*, 2004).
6 The evidence to support the case for the benefits of integrated services is not as strong, particularly in terms of cost-effectiveness (Penn *et al.*, 2004).

Waldman *et al.* (2008) then considered the best way to approach and support the engagement of family members, especially parents and carers, in young children's learning. They found that:

1 Effectively engaging parents is the first step in addressing problems. Yet parents most in need of family support services are often the least likely to access them (Quinton, 2004; Katz *et al.*, 2007).

2   It is important for staff to establish trusting relationships with parents and carers and to support them by getting to know individual families and maintaining this through regular contact about children's progress and learning (Moran *et al.*, 2004).
3   Early childhood education practice must be sensitive to differences in home culture and work to the strengths of these differences, supported by the evidence for culturally specific programmes for improving attendance for families of different ethnic groups (Dutch, 2005).
4   There is a positive impact on a child's development when parents are actively engaged in simple 'educational' activities such as teaching songs and nursery rhymes (Melhuish *et al.*, 2006).
5   Minimum levels of intervention and voluntary rather than compulsory approaches are recommended (Scottish Government, 2008a, 2008b).

Finally, Waldman *et al.* (2008) considered how support needs might differ for different groups of parents and carers, such as low-income families, fathers, mothers, other family members/carers, and parents/carers from black or other minority ethnic groups. Their conclusions were:

1   Minority ethnic parents are likely to be disproportionately affected by barriers such as a lack of time, travelling distances, costs and language, especially when English is a second language (Page *et al.*, 2008).
2   Parents with disabilities may experience a sense of isolation and exclusion if their needs are not considered and met. Cultural institutions and structures can act as barriers to participation in services by families from minority ethnic backgrounds (Katz *et al.*, 2007).
3   Locally based early childhood services are important to all parents but are more difficult to access for those living in rural areas (Katz *et al.*, 2007).

What works in parenting support?

A review of all the international evidence into the question of what works in providing support to parents undertaken by Moran *et al.* (2004) for the Department for Education and Skills is also well worthy of our consideration. They found that approaches that work well in practice include:

1   Both early intervention and later intervention. Early intervention normally works better as a strategy and generates more durable outcomes for children. However, late interventions are better than none at all and may help to facilitate parents under stress.
2   Interventions with a strong theory base and clearly articulated model of the predicted mechanism of change. However, services need to know both where they want to go and how they propose to get there.

3 Interventions that have measurable, concrete objectives, as well as overarching aims.
4 Universal interventions. These include those aimed at primary prevention among whole communities for assisting with parenting problems and needs at the less severe end of the spectrum of common parenting difficulties. Like Desforges and Abouchaar (2003), Moran *et al.* (2004) found that these types of interventions require more and better evaluation in order to determine their effectiveness.
5 Targeted interventions. These include those aimed at specific populations or individuals deemed to be at risk of parenting difficulties in order to learn how better to tackle more complex types of parenting difficulties.
6 Interventions that pay close attention to implementation factors. These include those for getting, keeping and engaging parents in practical, relational, cultural, contextual, strategic and structural domains.
7 Services that allow multiple approaches and referral routes with families.
8 Multi-component interventions (i.e. those with more than one method of delivery).
9 Group work, where the issues involved are suitable to be considered in a 'public' format and in which parents can benefit from the social aspects of working in groups with peers.
10 Individual work in which problems are severe or entrenched. Often, these parents are unable or unwilling to work in group situations. These often involve an element of home visiting as part of a multi-component service and/or providing one-to-one tailored support.
11 Interventions delivered by appropriately trained and skilled staff, backed up by good management and support.
12 Interventions that include manualised programmes where the core programme delivered is carefully structured and controlled to maintain 'programme integrity'.
13 Interventions of longer duration, with follow-up and/or booster sessions for problems of greater severity or for higher risk groups of parents.
14 Short, low-level interventions for delivering factual information and fact-based advice for parents. These often increase their knowledge of child development and encourage change in 'simple' behaviours.
15 Behavioural interventions that focus on specific parenting skills and practical 'take-home tips' for changing more complex parenting behaviours, as well as impacting upon children's behaviour.
16 'Cognitive' interventions for changing beliefs, attitudes and self-perceptions about parenting.
17 Interventions that work in parallel, although not necessarily at the same time, with parents, families and children.

Therefore, as Harris and Goodall (2008: 281) have written:

> *The evidence about interventions and programmes aimed at improving parental engagement is patchy, anecdotal and often based on self-report. Consequently, we do not know enough about how to design programmes of intervention that work with different groups of parents in different settings. Creating such knowledge of design requires more in-depth research into parental engagement that captures the voices of parents and students in a serious and authentic way.*

Providing services to parents

A similar picture emerges from research into the work of the services with families in their intervention strategies and endeavours. For this reason, Pugh (2010: 3) prepared a list of ten principles for local authorities (LAs) and national organisations to become involved with parents and to put themselves in a position where they could evaluate and improve their engagement with families. These principles were that successful and sustained engagement with families:

1. is maintained when practitioners work alongside families in a valued working relationship;
2. involves practitioners and parents being willing to listen to and learn from each other;
3. happens when practitioners respect what families know and already do;
4. needs practitioners to find ways to actively engage those who do not traditionally access services;
5. happens when parents are decision-makers in organisations and services.
6. occurs when families' views, opinions and expectations of services are raised and their confidence increases as service users;
7. is where there is support for the whole family;
8. is through universal services but with opportunities for more intensive support where most needed;
9. requires effective support and supervision for staff, encouraging both evaluation and self-reflection; and
10. requires an understanding and honest sharing of issues around safeguarding.

Parents with needs are often engaged with a whole array of additional services at the same time as liaising with their children's schools. Often, this engagement is with multidisciplinary, interdisciplinary or specialist teams. Pugh (2010) considers that parents' views and voices in the development of services and their evaluation are crucial to the solution of finding good practice that works effectively. These developments have been taking place alongside the progression of National Occupational Standards (NOS) within the caring professions such as social work and educational welfare (Lifelong Learning UK, 2005).

Summary

In this chapter, we have examined some of the most significant research into children, families and schooling. We will now develop these themes further in the next two chapters by looking more closely at life within one-parent families, as well as the link between children's schooling and learning, followed by some ideas on how best to engage with the families of our schoolchildren.

Chapter 3

One-parent families, schools and raising achievement

In this chapter, we will consider such issues as life within one-parent families given the fact that this is the fastest rising category in modern-day family life according to recent national censuses. Within this context, we will consider such issues as stigma, the role of fathers and children in one-parent families. We will then develop this theme, first by discussing the role of parents in interacting with their children's schools and then, in the following chapter, by considering how parents can help their children achieve successfully at school through meaningful participation and engagement. The specific topics covered in this chapter are:

1   changing family patterns and one-parent families;
2   children in single-parent families;
3   stigma and one-parent families;
4   fathers and single-parent families;
5   parents and schools including barriers to achievement;
6   schools and one-parent families;
7   engaging parents in raising achievement;
8   parents and their children's literacy; and
9   some practical tips for parents.

Changing family patterns and one-parent families

The most popular living arrangement in British society is still the traditional marriage. However, it is now just one of a number of options. Fewer people are actually marrying. Another important change is that marriage is more easily broken up today compared with three or four decades ago. There are now fewer church weddings and more civil marriages in Britain. The increase in cohabitation reflects fewer constraints now on long- or short-term relationships that are not sanctioned by marriage. Many more relationship patterns are casual or transient.

No one knows precisely how many one-parent families exist in the UK or US or in some other Western countries. Nearly 1 million families in the UK were headed by one parent by the early 1980s. Latest estimates are that this figure may have doubled over the last 25 years, and this category saw the sharpest rise in the last census in both the UK and US, with some interesting regional differences. So, by the early 1980s in the UK, more than one family in seven was a one-parent family, involving some 1.5 million children under the age of 16. Almost 80 per cent of one-parent families arise through loss in the form of death, separation or divorce. A significant number of women enter into single parenthood by choice, while some girls become pregnant accidentally. Many are reluctant to have an abortion, perhaps on religious grounds or because of a subconscious wish to have a baby.

Most early writers and workers in this field (Bowshill, 1980; Cashmore, 1985) saw contributing factors to changing family patterns in the interaction of two different systems: on the one hand, the social, environmental, external system and, on the other, the internal, private system of the marital relationship itself.

The external system

Reid (1989c) has written that the following factors are identified within the external system:

1 The extended family lends less support in modern British society because families are more scattered. Intimacy with and support from other family members can no longer be maintained to the same degree as before. Marriage partners therefore put much greater emotional demands on each other for companionship and fulfilment.
2 Divorce is increasingly regarded as an acceptable solution to marital unhappiness and this response is supported in changes in the law governing divorce. For example, divorce in Scotland almost trebled between 1970 and 1983 and has at least doubled again since then. Divorce is now less technically complex and less publicly traumatic for the individuals concerned.
3 Within conventional marriages and in more casual living patterns, there is considerable blurring of firm roles and obligations that, traditionally, have served as guidelines. There is now more role sharing and role reversal.
4 There are more 'dual-career' marriages across all occupational levels. Spouses are faced with problems of managing competitive feelings, and of dealing with multiple-role demands, while, paradoxically, their material expectations and aspirations remain those characteristic of the traditional mood of marriage. In this mood, the husband is expected to be the main provider of economic support and material comforts for the family, and the wife is expected to take care of the emotional needs of husband and children by creating a supportive and comfortable domestic environment.
5 Women have more economic and general independence and therefore more opportunities to grow away from their husbands. Wives now have more sources of personal affirmation beyond the house and develop a separate identity less likely in earlier decades. This often contributes, among other factors, to changes in value stances between individuals and spouses.

6   Studies into the characteristics of those who divorce refer to the significance of the place of ritual in the transition from a single to a married state. The studies demonstrate a higher incidence of divorce in marriages that had a lack of ritual preparation, in the absence of formal engagements, church weddings and honeymoons. A more ritualised transition, it is claimed, gives the partners a stronger sense of their own new identity, and a more stable family base.
7   It is increasingly acknowledged that the increase in mental illness associated with stress and the general increase in violence in society is mirrored in a larger percentage of marriages than in previous generations.
8   There is a perceptible shift from institutional to community care. Families are expected to undertake more caring for dependent relatives without a matching increase in supportive public services.

Internal system

In looking at the internal, private system of the marital relationship, it is helpful to acknowledge the four phases in marriage, which are separated from each other by crises of transition. Each of the four phases is characterised by a change in family structure, when some major reorientation is required. When this is successfully accomplished, marriages normally survive. When this is not achieved, marriages tend to become unstable.

The first phase of marriage takes place before the birth of children. Each person makes the shift from perceiving a parent as the most important person to him or her to perceiving the new spouse in this capacity. Some never make this shift. Teenage marriages are at particular risk during this phase, and difficulties in relationships are often exacerbated by economic and housing problems.

The second phase relates to the period when the children are at home. Each partner must accept that parental responsibilities will impose restrictions, and that each must permit the other to have the child or children as additional love objects.

The third phase is the period of the children's adolescence, and usually while they are in the process of leaving the family home. The parents will experience a range of other losses at this stage – the menopause for women, and for men perhaps a final recognition that career ambitions will remain unfulfilled. This is a time for enormous mutual support and empathy. The absence of such support can often be revealed in clear silhouette with the departure of the children. It is a time when extended family support and understanding is crucial, but is often unavailable.

The fourth phase is when the final readjustment to a private relationship between the partners must take place. This is frequently a period of declining health and fewer outside interests. The ageing period is perhaps the ultimate testing grounds of marital relationships.

Stigma

Although it is always difficult to assess the attitudes of a society to changing family patterns, there is a tendency to measure such patterns against the model of conventional marriage. The degree to which new patterns depart from conventional marriage will determine society's tolerance and approval. In addition, families that do not conform to this model or stereotype may be seen as being to blame for their situation. Such stereotyping and negative discrimination are the experiences of members of other minority groups.

Some families and children are keenly aware of discrimination. This discrimination increases their sense of stigma, inequality and social isolation in the community. The following are examples:

1. The family parented by a widow or widower is most likely to be accorded the sympathy and understanding of society.
2. Separated or divorced one-parent families experience considerable disapproval and single mothers endure a low rating of tolerance and approval.
3. Society's attitudes towards the more unusual forms of family patterns (which give rise to new values of equality and self-expression, in contrast to the old values of self-denial, conformity and obligation) are more difficult to assess. There is, as yet, little awareness of the extent to which such alternative patterns are replacing the conventional.

Stigma as experienced by one-parent families

Many one-parent families are automatically stereotyped as economic risks. For this and other reasons, the one-parent family is often allocated poor housing accommodation in run-down areas. The divorced, separated and unmarried constitute a large number of the hidden homeless in society. They are possibly three times more likely to be homeless than two-parent families. The single mother may never have had a home. The separated or divorced, even if they gain the matrimonial home, sometimes have to give it up because they cannot afford the mortgage payments.

Lone parents are also at a disadvantage in the job market. Employers perceive them as unreliable and irregular workers. Lone parents are severely disadvantaged financially. The average income of one-parent families is only half that of two-parent families. National income policies tend to take no account of the hidden extra costs in lone parenting associated with the loss of a handyman/woman in the home, with buying in day care or childminding facilities (assuming they are available), with restricted opportunities to take on overtime. Many such families face long-term poverty, although things have improved markedly in this respect in recent years.

Sometimes, professional assessment relating to one-parent families in difficulty is all-too-easily prejudiced by inappropriate labelling. For example, in one case cited by Reid (1989c), a child's lack of progress at school was attributed to the lack of support at home from the lone parent. It was later discovered that the child was blind in one eye. In another case, one of a group of four involved in a joint offence was taken into care, while the others were recommended supervision. This youngster came from a one-parent family with quite significant extended family support. In fact, a very high percentage of children in long-term care come from one-parent families.

Some feeling of stigma by lone parents arises from social slights, often unintended, from within the local neighbourhood. Former married friends give up trying to fit one-parent friends into their social circle and may indeed see a single woman (or man) as a threat to their relationship. For a variety of reasons, other social outlets become inaccessible and much stress builds up from growing social isolation. Lack of money and difficulty in obtaining babysitters isolate single parents. If the stress results in antisocial behaviour by the children, the family often spirals downwards to become categorised locally as a 'problem' family.

Children in one-parent families feel 'different' to others. This is particularly so in cases of separation and divorce, where the non-custodial parent is still around somewhere in the picture, and relationships often remain confused and unresolved for the children in the middle.

Lone parents can feel stigmatised and vulnerable because of dependence on public services such as social work. They guard their privacy wherever possible and so may deny themselves and their children support and understanding when it is needed. Lone parents may fear that if they are seen to be 'not coping' by social workers, their child/children may be taken away. For example, when made aware of a family situation, a school teacher might perhaps respond more appropriately to a child's difficulty. However, both teacher and parent may feel sensitive about 'prying'. One has to conclude from all this that some one-parent families must experience society as not only indifferent, but also somewhat hostile.

Children in a single-parent family

There are three ways of becoming a single-parent family: through death of a parent; through the separation of parents; or through being an unmarried mother. About four-fifths of single-parent families are headed by mothers. These families are not necessarily single-parent households. They often live with other relatives.

Between 10 and 20 per cent plus of children under 5, and up to half of all children under 16, do not live with their two natural parents, with major regional and national differences for reasons of culture, tradition, history and religious variations. We do not know precisely how many live with a parent and step-parent figure (i.e. married or cohabiting).

Parental separation, whether or not followed by divorce, brings practical and emotional changes to children.

After separation, the children are likely to:

- live in poorer-quality housing;
- have a lower standard of living;
- receive less parental care;
- receive more substitute care (especially those under 5);
- be 'latchkey' children (especially schoolchildren);
- take on more domestic responsibilities; and
- grow up a little faster.

There is also the possibility that:

- siblings will be divided;
- there will be several changes of home;
- there will be changes of principal carer (mother, father, grandparent, foster parent, etc.);
- there will be a step-parent (married or cohabiting);
- there will be different surnames within the family;
- children will acquire step-siblings; and
- children will acquire half-siblings (sharing one parent).

Many children take all these practical changes in their stride, but they may well lead to emotional problems, which are more upsetting and less tangible.

As a result of the emotional effects of parental separation, children are likely to:

- be distressed, confused, angry;
- be concerned for their parent(s);
- lose touch with one parent; and
- wish for parental reconciliation, even after parental violence.

Children will possibly:

- regress in behaviour (i.e. cling or bed-wet);
- need psychiatric help;
- lose touch with one set of grandparents;
- become delinquent;
- achieve lower educational standards;
- truant;
- become aggressive; and
- be embarrassed, hiding the fact of their parents' separation.

The lower the social class, the higher the rate of divorce. In some geographical areas, marital breakdown will be almost the norm, but can nevertheless be distressing to the children. In other areas, marital breakdown will be comparatively rare and bring a sense of isolation and stigma to children.

Some, perhaps many, children will experience several parental separations and several step-parental relationships. Some children will become confused about their own identity and about who are their own parents and siblings.

Fathers

Historically and traditionally, fathers have been much less involved than mothers in the upbringing of their children (Mosley and Thompson, 1995; National Center for Education Statistics, 1997). There have been several practical reasons for this. Fathers were, and to an extent still are, more likely to be in full-time employment, so have less time to spend with their children, especially young children.

Within society, despite increasing gender equality, there remain certain cultural pressures that tend to reinforce differences between men and women, boys and girls, and mothers and fathers. Explicitly, fewer men wash nappies. Fathers normally teach their sons to play football and often not their daughters. Likewise, men tend not to play with 'dolls' with their daughters. More men still tend to be the disciplinarian and hand out punishments: 'Wait till your dad gets home!' Mothers often remain the parent of choice when children are either ill or hungry!

But events are changing, especially with increasing parental rights over issues such as maternity and paternal leave. So are some of the complexities. For example, as more mothers go out to work, there is an ever-increasing demand for childcare arrangements, especially as many grandparents live in different towns or regions or are still in employment. Therefore, for practical reasons alone, more men are engaged in housework or cooking. In addition, more fathers wish to be involved with their children from the start and it is now normal for dads to be present when their children are born (Williams, 1997).

Fathers continue to play a vital role in their children's development as role models for both their sons and daughters. The evidence is mounting that most men can be every bit as competent as women in every aspect of bringing up children, even if this is not always appreciated by everybody! But variations remain between cultures, nationalities and religions, and the status of women and daughters remains an issue more in some countries, religions and traditions than others and can be a grey area in terms of achieving truly integrated multicultural societies. So, in some religions, there is less distinction between the role of mothers and fathers than in others and the amount of time fathers spend with their sons and daughters.

Fathers and single-parent families

Fathers in single-parent families

Some interesting facts: up to around one in five single-parent families (dependent upon regional and international variations) are headed by a man. Over 60 per cent of these men are separated or divorced. About one quarter are widowed, although in some cases, for a whole variety of reasons, the mother may have chosen to move on in her life, as increasingly mothers win custody of the children except in exceptional circumstances.

What challenges do these fathers face? What satisfaction do they encounter?

To work or not to work?

Approximately two-thirds to three-quarters of single-parent fathers who head a family work full time. This compares with around one-third of mothers, although there are major differences dependent upon the age of the children. As a result, many male-headed single families can be better off financially than single-parent mother-led families.

Like mothers, single-parent fathers have some difficult decisions to make. Do they stay at home in order to spend more time with their children and so lose out financially and in terms of adult company and job satisfaction, status and interests, or do they continue to go to work? Some elements within society tend to disapprove of a man not working. Coincidentally, the same people might disapprove of a single mother who does work, believing 'a mother's place is in the home'. Men who decide to continue to work may have to change their hours to avoid certain shifts or to take their holidays out of term time. They may therefore find it harder to liaise with their children's schools. They may also need to make arrangements for the care of the children before and after school, during holidays and when one or more of their children is sick. Being a single parent is never easy, whether you are male or female!

Housework

Most single fathers have to get used to doing more household tasks than before. These include the washing, ironing, cooking, sewing, household repairs, putting the children to bed and reading and playing with them, hoovering, gardening, fetching and carrying them back and forth to wherever and whenever it is needed (clubs, appointments, parties, school), etc. Normally, the only time they get respite from the children is when they are asleep, and not always then! Discovering that all your white shirts have either shrunk or turned pink in the wash may be funny in some situations but it can be dispiriting, costly and feed your ongoing battle against depression! In reality, it is almost impossible for one parent to attempt to be both father and mother to his children. Some fathers inevitably run the risk of breaking down or developing mental health problems.

Childcare

Inevitably, some fathers may find certain aspects of childcare more difficult than mothers, although this is no longer always the case, as many fathers these days are now much better and more helpful than in previous generations. Nevertheless, as the children grow older, new challenges often lie ahead. These may include shopping trips with teenage girls and trying to appear 'cool' for the sake of your children when they are with their friends.

Social life

Single-parent fathers, like single-parent mothers, often feel isolated and vulnerable and quite often find it difficult to get out and meet other adults. It can be especially difficult if they wish to start going out with another woman and vice versa. When do you tell the children? How?

Fathers who no longer live with their children

Research over the last 20 or 30 years consistently shows that one of the most serious consequences of divorce upon children is that they may soon lose contact with their dad, especially if he moves away to a different part of the country or begins a 'new life'. Children often either secretly or openly worry about their absent father. Children who maintain regular contact with their fathers normally make better progress at school and in their everyday lives than those who do not or those who have irregular, infrequent or unpredictable contact.

Research into the effects of divorce on men (American Association of Single Parents, 2012; National Society for Children and Family Contact, 2012; Single Parent Action Network, 2012) shows that they are often devastated by their marital break-up, and by the subsequent bitterness, as well as the outcome of the legal process. After losing his wife and children, a man often faces losing his home, his possessions (e.g. pets) and his mutual family friends, as well as a significant part of his existing and future income and pension entitlement. Like women, their whole sense of purpose, self-esteem and personal identity and private space may be shaken.

As a consequence, many men suffer ill health after separation or divorce. Some find it difficult to concentrate, especially at work; some even lose their jobs or feel the need to start a new life elsewhere; some begin to drink heavily. It is always important for divorced fathers to feel that they can have easy, pleasant and regular contact with their children.

But being a part-time father or a 'Saturday parent' is very different from living under the same roof as your children and joining in with their everyday activities. It is always important (unless there are child safety issues) to find ways of keeping the father–children relationship alive in a constructive and meaningful way. Indeed, some fathers (and mothers) feel that they have a better relationship with their children after a separation or divorce.

Parents and schools

Parent involvement in schools is key to both children's learning and behaviour (Evans, 2000). Feinstein (2003) found there is already a social class differential at 22 months between children from disadvantaged backgrounds and those from advantaged backgrounds in the UK. This gap widens as children get older. However, it is possible to change and improve this situation. Blanden (2006), who used the same data base as Feinstein, found that parental interest in children's learning enables some children to buck the trend and do well despite their inherent disadvantage.

Governments in the UK have been keen to facilitate parents in helping with their children's learning and in them supporting their children's schools. As early as the late 1960s, the Plowden Report (1967) acknowledged both the importance of the parents' role and the need to engage parents respectfully in the supporting services. Ball (1994) argued for a new kind of partnership between parents and professionals. Sylva et al. (2004), in their important study, coined the phrase that 'what parents do is more important than who the parents are'. This process has now rapidly progressed to the point in which parents' and children's rights and voices have become central within the process of education and schooling (Pugh, 2010).

Barriers to engagement

There are several reasons why some parents do not engage with their children's schools. These include work commitments, lack of time or interest, childcare difficulties and parents with low self-esteem or those who may have had bad experiences themselves while at school. Single parents often feel very restricted in this regard, as do parents of disaffected, disengaged pupils or those with special or additional learning needs (Reid, 2012a).

The relationship between some parents and teachers is not always smooth or easy. For example, Williams et al. (2002) reported that 16 per cent of parents were wary of overstepping some unwritten mark in their relations with teachers. Parents' evenings are a particularly well-documented source for creating parental confusion and frustration (Harris and Goodall, 2008). Although there is broad agreement among scholars that most parents seek more and better involvement in their children's schooling, there are clearly material (time and money) and psychological barriers that operate differentially and discriminatingly across the social classes and individual differences among parents that operate within social classes (Harris and Goodall, 2007).

Parents tend to get involved in their children's schools if they see it as part of their 'job' as a parent or if they feel they have the capacity to contribute (Hoover-Dempsey and Sandler, 1997; Hoover-Dempsey et al., 2001). While the literature highlights that parental engagement with their children's schools makes a significant difference to educational achievement and learning, as we will discover shortly, we still need to know more about the ways in which parental engagement can be facilitated across different sectors of society (Epstein, 1992; Sammons *et al.*, 1995).

Thus, a lack of research into identifying successful strategies (Moran *et al.*, 2004) about how to raise children means a lot of teachers tend to believe that not enough is being done to help improve children's lives beyond the school gate. This issue is of even greater significance for children from deprived socio-economic backgrounds, given the evidence from Waldfogel and Washbrook (2010), which suggests that parental income is likely to have a significant impact upon their children's development.

This is one of the reasons why school inspectors are increasingly stressing the importance of involving parents more in school life, of being aware of their views and opinions and of schools becoming more engaged and involved within their local communities. School inspection frameworks are also now stressing the importance of parents and parental views in their internal self-assessments and in their well-being strategies (Ofsted, 2010). We need to appreciate, for example, that some parents have similar concerns to their children's teachers on some issues, such as the amount of time their children spend in front of the television or computer screen or the amount of junk food that they consume in their own time.

Schools and one-parent families

Reid (1989c) suggested that schools can help single parents and their families in a number of ways:

1 Schools should ensure that information on the child's home circumstances is regularly checked and updated in conjunction with the parents. Where the parents have separated, the school should have details of custody and access arrangements.
2 Where a child's parents have separated or, in the case of a single mother or father, where both parents are involved, schools can help by establishing procedures for keeping both parents informed of the child's progress and school events. An exception to this might be where violence is involved, when the school should ensure that the mother's safety is protected. If possible, make a comfortable room available for meetings with parents to discuss any problems or disagreements.
3 Schools should know their education authority's policy and discuss their own policies for dealing with problem situations (e.g. dealing with possible disputes between parents). It is helpful if children are consulted when disputes arise.
4 Children can be helped if they and their parents feel able to confide in their class teachers, and are assured that any information given will only be passed on with their consent.

5   Staff should be sensitive to significant changes in a child's behaviour or attitudes (e.g. worsening temper, aggression, lack of concentration, depression, loss of appetite and truancy). Such changes may not relate to a change in home circumstances, but can do so.
6   Schools should, as far as possible, cater for a child's practical needs (e.g. trying to ensure that they eat well and are kept busy without creating pressure).
7   Schools can help to break down the stigma felt by many single parents and their children by ensuring that books portray a variety of family structures and that classroom exercises do not assume a 'nuclear' family (e.g. making Mother's Day or Father's Day cards may not be appropriate). A booklist is available from the National Council for One Parent Families. It is also important to make sure that problems are not inappropriately related to the family situation.
8   Children from single-parent families should receive the same encouragement as everyone else. Research shows that, once social and economic factors are allowed for, the family situation itself has very little effect on school performance. However, some children have found that teachers expect less of them because they come from single-parent families.
9   Schools should make information available on sources of financial assistance for single parents and on relevant organisations in the area that may be able to provide support and help.
10 It is important to be aware of the potential difficulties single parents may have in obtaining after school care and babysitting, so, where necessary, provide after school care and crèches for parents' meetings. Organisations such as the Council for Single Parents can provide information on this. It is also helpful if schools can give parents adequate warning of early closure to assist working single parents.
11 Parent involvement should be encouraged. If appropriate, this might include establishing a regular parents' group for mutual support. It is important that teachers talking to groups of parents do not assume a two-parent family. If at all possible, meetings should be held at times convenient to working parents and teachers.
12 All pupils can benefit from education on the growth and development of children so that they grow up with a realistic idea of what parenting involves.
13 Schools can play an important role in encouraging girls to pursue subjects that are likely to make them more financially independent when they grow up. The majority of single parents are women, many of whom struggle to support their families on the low wages paid in many traditional women's occupations.

Engaging parents in raising achievement

Harris and Goodall (2008) have reported on their findings relating to a sponsored research project to evaluate and explore the relationship between innovative work with parents and its subsequent impact upon student achievement. One of the key aims was to capture and explore the views and voices of parents, students and teachers about the barriers to parental engagement and the respective benefits to learning. Their research findings highlight a number of barriers facing certain parents in supporting their children's learning. It is clear that powerful social and economic factors still prevent many parents from fully participating in schooling. Their research showed that schools, rather than parents, are often 'hard to reach'. The research also found that, while parents, teachers and pupils tend to agree that parental engagement is a 'good thing', they also hold very different views about the purpose of engaging parents. It became clear that there was a major difference between involving parents in schooling and engaging parents in learning. While involving parents in school activities has an important social and community function, it is only the engagement of parents in learning in the home that is more likely to result in a positive difference to learning outcomes.

Therefore, as Deforges and Abouchaar (2003) reported, it is parents' engagement in children's learning within the home that makes the greatest difference to student achievement. While most schools are involving parents in school-based activities in a variety of ways, all the evidence shows that this has little, if any, impact upon children's subsequent learning and achievement.

The study by Harris and Goodall (2008) showed that some of the real values gained from parental engagement included:

- moral support;
- a better valuing of education;
- better behaviour from pupils; and
- a better standard of homework.

Parents and literacy

We will now conclude this chapter by focusing upon one of the key issues for involving parents in their children's schools by way of an exemplar before considering its implications. This will be on the importance of parent involvement in their children's literacy practices. We have chosen this field because of the overwhelming evidence that, once pupils fall behind with their reading and literacy skills, they generally fall further behind with age in terms of attainment, behaviour and school attendance (NBAR, 2008).

In fact, evidence from research shows that parent involvement in their children's learning per se positively affects the children's academic performance (Fan and Chen, 2001) in both primary and secondary schools (Feinstein and Symons, 1999), which in turn leads to higher academic achievement, greater cognitive competence, greater problem-solving skills, greater school enjoyment, better attendance and fewer behavioural problems at school (Melhuish *et al.*, 2001).

In terms of parent involvement with their children's literacy, similar traits have been identified. The key findings are:

1   Involvement with reading activities at home has significant positive influences not only on reading achievement, language comprehension and expressive language skills (Gest *et al.*, 2004), but also on pupils' interest and enjoyment of reading, which is extremely important. It also increases positive attitudes towards both reading and attentiveness in the classroom (Rowe, 1991).
2   Early reading experiences with their parents help to prepare children for the subsequent benefits of more formal literacy instruction at a later time. Parent involvement in their children's reading has been found to be the single most important determinant of language and emergent literacy (Bus *et al.*, 1995).
3   Parents who introduce their babies to books give them a head start in school and an advantage over their peers throughout primary school (Wade and Moore, 2000).
4   Parent involvement in their children's literacy practices has been found to be a more powerful force than other family background variables, including social class, family size and levels of parental education (Flouri and Buchanan, 2004).
5   Research also indicates that the earlier parents become involved in their children's literacy practices, the more profound the results and the longer-lasting the effects (Mullis *et al.*, 2004).
6   Of all school subjects, reading and literacy have been found to be the most sensitive to parental influences (Senechal and LeFevre, 2002). In turn, success in reading has been found to be the gateway for other academic success (Jordan *et al.*, 2000).
7   While parent involvement has the greatest effect in the early years at home and at school, its importance to children's educational and literacy outcomes continues into both the teenage and adult years (Desforges and Abouchaar, 2003). Feinstein and Symons (1999) found, for example, that interest in their children's education was the single most powerful predictor of achievement at the age of 16.

Beyond these points, we should be aware that the benefits of parent involvement in their children's early reading, schools and general development extend well beyond the realm of literacy and educational attainment and achievement. Studies indicate that children whose parents are involved with them in their learning at home are often more committed and show greater social and emotional development than their peers (Allen and Daly, 2002). This includes:

- more resilience to stress;
- greater life satisfaction;

- greater self-direction and self-control;
- greater social adjustment;
- better mental health;
- more supportive relationships;
- greater social competence;
- better and more positive relationships with peers;
- having more tolerance;
- having better and more successful marriages; and
- manifesting fewer challenging behaviours (Desforges and Abouchaar, 2003).

Tips for parents

It is most important that both teachers and parents fully understand and appreciate the significant contribution that parents, carers and extended family members can make to their children's learning, development, reading and attainment. They can achieve this best by providing a stimulating environment around language, reading and writing, as well as supporting at home a school's literacy agenda, not only during the early years, but later in the primary and secondary phases as well.

Eleven tips

We conclude this chapter by providing a list of eleven practical 'tips' for parents for you to use in your professional activities.

1. Provide a loving and supportive home environment.
2. Practice active listening, hold conversations and show that you are interested in what your child has to say.
3. Send your child to school for the day with a good breakfast and a good night's sleep.
4. Keep your child informed of any changes in his or her home life that might affect his or her progress at school.
5. Work with teachers, staff and other parents in a cooperative way.
6. Learn as much as possible about the school.
7. Provide good parental leadership by participating in relevant parental groups.
8. Contribute your service in whatever way you can towards the child's total understanding and enrichment of the school and his or her learning.
9. Offer constructive criticism, if necessary.
10. Become involved in school and local community programmes that help to improve the academic and social health of those involved.
11. Listen to your child read as often as possible and as soon as possible in the early years. Show your child your own interest in reading and in books. When your child is very young, start reading aloud to him or her as soon as possible.

Summary

This chapter has provided a concise summary of some of the main findings and key studies that have been undertaken into families and their children's schooling and learning over recent years. All these findings helped to influence our thinking as we planned our Family Values Scheme and took them into account; albeit we were starting from a situation of working within a deprived community with low income, low social class parents and homes in which children found that reading, books and learning were often not fully appreciated. We will now begin to move forward and start to consider in more detail how to engage families and begin to instil sound values into them.

Chapter 4

Engaging with parents

> *School success must look beyond the school door. During the last 15 years education has concentrated on course curriculum, instructional methods and teacher training. Academic achievement is shaped more by children's lives outside the school walls, particularly their parents and home life. When parents and families are involved in school life there is a higher likelihood of better performance and a more positive attitude to school life.*
>
> (Bogenschneider and Johnson, 2004)

Introduction

In this chapter, we will consider a number of issues relating to involving parents and families in better and closer relationships with their children's schools. These include:

1. how teachers and schools can provide more effective links with parents and involve them better in school life, as well as the benefits of doing so;
2. how to engage different kinds of families, including hard-to-reach parents;
3. the ten truths about parent involvement;
4. sound home–school family initiatives;
5. a sample school's parent involvement policy; and
6. some practical ways to engage parents and families.

Teachers and pupils are two of the key components in learning and schooling. But there is a third party in the equation: their parents and families. Parents are the child's first and most influential teachers. Therefore, engaging parents and the children's wider and extended family is a very powerful tool in helping to build a child's success both in school and at home. Research shows that excellent home–school links have a significant and positive impact on a child's performance at school (Fan and Chen, 2001). The involvement of parents or carers in their children's learning leads to greater problem-solving skills, more enjoyment of school, better attendance, fewer behavioural problems and a better, more natural development (Melhuish *et al.*, 2001). A child's life is greatly influenced by his or her parents, grandparents and other family members, including siblings.

Before we develop this chapter, it is first necessary to give it some context. Family life in the UK, the US, Canada, Australia and many other parts of the world is very different from, say, 100 years ago. The influence of the extended family can be much less in some homes, although cultural traditions still differ widely. Divorce and parental separation have increased several times over since the 1950s when divorce was rare. The number of children being brought up in single-parent families seems to increase in every new survey and census. In fact, it is probably no longer possible to describe the typical family, as so many different versions apply. Likewise, while it was unusual for both parents to work in the 1940s and 1950s, there has been a gradual change and increase to the point that it is the norm for both parents/carers to work in order to support the family home and lifestyle. Significantly, more women than ever before now work, and in an increasing number of families it is the mother who is the major earner. In most single-parent families, the mother is both parent and breadwinner.

Because of all these issues, among others, it has become even more important for the school to be aware of the home circumstances of each of their enrolled pupils for several reasons:

1   because of potential health and safety issues;
2   for reasons of contact as when, for example, pupils miss school without good reason (therefore, the head teacher and/or local authority are aware of whom the initial contact person for the home is and they are also aware of the daily home collection arrangements); and
3   in order to comply with both the law and local authority regulations such as the Children's Act, 2004.

This chapter is about schools and teachers and their relationships with parents, carers and extended family members. These relationships occur more naturally and are often better in some schools than others. Sometimes this is because some head teachers and their staff have better basic communication skills and are naturally more professional and empathetic than some of their peers. Some head teachers and individual members of their teaching staff tend to hide behind formalities and often do not feel sufficiently at ease with parents and carers. Conversely, some parents and carers do not feel at ease when visiting schools, sometimes because they remember their own bad experiences while at school.

Desforges and Abouchaar (2003: 2) recognised the importance of good parenting within the home as:

> *including the provision of a secure and stable environment, intellectual stimulation, parent–child discussion, good models of constructive social and educational values and high aspirations relating to personal fulfillment*

and good citizenship; contact with schools to share information; participation in school events; participation in the work of the school; and participation in school governance.

It is encouraging to know that the majority of parents are interested in their children's education, and recent research of parents surveyed in England showed that they wanted more involvement. In the past 35 years, the time British parents spend helping their children with homework or reading with their children has increased four times (Gershuny, 2003). However, recognition needs to be given to those parents who have work commitments and also single parents who find it difficult to devote substantial amounts of time and energy to their children's educational activities and school. Jean Gross, a UK government adviser, reported that she found middle-class children were struggling to learn how to talk because their working parents were unable to offer them the quality time that was crucial to their speech development (Gross, 2011).

Masters (2004) carried out a review of research gathered from around the world that identified the characteristics of good to outstanding schools. He found that the effective schools, regardless of family background and socio-economic status, had a number of similarities, one of these being a high level of parent, family and community involvement. It was the parent involvement element that is the most strongly connected to the successful attainment of children (Feinstein and Symons, 1999).

Involving families in school life

Epstein (1996) believed that schools and organisations should share the responsibilities for the socialisation of the child. This theory is based on the three most important contexts in which children develop and grow:

- family;
- school; and
- community.

Epstein stated that, for teachers to formulate good relationships, they need to be actively involved not only with their schools and organisations, but also with the family unit. She devised a framework of six ways that teachers can be involved in school life. These were:

1   *By supporting families with parenting*, helping them to understand their child's development and by being aware of their home conditions. Below are some examples:

- running workshops on helping parents to 'understand their child';
- providing resources to help support good parenting (e.g. online resources, DVDs, books);

- informing parents about available support to help with issues such as health and nutrition;
- ensuring all information available to families is clear, easy to read, age appropriate and relevant to their children's needs and achievements; and
- encouraging family members to participate in adult learning programmes.

2 *By communicating effectively with families* about the curriculum and by keeping parents up-to-date with their children's progress through parents' evenings, open days, after school activities, newsletters, etc. Below are some examples:

- inviting parents into school at least once a year to discuss their children's progress and, if needed, follow up meetings can be arranged;
- sending home a sample of their children's work for parents to read, review and comment on their progress and achievements, as well as providing an understanding of what their children are learning at school;
- keeping parents up to date via newsletters, texts, phone calls, emails, letters, etc.;
- asking parents to give feedback on aspects of school life, such as welcoming ideas on how to improve forms of communication (e.g. schools can add a feedback page on their school website or at the end of a report); and
- ensuring that all correspondence sent to parents meets disability requirements in compliance with the Disability Discrimination Act 1995 (e.g. newsletters available in large print).

3 *By involving parents in school activities* such as by encouraging them to be engaged as volunteers or by providing appropriate training to improve their parenting skills or knowledge. Below are some examples:

- making families aware of any voluntary activities/positions within the school;
- sending out a regular survey to ascertain families' talents, interests and availability; and
- sending out a monthly calendar of events that families can take part in (e.g. concerts, assemblies and sports days) to enable working parents to plan in advance.

4 *By involving families with their children* in learning activities at home, including homework and other curriculum-linked activities. Below are some examples:

- supporting families to enable them to help their children complete their homework activities;
- informing families how they can help to improve their children's skills and knowledge; and
- providing regular fun activities for families to undertake at home.

5   *By including families as participants* in the decision-making of the school through membership of the parent–teacher association (PTA), school councils, committees and other parent-led organisations. Below are some examples:

- offering representative positions to parents from all racial, ethnic, socio-economic and other groups in the school;
- providing ongoing training to ensure parents have the skills to carry out their appointment; and
- encouraging active participation in the school's PTA and/or other parenting organisations.

6   *By coordinating resources and services* to families, pupils and the school with businesses, agencies and other interested support groups, and by providing appropriate services *for* the community. Below are some examples:

- planning community activities (e.g. summer schools for pupils);
- getting involved in school-business partnerships;
- informing parents about community events, programmes and services; and
- working on voluntary community projects (e.g. litter picking).

Questions to ask about school equity

Epstein (1996) suggests that head teachers should ensure that their schools ask themselves the following seven questions in their quest to treat all parents, children and their families equally:

1   Does the school communicate with parents in their home languages?
2   Does the school involve parents in decision-making about how to run the school?
3   Does the school work with community groups on school and community events?
4   Does the school keep parents well informed about their children's behavior and progress in school?
5   Does the school keep parents well informed about school events?
6   Does the school hold programmes for parents on educational and parenting issues at times and places convenient for parents?
7   Does the school involve parents in everyday school activities?

Benefits of involving families in school life

Family participation in their children's schooling has many benefits. These include:
For the child:

- positive child–parent relationships;
- improved emotional literacy skills;

- improved basic skills in reading, literacy and numeracy;
- more opportunities to take part in activities inside and outside school;
- increased self-esteem as the family take an active interest in his or her learning and schooling;
- improved academic achievement;
- a more positive attitude towards school, teacher–pupil relationships, his or her peers, and cultural and aesthetic activities; and
- a better sense of security and well-being.

For the family:

- improved parent–child relationships;
- improved parent–teacher relationships;
- better networking with other families, often particularly helpful for mothers;
- promoting more positive attitudes towards school and teachers;
- a better understanding of the school process;
- improved confidence in their own skills to help their child at home;
- the satisfaction of knowing that they are contributing to their child's education;
- fostering a positive learning environment at home; and
- providing encouragement for family-based learning.

For the school:

- improved child behaviour, attendance and academic achievement;
- benefit from the parents' skills and expertise through volunteering and other forms of school-based and external supportive activities, including fund-raising, etc.;
- by providing more support within the classroom and for school/class trips, events, etc.;
- through parents or carers being involved with homework;
- by developing a better understanding of the local community; and
- an increased and better interaction within the family support unit, including good home–school communication and cooperation.

It is generally agreed that if parents are involved positively in activities associated with children's learning then the school outcomes for their children are likely to be enhanced. As a result, education practices that address inequalities in school attainments are designed more and more to involve parents in the learning experiences of their children, at home and at school . . . . [and] teachers are being encouraged or directed to recognise the importance of parents as partners. It is an expectation that such partnerships will be associated with the formation of more enriched learning environments, which in turn will be related to more positive school attitudes and associated with improvements in children's academic performance.

(Marjoribanks, 2002: 1)

Partnerships between home and school

According to Epstein (1996), there are four ways in which partnerships between home and school can be created:

1 Approach

The approach is the framework for schools to work with families to achieve a shared goal (e.g. successful educational outcomes for the children). This type of framework involves:

- effective communication between home and school; and
- problem-solving between home and school.

2 Attitudes

Attitudes are the perceptions that families and schools have of one another. It is important to identify and acknowledge each other's strengths for taking responsibility for the education and the children.

3 Atmosphere

Schools and organisations need to become 'family-friendly' communities, creating an atmosphere that welcomes all families and encourages active involvement. A welcoming atmosphere can be created by:

- regular home–school communication;
- using formal and informal methods of communication;
- encouraging activity and event participation; and
- showing an appreciation towards family diversity.

4 Actions

Implementing the correct approaches, attitudes and atmosphere will lead to positive learning occurring naturally, which will actively benefit schools by involving parents more easily into everyday life in their children's schools.

Engaging families

Not all parents are the same

There are many different types of parents to take into consideration when schools attempt to find effective ways of engaging with parents. Research by Smit and Driessen (2007) carried out in 500 schools identified six different types of parents and their characteristics:

1   supportive parent;
2   absentee parent;
3   politician parent;
4   career-maker parent;
5   tormenting parent; and
6   super parent.

1 Supportive parent characteristics

This type of parent is satisfied with the school or organisation. He or she is always readily available and likes to be involved in his or her child's education.

2 Absentee parent characteristics

This type of parent does not like to make a contribution, is impossible to contact and is often introverted and unapproachable.

3 Politician parent characteristics

This type of parent loves to be involved and make decisions, and is often a school governor.

4 Career-maker parent characteristics

This type of parent is business-like and loves responsibility, but generally does not have time for school events.

5 Tormenting parent characteristics

This type of parent can be cold, aggressive and impatient.

6 Super parent characteristics

This type of parent is loyal, inspiring to others and very good at communication. He or she contributes to events and usually has good ideas.

Engaging fathers

Fathers play a vital role in their child's development and attainment, particularly when fathers take an interest in their child's education. Pupils are then more likely to engage in positive behaviour and achieve better exam results. This is not dependent on whether the father lives with their child/children but is dependent on the quality of their involvement and their ability to set appropriate interventions (e.g. rules and boundaries to promote positive behaviour; Pleck and Masciadrelli, 2004; Flouri, 2005; Sarkadi et al., 2008).

US research (National Center for Fathering, 2009) reports that, while 32 per cent of fathers never visit their child's classroom and 54 per cent never volunteer at school, the trend for their involvement is upward. Over the past 10 years, the percentage of fathers taking their child to school has risen from 38 per cent to 54 per cent; attending class events from 28 per cent to 35 per cent; volunteering at their child's school from 20 per cent to 28 per cent; and attending school-based parents' meetings from 47 per cent to 59 per cent.

Engaging grandparents

Grandparent involvement in family life is a key ingredient to a child's healthy development. Grandparents not only provide good role models, but also provide the child with love, time and consideration, all of which make them feel cared for better. There are numerous activities in which grandparents can become engaged. Below are a few examples:

- reading, improving the basic skills;
- playing, understanding key skills such as turn-taking and sharing;
- cooking, developing numeracy skills;
- assisting with other household chores (e.g. gardening);
- visiting local attractions (e.g. museums, displays);
- trips to the park;
- having a picnic with other family and friends;
- taking them on holiday or for a long weekend; and
- sleepovers, helping the child to prepare for future sleepovers with peers and therefore promoting independence, and also giving parents a bit of a break.

In the study by Buchanan et al. (2008: 19), children were asked the following: What can grandparents do to be closer to their grandchildren? The response was that they:

> *wanted their grandparents to be actively involved in their lives. Being close was not enough. The first criteria was that grandparents had to keep in touch. This could be through email, telephone, and letters. The second was by doing things together and giving practical support. This could take the form of financial help, gifts, helping with education and homework as well as caretaking. Closely behind this, young people rated spending time listening to, and supporting them as important.*

In many Catholic countries in places such as Europe, the role of the grandparents and extended family members is often viewed more importantly than in some parts of the UK and US, where familial disintegration has occurred much more quickly.

Hard-to-reach families

Unfortunately for some families, engaging with school may not be as straightforward as it may seem due to a number of influencing factors. Desforges and Abouchaar (2003) identified the following factors as having an influence upon home–school relationships: social class, maternal level of education, material deprivation, maternal psychosocial health, single-parent status and, to a lesser degree, family ethnicity. It is important that schools are persistent when wanting to involve hard-to-reach parents (Aronson, 1996), understand these barriers and are able 'to see the world through the eyes of parents who do not fit the norm' (Crozier *et al.*, 2005: 158) in order to create effective partnerships to aid their children's education.

There are many misconceptions in the general public and teachers' minds about why some families are regarded as being 'hard to reach'. Below, we illustrate a few of the kinds of stereotypical statements that some people are inclined to make:

- Her mother was hopeless at school so what can you expect?
- If parents don't attend school events, it shows they don't care about their child's education.
- Parents who are illiterate and/or unemployed can't help their child.
- Children from working-class backgrounds and certain estates are all troublemakers.
- Considering how Amy performed in school, is it any wonder that her sister's academic performance is so dreadful?
- Families who are non-English speaking in the home don't understand how to help and support their child's learning.
- It is acceptable only to contact families when a child has misbehaved.

These kinds of statements typify the low expectations that some teachers and members of the general public can hold about certain families when challenging situations occur. These views tend to be held by professionals who always blame pupils' or their parents' shortcomings on the home rather than questioning their own or their school's actions. Research has consistently shown since the work of Rutter *et al.* (1979) that what happens inside individual schools and classrooms really matters and makes a significant difference to the performance of pupils. At the same time, Dalziel and Henthorne (2005) did find that certain families, such as those containing a persistent school absentee, held more negative views towards teachers and their schools and made fewer voluntary visits to schools to foster and promote good home–school relationships.

Research found that children were disadvantaged not by social class, but rather by lack of parents' interest. It is clear from all the research that the biggest factor in pupil attainment is parent involvement. It is not child poverty that creates low achievement, but the level of parent involvement that makes the difference (Feinstein, 2003).

The ten truths about parent involvement

The National Community Education Association (White-Clark and Decker, 1996) put together a list of ten truths about parent involvement. These are:

1 All parents have hopes and goals for their children. They differ in the ways they support their children's efforts to achieve those goals.
2 The home is one of several spheres that simultaneously influence a child. The school must work with the other spheres for the child's benefit, and must not push them apart.
3 The parent is the chief contributor to a child's education. Schools can either co-opt the parent's role or recognise the parent's potential.
4 Parent involvement must be a legitimate element of education.
5 Parent involvement is a process, not a programme of activities. It requires ongoing energy and effort.
6 Parent involvement requires a vision, a policy, a framework and a consensus.
7 Parents' interaction with their own children is the cornerstone of involvement. A programme must recognise the value, diversity and difficulty of this role.
8 Most barriers to parent involvement are found within school practices, not within parents.
9 Any parent can be 'hard to reach'. Parents must be approached individually; they are not defined by gender, ethnicity, family situation, education or income.
10 Successful parent involvement nurtures relationships and partnerships. It strengthens bonds between home and school, parent and educator, and school and community.

Family initiatives

There are many initiatives that involve families in sound home–school links. Desforges and Abouchaar (2003: 2) state that the following are all important:

> *good parenting in the home, including the provision of a secure and stable environment, intellectual stimulation, parent-child discussion, good models of constructive social and educational values and high aspirations relating to personal fulfilment and good citizenship; contact with schools to share information; participation in school events; participation in the work of the school; and participation in school governance.*

Parent involvement policy

Developing a parent involvement policy (PIP) is a great way to ensure a sustainable and effective approach to engaging all different kinds of families. The policy should include information on how the school will address the following issues:

communication, parenting, skills, children's learning, volunteering, school decision-making and community involvement.

Communication

Implementing effective communication channels between the home and the school in order to provide information about the children's curriculum, progress, behaviour, attendance, interests, activities and other school-based events, including any external trips or visits.

Parenting

Providing information and training for families about how to create a positive learning environment at home, as well as the best ways of supporting their school and schooling.

Children's learning

Providing information and training for families to help with their child's education on such issues as, for example, homework.

Volunteering

Creating opportunities for parents or carers to volunteer through participation in supportive roles, activities and events at the school.

School decision-making

Good decision-making is about providing opportunities for parents or carers to become involved in educational advocacy and decision-making on issues that affect their children's education, such as invoking and implementing new school policies.

Community involvement

Creating links with community support groups, agencies and initiatives to help strengthen family and school partnerships.

Overleaf is an example of a primary school's parent involvement policy. This is fairly typical of the type of policy that is used in schools and by local authorities.

Priestthorpe Primary School parent involvement policy

At Priestthorpe Primary School, we recognise the importance of ensuring we have a strong partnership with parents and value parent involvement in the life of the school. Throughout this policy, the term 'parent' is used to refer to parents, guardians and carers. We believe that education is a collaborative enterprise involving, among others, parents, staff and children. It is known that parents are the most important influence in a child's life. Parents need to be able to provide the educational and emotional support that children need if they are to succeed.

As a school, we are therefore committed to establishing and maintaining an effective and purposeful working relationship between the school and home.

Aim

- To promote parent involvement in children's learning and the life of the school.

Objectives

To foster an ethos and atmosphere where all parents feel welcome and valued, we will:

- create an atmosphere that is respectful and positive towards parents, children and everyone in school;
- maintain an 'open door' approach for parents to contact and visit the school;
- work with parents in promoting positive behaviour at home and at school; and
- seek to provide a range of opportunities throughout the year to invite families into school (e.g. Harvest Festival, carols around the tree, thank you assembly, good work and achievement assemblies).

To have good communication and mutual dialogue between home and school, we will:

- provide as much information as possible in timely, specific, targeted and accessible ways so that parents feel confident and knowledgeable about what is happening in school; and
- use a variety of methods of communication: written communication, school prospectus, home–school agreement, half-term head teacher's news, weekly newsletter, key policies in family information sheet format, family involvement news, curriculum letters, pupil progress information letters, informal and formal meetings, home visits, assemblies, texts,

school notice boards, email, telephone, and the school website/learning platform will also be used as appropriate.

To actively involve parents in their child's learning and progress, we will:

- hold parent consultation meetings with teachers of each class;
- send an annual report home;
- hold annual workshops on reading/literacy, numeracy and handwriting where parents can learn about, and are encouraged to discuss, how to support their child; and
- encourage parents to recognise the importance of the support they give their child at home.

To make good use of parents' expertise and willingness to enhance their own learning and that of their own and other children and to actively involve them in school life, we will encourage parents to:

- volunteer to support with reading in class, to help with 'Wonderful Wednesday' creative workshops, to assist on school trips and to become involved in school projects (all subject to the school's child protection procedures);
- attend 'Friends of Priestthorpe Primary School' meetings and support the group's fund-raising activities; and
- become parent governors.

To provide good induction and transition for all groups of parents, we will:

- provide opportunities for all prospective parents to find out about the school via individual visits and/or annual meetings for nursery and reception; and
- provide opportunities for parents to discuss transitions by holding an annual 'Shuffle Up' day for all classes and a secondary school transition event for Year 6 pupils and parents.

To establish the views and opinions of parents of the school and act upon these, we will:

- conduct an annual parental questionnaire and inform parents of the results;
- seek parental consultation on key issues and policies in school; and
- seek parental feedback on key events in school.

In employing a parent involvement worker, Priestthorpe Primary School seeks to build on and further develop opportunities for parental and family involvement in all aspects of school life. The parent involvement worker will:

- seek to provide a range of activities and workshops to promote parent involvement in children's learning, and also lifelong learning for both children and adults (e.g. sports/fun/craft activities at mum's nights and

dad's nights, family learning events such as healthy lifestyles and child safety, etc.); and
- seek to provide parenting and family support (e.g. providing information about holiday activities, childcare, local community events, parenting courses, e-safety, providing support and encouragement for families suffering difficulties/crises or barriers to involvement, being accessible and approachable to parents to voice their concerns, issues and opinions).

The school recognises the fact that some parents are restrained from participating in the life of the school owing to other commitments. The staff understands that this does not mean they are not interested in their child's education. Therefore, it is necessary to provide opportunities for parent involvement on a variety of levels so that parents can participate at a level to suit their individual needs.

Monitoring and review

The head teacher, who reports to governors about the effectiveness of the policy on request, monitors this policy on a day-to-day basis. This parent involvement policy is the governors' responsibility and the school improvement committee will review its effectiveness annually. They do so through discussion with the head teacher.

Signed: .... (head teacher)

Signed: .... (governor)

Practical ways to engage families

It is important to make all parents or carers feel valued, as some may have reservations about their own ability, participating in school life and the response they may be perceived by members of staff. Below is a bank of suggestions to help engage parents, carers and their wider families in their home–school links.

Effective home–school communication

There are various ways to communicate with family homes and keep parents or carers updated about events, activities and other information. Within a minority of homes, some parents' poor language skills and their inability to read can prove a barrier to good home–school communications. This can be overcome in a number of ways (e.g. by phoning the home or videotaping the message). Home visits are also very effective. Written communication such as newsletters needs to be brief, jargon-free and, whenever possible, use bullet points. It is good practice to involve parents in improving the design and content of written communications and it is always wise and good practice to advise them of the home–school communication policy when their children start at the school. In some parts of the country, it may be necessary to provide a translation service to assist non-English-speaking families.

Here are a few suggestions about approaches to manage effective home–school communication:

- face-to-face (parents' evenings, open days, home time, special events);
- telecommunications (telephone, mobile, text messaging, radio services);
- online (school website, group/individual email, invitation-only social networking sites, PowerPoint presentations in foyer);
- printed materials (brochures, message board inside/outside school, newsletters, flyers, letters, personalised invitations, reports, newspapers); and
- ask parents or carers for their preferences and whether they have any particular specific or special needs.

Welcoming new parents: a school welcome pack

Making new families feel welcome and supported is very important for any school. A school welcome pack can provide key information on the school, its organisation, rules, activities and achievements. These can include:

- the school brochure;
- a copy of the home–school agreement;
- a calendar of events (e.g. school fete);
- a list of after school clubs;
- a list of activities taking place within the area;
- details about the family drop-in centre;
- related home–school activities (e.g. the Family Values Scheme); and
- guidance about how to become a school volunteer, parent governor, member of the parent–teacher association, etc.

Welcome back to school

At the beginning of the new academic year, organise a 'get-together' to help re-engage families. This event can be held at a convenient time to ensure a good turnout (e.g. during the early evening for working parents or in the afternoon during school hours). The event provides an ideal opportunity for families to meet the staff, take a look around the school and have an overview of the forthcoming year. It also provides an opportunity to re-establish the school's expectations on, for example, attendance, behaviour, uniform, equipment, etc. The event can be given a theme, such as:

- quiz hour;
- bingo and prizes;
- cheese and wine evening; or
- coffee morning.

Tell them about yourself

Introduce yourself to your pupils' families by creating a flyer informing them about your job, responsibilities and tasks within the school and any interests that you may wish to share outside school. You can also include a photo of yourself. This is a great way to break down barriers and make families feel more at ease, and you may also find you have a few things in common. If families feel they have an activity or interest in common with their child's teacher, they are much more likely to engage in conversation and form a good working relationship, and will feel more at ease when visiting the school.

Tell us about your family

It is surprising how many different interests members of a family have and share. By inviting them to complete a 'Tell us about your family' questionnaire, the data gathered can provide the school with a wealth of information. For example, by collating the information, the staff may decide to establish to:

- help set up and maintain a community garden;
- help choreograph the school play;
- paint a mural in the school hall;
- talk to a class about being a sanctuary for injured hedgehogs;
- help design and build a role play area (e.g. a Viking ship); and/or
- coach a football/rugby/netball team.

Home time

The end of the school day is an ideal time to interact with families. Informing them of their child's achievements on the day helps to lower barriers and encourages engagement. Some parents have formed barriers due to receiving negative comments regarding their child and also their own level of parenting. These barriers take time to break down but it can be done by greeting a parent with, for example, 'Hi Mrs Harris, Jenny has had a great day with all her friends and during one of her lessons she created a very colourful flower out of plasticine'. Such little titbits of easily relayed conversation can make a big difference and ease the process of relationship building.

Class/school assemblies

Whole school and/or class assemblies are another great way of brining everyone together, including families, thereby creating a sense of community. There are a number of ways to engage families in an assembly. Here are a few simple suggestions. Why not invite families:

- to an end-of-term/-year celebration of their child's work;
- to talk about their job and/or interest; and/or
- to watch their child, for example, perform or recite a poem.

Special events

A range of different events can be arranged in order to target different members of the family at different points of the day, term or year. The timing of these events is important to take into consideration. For example, dads are often more likely to attend in the evening, and so offering soup and a roll with the activity may make it more tempting. If the school is located in a multicultural community, such events can also include different food, costumes, traditions and heritage. Here are a few suggestions for possible school-organised activities:

- afternoon tea;
- historical talks;
- vegetable growing;
- orienteering;
- jewellery making;
- henna designs;
- international dinner;
- World Book Day; and
- meet your child at the local library.

We will now consider some of these ideas in more detail.

Open days

Invite families into school to see their child's work and meet the staff and other parents. Invitations can be written by their child so that they are personalised. These open days can also involve the families participating in an activity such as:

- building the tallest tower using newspaper and masking tape;
- creating a bookmark using beads, ribbon and card; or
- using ICT to research origami.

At the end of the open day, the families can be sent a thank you note from their child, teacher or whole class. The note can also include information regarding the next activity/event on the school calendar.

Mega challenge evening

Once a month hold a mega challenge evening and involve the families in a series of fun and exciting activities they can also do at home. To create an inviting atmosphere, provide refreshments and music. At the end of the mega challenge, hand out certificates for all those who participated. Here are some ideas for a mega challenge evening:

- obstacle course;
- board game challenge;
- treasure hunt – using map-reading skills;
- fashion show – create an outfit from recycled materials;
- create a family crest – using paint, paper, card, glitter, etc.; and
- kite making – using ICT to establish a design, then making and flying the kite.

Get creative for parents' evening

To ensure a good attendance for a parents' evening, invite parents/carers to an art exhibition at the school where they can view and buy their child's work. Choose a school/class theme such as a sunset for the children to paint. These works of art can then be framed and displayed with the child's name engraved upon them.

My portfolio

At the end of the week, month, term or year, pupils can compile a selection of their best work, which can be displayed in a portfolio and taken home to show their family. The portfolio can include work from all subjects, including written documentation, photographs (of models made), drawings, etc. For children whose families have never seen their work, this provides a great opportunity for the child:

- to have their efforts acknowledged within the home;
- to talk to their family about what they have learnt;
- to recognise their achievements and develop self-esteem; and
- to internalise what it feels like when their family takes an interest in their education.

Your child is a star!

Rewarding positive behaviour does not have to be time consuming or expensive. A simple positive note or phone call home can make such a difference for the child and family. Some families sometimes perceive a phone call from the school as likely to contain negative content. Therefore, receiving a positive communication helps to break down these perceptions. It also shows that the school cares about their child and the family and that they value the family's involvement.

Family drop-in service

There are occasions when families need to use a computer, find out information or just have a chat. School is a great place to capitalise on this need. Enlisting the help of a volunteer coordinator to be available at certain times of the day to facilitate parents, carers or other family members and, if possible, providing a readily accessible room equipped with a computer, leaflets and information about organisations, local initiatives, charities and support groups all helps. This service can also offer resources that allow users to borrow items such as books, games, DVDs and CDs to help with family learning.

Information evening

Why not send out a questionnaire to establish what families are interested in or would like more information about on the school? For example, such issues might include: homework strategies, healthy eating, behaviour management, Internet safety and adult learning, to name but a few. This can be achieved by either arranging an evening once a month with a guest speaker to present practical information on each chosen subject or by arranging with the local authority to set up an adult learning centre within the school. Here are some suggestions:

- understanding my child, stages of child development, parenting strategies, etc.;
- reading with my child, strategies, tips, etc.;
- helping my child through divorce, bereavement, remarriage; or
- being a single parent/co-parenting.

Getting involved

Encouraging families to volunteer at school provides a potentially useful and supportive resource and also demonstrates to the children the value and importance of participating in the larger community. Informing families on how they can get involved in the running, organisation and supervision of the school is an essential part of the process. Whether this means encouraging them to get involved with the parent–teacher association or by becoming a classroom assistant or by applying for a position as a school governor are among a wide range of potential options. Parents can also get involved by contributing to other school schemes, campaigns and collections. Here are some possible examples of these potential options:

- collecting vouchers for schools from local supermarkets and petrol stations;
- being a classroom helper;
- helping to organise a fund-raising event;
- being a playground supervisor;
- becoming a school/class trip helper;
- organising and/or assisting after school clubs (e.g. chess);
- coaching the school team (e.g. football, netball);
- becoming a library assistant;
- working with the school orchestra choir;
- participating in the walking bus scheme;
- helping administration staff (e.g. with press releases);
- helping to judge competitions;
- speaking at events on a specific subject (e.g. the Second World War);
- helping with art and craft projects; and
- creating costumes for school performances.

Volunteer training programmes

A volunteer training programme can be run at certain times of the year to provide on-site training for members of the family who are interested in supportive roles such as being a library assistant, reading buddy, classroom assistant, playground supervisor or family drop-in service coordinator. The training would provide them with key skills, confidence and an insight into each role. Once trained and experienced in their role, they can then be invited to become a contributor or trainer on future programmes. This type of training ensures retention and job satisfaction for all involved.

Crèche facilities

Some families are restricted due to the lack of childcare provision available. For key activities and events, a crèche service is key.

Parent governor

Parents can express their interest in becoming elected as a parent governor. Provide accessible information regarding the application process. The parent governor has many roles, such as making sure all communications with parents are informative, accessible and easy to read.

Support for parents

Schools can provide a hub of support and provision for children, parents and families (e.g. a drop-in facility at the school where they can receive advice and/or by erecting signposting to their services). In this regard, the Solihull Approach parenting programme (Douglas, 2004) is one of the best programmes available.

Adult learning

Schools can focus on providing parents with the knowledge and skills needed to help their child work with homework, as well as developing other skills such as ICT. It is evident that, when parents know how to help with homework, the result can raise pupil performance (Balli *et al.*, 1998). A survey carried out by the Basic Skills Agency (2001) found that 34 per cent of parents said they had difficulties reading from a children's book, and 18 per cent said they found it difficult to understand and recognise numbers.

Feedback

Encouraging families to feed back on different aspects of school life not only provides valuable information on what the school is doing well and on what needs to be improved, but it also encourages families to be actively engaged with the school. Opportunities to provide feedback can be displayed on the school website, in a suggestion box, newsletter, and in other documentation and correspondence.

Summary

In this chapter, we have presented and considered some ideas for engaging with parents appropriately and effectively. The four core sections have been on involving families in school life, considering different parental and family needs, some sensible family initiatives, including the role of parent involvement policies, and some practical ways to engage families; a sensible precursor to our Family Values Schemes.

We will begin our journey towards a consideration of the Family Values Scheme per se in more detail by first discussing how to use values-based education to promote positive learning in the next chapter.

Chapter 5

Values-based education
Values, morals, ethics

A good starting point to introduce values-based education is first to define what we mean by values, as it is often confused with the terms 'morals' and 'ethics'. They do all have one thing in common in that they provide us with a daily set of rules or boundaries. However, there are significant differences between the three terms.

Values

Values are principles and qualities that we want in our life. They are not things that we want on a materialistic level, but something that we need in our life so that we can be true to ourselves. The good thing about values is that we are able to identify the values that are important to us on a personal level and, once we have done this, we can then utilise them according to our individual needs. To sum up, our values will differ in priority depending on the situation that we find ourselves in at different stages of our lives. The term values goes much further than defining what is right and wrong, but includes expectations of how we need to behave socially in order to have the caring, nurturing society that we strive to create.

Morals

When we think of morals, we always think of the traditional stories that we are taught at a young age used to reinforce what is good and bad. The most well known of these is Aesop's *Fables*, with the characters featuring animals to reinforce the moral code of good and bad. These stories are very short to help children understand what happens if we do not make the right choices. Morals are limited to teaching children just about good and bad, in comparison with the teaching of values, which are personal and come from within.

Ethics

The term ethics is normally associated with a group of people rather than an individual. They are a set of rules usually adopted in a workplace to help people behave professionally. We often hear that people or a workplace behaved unethically or unprofessionally.

What do we mean by values?

Our values are something that we are born with; ideas and beliefs that we inherit from our parents as soon as we arrive in the world. These ideas and beliefs from our parents are passed down to us so that we can continue to live these same values in our own lives. To sum up, values are what we are, how we behave to others and how we expect others to treat us. As we grow and develop from childhood into adulthood, other factors shape the values that we live our lives by, such as family, home and school. However, the biggest impact on the child is his or her parents and the family home. It is crucial that these values are nurtured in the right way by these factors if we are to create a society that is caring and nurturing for future generations. This may sound dramatic, but if we are to have an impact on society in the right way values need to be intrinsic to the way that we conduct ourselves everyday.

Where did values come from?

According to Massey (1976), values are developmental and differ according to age. He defines three significant stages, starting from the minute we are born until we reach early adulthood:

- imprint period (0–7 years);
- modelling period (8–13 years); and
- socialisation period (13–21 years).

The imprint period

This stage occurs from birth to the age of 7. Massey says that, at this age, our brains are like sponges, soaking up everything around us and accepting from our parents what is given or said to us without giving an expression or opinion. If our parents do not provide the correct role models, the behaviours that we want to see have little opportunity to develop, and this can have implications for the child later on in life. Therefore, this stage is crucial in creating the foundations for well-rounded confident adults. The emphasis at this stage is to focus on the basics of right and wrong and to develop social skills such as sharing and taking turns in a small-group situation.

The modelling period

The second stage builds on from the imprint period and formulates between the ages of 8 and 13 years. At this stage children are beyond the pure acceptance of what is said or given to them by their parents and start to extend these influences to a wider scale, namely school and their peers. This period is associated with children developing their own sense of who they are through a choice of fashion, hobbies, peer groups and the media.

The socialisation period

The final stage is from 13 years to 21 years, and the biggest influence during this period is not the parent, but their peers. How they are perceived to others is an important characteristic during this period. The values instilled in us during the imprint period by our parents is reaffirmed during this period, when we normally associate with people who share the same values that our parents influenced us with from birth.

Our early childhood has an impact on the values that we choose later in life. They help us to overcome challenges that we may face on a day-to-day basis. Our personal values shape who we are and what we want to become. This personalisation helps us to make a valid contribution into a culture that has a common set of values. A society without values is a society that is deprived and one we would find it difficult to measure our own values against. When we are faced with difficult circumstances, we very often refer back to our values to help us make the right decision. It is clear, therefore, that the biggest influence on our lives is our parents and our families.

Personal values

Every person has his or her own set of values that are unique and personal to him or her. Although we may share the same values as others, how we use them and articulate them will be different to the next person. If we can take the time to clarify our values individually, life will have more of a focus and more meaning. It will reduce anger, resentment, frustration and stress, and will make us become more self-aware of our capabilities and what we need to do to achieve them. There is no doubt that there are benefits to identifying your own set of values. It helps us to make the right choices and influences our decision-making and thought processes. Continually reaffirming our values makes us more self-reflective and less critical of others.

Discovering our values

Think about the last time you were faced with a challenging situation and then consider how you dealt with it. What values did you use to resolve the situation? How did you feel when faced with this level of challenge? Did you feel exhilarated, angry, frustrated? It is only at this level of personal challenge that we are able to really return to our values. What values did we personally rely on to get us through the situation? Was it honesty, respect, trust or cooperating with others. Following is an extensive list of personal values for your perusal. Identify your top ten personal values and then prioritise them in order of importance to you. You can even give them a score on a scale of 1 to 10, with 10 being the highest.

A personal values list

Achievement	Health	Recognition
Adventure	Helping	Reliability
Affection	Honesty	Respect
Altruism	Hope	Revolution
Autonomy	Humour	Risk taking
Caring	Inclusivity	Romance
Challenge	Independence	Safety
Community	Innovation	Saving
Completion	Integrity	Seeking truth
Connection	Intimacy	Self-control
Creativity	Joy	Self-esteem
Doing the right thing	Justice	Self-expression
Doing things my way	Keeping things	Self-mastery
Elegance	Leadership	Self-reliance
Emotional health	Learning	Self-respect
Empowerment	Leisure time	Sensuality
Enlightenment	Looking good	Service
Entrepreneurship	Love	Setting example
Equality	Loyalty	Simplicity
Excellence	Mastery	Socialising
Excitement	Maturity	Solving problems
Fame	Nature	Spiritual growth
Family	Nurturing	Spirituality
Feeling good	Openness	Spontaneity
Financial security	Opportunity	Strength
Fixing things	Orderliness	Synergy
Frankness	Partnership	Team spirit
Freedom	Passion	Teamwork
Friendship	Peace	Trust
Fulfilment	Personal growth	Truth
Fun	Playfulness	Uniqueness
Getting there	Pleasure	Vitality
Giving	Power	Wealth
Happiness	Privacy	Winning
Harmony	Quality	Wisdom

This list is not exhaustive and can be added to depending upon circumstances.

Traditional family values

A strong family unit will provide stability, trust and openness for all its members to develop and grow in a positive way. Traditional family values are a set of social standards and expectations that have been passed down from generation to generation, which provide the social and emotional characteristics that families need if they want to create this strong family unit. These traditional family values are vital if we want our children to become confident, well-adjusted individuals in society. In our busy lives, we often find it difficult to obtain a balance between individual, family and work goals, and this can have a detrimental effect on the amount of time that we spend together as a family. However, if we can create this balance, our lives will become more purposeful and have clear direction. Values will help give us this sense of direction, and it may mean a different set of values for each family. It is more important that families choose values that they feel are relevant to them. In this way, every family member can take ownership of the values and feel a sense of belonging.

Studies show that families spending quality time together can affect learning by 60 per cent. To reiterate, it is the things that families actually do together that achieves the best environment for learning. This process is described by Sheridan and Kratochwill (2007) as the 'curriculum of the home'. This clarifies that parents who are actively involved in their child's development and learning are a major contributor to creating a positive learning environment. It is important that this is supported by continuity (i.e. 'closing the gap' between home, school and community). The integration of values as a way of narrowing this gap is one that has the greatest influence on learner's achievement.

Epstein (1996) and Sheridan and Kratochwill (2007) reinforce this concept through their effective partnerships model. Epstein (1996) believes that schools and organisations should share the responsibilities of the child. This theory is based on the three most important contexts in which children develop and grow:

- family;
- school; and
- community.

Epstein believes that, for parents to formulate good relationships, they need to be actively involved not only with their schools and organisations, but also within the family unit.

Values and education

It was the founder of the International Values Education Trust, Dr Neil Hawkes, who was a pioneer of the idea of bringing values into the school setting in order to create values-based schools. He was the head teacher of West Kidlington Primary and Nursery Schools in Oxfordshire, when he, actively supported by the staff and community, conceptualised the theory of values-based education with young people and adults. His ideas provide a vision for the school in which the basic human values can be taught not just as part of the curriculum, but one in which values could become an intrinsic part of school life. His research at Oxford University looked at the positive effects of giving an ethical vocabulary to a school community to develop ethical intelligence. Working with the Association of Living Values (ALIVE), of which he is a founder member, the following statement was formed:

> *Values is a way of conceptualizing education that places the search for meaning and purpose at the heart of the educational process. It recognizes that the recognition, worth and integrity of all involved in the life and work of the school are central to the creation of a values-based learning community that fosters positive relationships and quality in education. Behind my thinking lies an understanding and assumption that values-based education is far more than a process of instilling values in pupils. It is concerned with the very meaning and purpose of education; a statement about the quality of education that can be achieved and the impact that this can have on society and the world. With this view of the role and purpose of education, schools that adopt a values-based approach can positively influence the development of positive values, which sustain a civil, caring and compassionate society.*
>
> (Dr Neil Hawkes, ALIVE 2007)

His philosophy and practice of valuing was created in response to a real concern about the way that people interacted with each other in their daily lives. The world since time began has always been faced with periods of violence, drugs, alcohol abuse and economic and social deprivation, and the role of the adult has been instrumental in how these issues have impacted on society. It is clear from these issues that society has lacked an emphasis on values. For whatever reason, the lack of the core values of honesty, trust and respect have resulted in a breakdown in some areas of society. Caring for each other and the world around us is not consistent practice for everyone!

Dr Hawkes clearly puts the emphasis of the responsibility for the nurturing of young people with the adult. It is through this fostering role that values can be introduced to children at a very young age and carefully nurtured through to young adults. It is by adults role modelling positive relationships to each other that values-based education is at its very best. Young children need positive role models if they are to become confident, well-adjusted adults ready to take on whatever they may face in the world. Young people who are exposed to adult behaviour that is not positive adopt characteristics that may hinder them later in life.

Values-based education embraces a climate in which people are valued and, in turn, they learn to value others. If we seek to achieve this goal, we will allow children to develop by receiving the very best guidance and learning through good social and educational role models.

In 1996, Hawkes was part of a team of 30 global educators who were invited by UNICEF to discuss the possibilities of using values-based education to help resolve some of the issues that he felt were damaging society. The discussions led to the creation of a framework (Living Values) that uses values to show how young people could be educated to become good citizens of the world. The Convention on the Rights of the Child was part of the framework to be used to create a vision for the future in which values would be practiced in all countries in order for everyone to achieve this common goal.

Using values to educate young people and adults in this way is reinforced by UNESCO's Commission Report into *Learning: The Treasure Within*, headed by Jacques Delors, which states:

> *In confronting the many challenges that the future holds in store, humankind sees in education an indispensable asset in its attempt to attain the ideals of peace, freedom and social justice. The Commission does not see education as a miracle cure or a magic formula opening the door to a world in which all ideals will be attained, but as one of the principal means available to foster a deeper and more harmonious form of human development and thereby to reduce poverty, exclusion, ignorance, oppression and war.*

Living Values (LV) now operates successfully around the world and holds regular training sessions through its volunteer workforce to share with schools and parents how to use values effectively in their daily lives.

Earlier, we described values-based education's principles and philosophy through Dr Neil Hawkes. His work at West Kidlington School became the gold standard for the Australian Government's Values Education Initiative influenced and researched by Professor Terry Lovat and his colleagues at Newcastle University, Australia. They have researched the effects of the Australian Government's Values Education Initiative. The university published its final Report for the Australian Government, which considered all the evidence related to the impact of introducing and developing values-based education in schools (Lovat, 2009).

The research describes how values-based schools give increasing curriculum and teaching emphasis to values-based education. As a consequence, pupils become more academically diligent, the school assumes a calmer, more peaceful ambience, better pupil–teacher relationships are forged, pupil and teacher well-being improves and parents become more engaged with the school.

The explicit teaching of values provides a common ethical language for talking about interpersonal behaviour. It also provides a mechanism for self-regulated behaviour. An important outcome is a more settled school, which enhances quality teaching and enables teachers to raise expectations for their pupils' academic and personal development.

The values for education

Here is a list of the values as identified by Hawkes (2009).

A list of the values for education

Appreciation	Hope	Simplicity
Caring	Humility	Thoughtfulness
Cooperation	Love	Tolerance
Courage	Patience	Trust
Freedom	Peace	Understanding
Friendship	Quality	Unity
Happiness	Respect	
Honesty	Responsibility	

Appreciation

Appreciation is to be thankful for something that has been done for you. Appreciation is a feeling you experience when you realise something good has happened. It is important to be thankful for the things we have in our lives that we appreciate and to show our appreciation when people do something for us.

Caring

The value 'caring' means loving one another as well as yourself! It is important that you do not take each other for granted just because you are members of the same family. Even individual family members need to know that everyone in their family cares for them, and it is good to make time in your busy lives to tell your nearest and dearest just how much they mean to you. Showing concern for others and making that person feel very special is important to how close you are as a family. Being part of a family and taking an interest in something or someone shows that family member that you really do care! Remember, a hug costs nothing!

Cooperation

When there are lots of family members, we need to demonstrate this value more readily. If we are cooperating well, it should be without effort! Remember that you are all working towards the same goal – to achieve happiness and harmony in your family. Cooperate with each other by listening to each other's points of view without making unfair judgments.

Courage

To have the courage to try something that is different and that you are not familiar with is a real challenge in itself. Courage is not something that you are born with, as it comes from within, but it is very easy to care for. Having courage is persevering when things maybe do not turn out as they should, or it could be having the confidence to stand up to someone or something you believe in.

Freedom

Freedom means to be independent and choose your own actions. Freedom comes with the responsibility to make choices for yourself but also being held to the consequences of your choices. To have freedom means you should be released from ties or constraints that are placed upon you to allow you to act freely as your own person.

Friendship

Friendship is a special gift that needs to be treasured every day. Being a member of a family is very special and, like friendships, families are always there when you need them. The best gifts have ribbons tied around them and their job is to keep things together so that the things inside do not fall apart. True friendship is the best present anyone can have because, if you look after it, you will have it forever!

Happiness

Happiness is feeling good about yourself and having that same emotion for the people around you. You do not find happiness, you make happiness! Making others laugh and smile should make you happy. What you do and what you say affects other people, especially if those things said are meant to hurt others. Family life is like a roller coaster – it has its ups and downs – but if you celebrate the good times and believe that you can achieve your expectations, you will reach happiness.

Honesty

Honesty means to be truthful. To be an honest person, you should always tell the truth. Being honest means that you are a trustworthy person. Sometimes it can be difficult to be honest if other people do not think the same as you. To be an honest person means that you have to accept your mistakes and be able to correct them.

Hope

We always aim to achieve the very best for our families. We set ourselves goals and dreams with the hope that they will be achieved. By working together, we can achieve those wishes if we have the confidence in ourselves and trust others with doing things that we ask of them. Families need high expectations so that they can plan how they are going to achieve them and then they can celebrate the success together.

Humility

Humility or humbleness is being truly happy with who you are instead of pretending you are someone you are not; feeling proud about what you have achieved rather than being boastful. It is being courteous and respectful of others. The value of humility is the opposite of aggressiveness, arrogance, boastfulness and vanity.

Love

Love is a warm, personal emotion that we feel for another person. When we show love, we also show kindness, compassion and affection. In families, we demonstrate and show our love for one another in lots of ways, such as by intuitively doing someone an act of kindness for your brother, sister or mother or simply by giving one another a hug. Love is like a fire – it needs to keep being rekindled or the fire will go out. It is important that families show and tell each other that they love each other every day.

Patience

To show patience is to wait for something or someone without getting agitated or angry. Patience is one of the values that can be the most difficult to show each other. It takes a lot of patience to wait for a child to get himself or herself dressed than to do it for them. However, we must learn to show patience in the same way that famous people such as Leonardo da Vinci painted the most intricate scenes lying flat on his back for hours on end. It also means not giving up when things get too difficult, but to have the patience to see your goals through to the end.

Peace

Peace means living harmoniously without conflict or hostility. Living peacefully means allowing individuals to have their own time and space without the intrusion of other members of the family. It is good to build quiet and still time into family life, and this can be a quiet minute to oneself or listening to music. Being aware of everyone's needs and respecting each other is the right way to achieve peace within your family.

Quality

This value focuses us on the words 'we can' and 'we will'. It makes everyone aware that to achieve excellence in our family life we must first of all think about the quality of our relationships with each other. If we help and support each other, relationships with each other will meet each other's needs and reach the quality that you are striving for. Go for excellence and support each other in enabling everyone to achieve their very best.

Respect

Respect is treating other people, places, and things the way you want to be treated. Valuing someone and his or her thoughts and feelings is also important. We can show respect in many different ways (e.g. listening to someone without interrupting, being polite by saying please and thank you, being truthful with them). We can act in many different ways that are considered respectful.

Responsibility

Responsibility is the commitment to successfully complete a task you agreed to undertake. When you have agreed to complete something, there is an expectation that you keep to your word. It is important that every member of the family has their own responsibilities. The older you get, the more responsibilities you will have.

Simplicity

Simplicity is what makes things beautiful! The environment around us in its natural state is simplicity. It is only when we try to change what is around us that things become complicated. In our family life, we can live quite happily on the basics, and we do not always need the luxuries and the frills to feel content. Keep things simple, plain and uncomplicated and we will achieve but without the stress!

Thoughtfulness

It is very easy to be selfish and not think of others, especially the ones we love and mean the most to us. We can so easily be caught up with busy routines in our daily lives that we start to take things and people for granted. Take a moment to be thoughtful and think how much our families mean to us and how we treasure the time we spend together. Work together as a family on being kind, considerate, unselfish and compassionate in the things we say and do.

Tolerance

Showing tolerance towards another person when that person's beliefs differ from your own can be difficult. The values of patience and cooperation need to be practised if the other person is to feel valued. If conflict arises, then the person causing the conflict is not being fair and just in their actions. Families need to work hard to be tolerant of others and make the time to listen to people's points of view with honesty and fairness!

Trust

Of all the family values, trust is one of the most important because it is what all good family relationships are based on. To trust each other, you need to be honest and not hold any secrets. Good family relationships are like building a house – without the foundations of trust and honesty being laid first, the walls and roof will not stay up but will come crashing down. Learning to trust each other gives everyone confidence to achieve success in everything they do. Work together to earn each other's trust and you will all reap the benefits.

Understanding

To know how another person is feeling without judging him or her requires you to understand his or her state of mind. It is important that we show sympathy and comprehend what that person is showing or telling us. Understanding one another is the right road for creating harmony within the family group. To do this, we need to make decisions together and have a recognition that everyone has a different personality. Show your understanding of others and they will really appreciate a listening ear!

Unity

Some might say that a family is a unit (i.e. we aim to work as one)! The word unity does not mean working individually and for oneself, but working together, supporting and helping each other. Family life is just like this – it is about working as a team to achieve happiness and harmony!

Implementing values-based education in schools

In practice, being a values-based school means establishing not just good relationships between staff, pupils and parents, but between themselves. A values-based school is one where the values are lived on a daily basis and this is shown in a culture that is open, honest and harmonious. As adults, we need to be the role models for the pupils in our care and, if staff show and demonstrate the values to each other, this strong message will be transmitted to the pupils. Establishing these relationships and showing with others that you trust and care for them are what we want our pupils to practise at school and at home.

To become a values-based school, there are certain elements that go hand in hand with its philosophies. A values-based school is defined by Dr Neil Hawkes as:

1. The over-arching focus on the holistic betterment of pupil achievement, defined in terms of:
   - academic development;
   - affective development;
   - moral development; and
   - spiritual development.
2. The quality of its teaching and learning practices.
3. The attitudes and practices of its staff.
4. The values-based curriculum, both explicit and embedded.
5. The physical, aesthetic and communal environment.
6. The involvement and support of parents and the community.

To satisfy the above credentials, here are a set of key indicators as defined by Hawkes (2007), which put values into practice in a school setting:

- The agreement to underpin all work with positive human values.
- Values-based education is considered an explicit element in the curriculum.
- The individual teacher is valued and all staff and pupils are shown care and respect.
- Staff morale is high as there is an emphasis on the caring for self and others. There is a constant striving to raise and maintain self-esteem for all members of the school setting.
- All staff have agreed to model the values, and a high level of consistency exists in adult behaviour.
- There is a focus on creating and maintaining positive relationships.
- Values-based education is seen as an integral part of school assemblies.
- Values underpin the ethos of the school and the climate is happy, calm and purposeful, and one that promotes quality teaching and learning.
- Space is given for silence and reflection. The school setting teaches reflection as a key approach to thinking and learning, and through this pupils develop the confidence to challenge, question and consider.
- There is an emphasis on developing pupils' self-esteem and ability to make decisions and to reflect on their feelings and emotions. Pupils are self-confident and know how to behave appropriately in different situations and scenarios.
- The focus for the curriculum is on the formation of caring, civil and well-educated people.
- The physical, aesthetic and communal school environment reflects the school's values.

- The school communicates the values to the parents and the wider community. The school works with and in the community.
- Values are an integral part of all school activities, including break times and extracurricular activities.
- Values are reflected in the schools aims, mission and vision statements.
- Values are explicit in the school's development/improvement plan.
- There is a focus on nurturing and developing pupils' emotional intelligence (e.g. through nurture groups, play therapy, massage, etc.).
- The core values are linked to other worthwhile programmes such as SEAL and Philosophy for Children.
- Governors are fully involved in developing the school from a values perspective.
- Pupils are able to articulate their thoughts using a values-based vocabulary.
- Everyone in the school setting recognises and takes responsibility for self-improvement and high levels of achievement.
- There is a culture of self-evaluation for the values scheme and its review and impact.

Values-based education quality mark

Schools have the opportunity to work towards a 'values-based education quality mark'. This mark is achieved following a successful validation of a school's commitment to values-based education and is signified by the school being allowed to show its unique values-based education logo in its publicity material, marketing and school badges. The benefits of achieving the quality mark are:

- to acknowledge and celebrate being a values-based school or setting;
- to recognise the school's commitment to high aspirations and to its culture of continuous improvement;
- to value the hard work that all staff engage in on a daily basis;
- to provide recognition of success to parents and the local community; and
- to contribute to a school's self-evaluation process.

Every stakeholder needs to recognise and reflect the philosophy of values-based education if it is to be effective. This includes:

- the head teacher;
- all of the teaching staff;
- non-teaching staff;
- pupils;
- governors;
- parents;
- visitors; and
- the values coordinator.

The evidence needed to provide the backdrop to a successful validation for the values quality mark includes:

- displays;
- photographs;
- children's work;
- school self-evaluation;
- inspection and other monitoring reports;
- school development/improvement plan;
- senior leadership minutes meetings;
- values policy or statement;
- sample annual report to parents;
- school prospectus;
- details or reports of values-based events;
- examples of newsletters;
- governor body meeting minutes;
- evidence of family learning activities;
- parent questionnaire responses;
- home–school partnership agreement;
- discussion with staff, pupils and parents; and
- DVDs of school events/assemblies.

The application process

- Contact Dr Neil Hawkes at Neil.Hawkes@btinernet.com.
- Complete a self-assessment.
- Arrange school validation visit.
- Await confirmation of award.
- Celebrate the award.
- Review the award annually.
- Renewal of application process every 3 years.

The work carried out by both Hawkes (2009) and Lovat et al. (2009) influenced the thinking behind the creation of the Family Values Scheme. The desire to respond to a breakdown in society in which core values such as trust, honesty and respect have been lacking and the desire to create a vision for a world that is not only caring, but one where individuals value each other, has been at the heart of the drive for the creation of the scheme. The scheme mirrors the philosophy of values-based education in that the role of the adult is a crucial factor in its success. How an individual adult behaves determines how others around that person interact and communicate with others.

These ambitions should be reflected within the family unit as the scheme encourages family members to use appropriate values to create positive relationships with one other through a series of fun-related and interactive activities.

Therefore, good behaviour is modelled by the adults within the family and this behaviour is learnt by younger members thereby creating a positive cycle which has clear benefits for everyone!

The research of both Hawkes (2007) and Lovat et al. (2009) clearly identifies the benefits gained by placing values at the heart not just within the school setting, but also within individual members participating in the scheme. They argue that the '*explicit teaching of values provides a common ethical language for talking about interpersonal relationships*', and this common language is vital if families are to make a valid contribution to society. As their research indicates, the emphasis placed on using values as a part of everyday language is not to be underestimated. The Family Values Scheme builds on the pioneering philosophy and development of the values-related goals of Hawkes to bridge the gap between the school and the home.

Summary

In this chapter, we have begun our journey towards an outline of the Family Values Scheme by first considering the concepts behind values-based education and then tracing the key pioneering work of both Hawkes and Lovat in this emergent field. We will now develop some of these ideas further in the next chapter as we begin to outline the detail of our own Family Values Scheme.

Chapter 6

How the Family Values Scheme works

Key principles

The preceding chapters of this book have discussed the meaning of values and the relevance of values not only in society, but also in educational settings. In this chapter, we take values one step further by explaining how values can be used to bridge the gap between home and school in order to form effective partnerships.

The development of the Family Values Scheme began in 2009 after a realisation that values-based education had made an impressive contribution to creating a positive learning culture at Coed Eva Primary School in south Wales. The idea of the scheme was quite simply to use the values that were practised within the school environment to help form effective partnerships with its parents and carers. The possibility of creating a scheme to enable this to happen was an exciting prospect, but we had to be certain our ideas were well researched and evidence-based if it was to be sustainable. Therefore, we will now divide our account across the next two chapters on the FVS to provide the relevant background information. The first part is included in this chapter, which describes the key principles and explains how the scheme is underpinned by theoretic principles and practices. This is followed in the next chapter by a description of how the FVS operates in practice on a daily basis in an educational setting.

About the Family Values Scheme

As explained in the introduction, the scheme was created and devised specifically to use values to formulate effective partnerships between home and school, and also to enable families to use values to celebrate family life by spending some quality time together. The scheme is highly successful in creating partnerships in a fun and active way, and is based on the philosophy of values-based education as previously explained in Chapter 5. It is through these approaches that the Family Values Scheme is founded. The values themselves permeate the scheme and make it an effective tool for any school or organisation to use. Schools that are not values-based should also find the scheme just as productive to use in their own setting. Research (see Chapters 2 and 3) has shown that healthy families spend quality time together, listen to one another, provide encouragement and

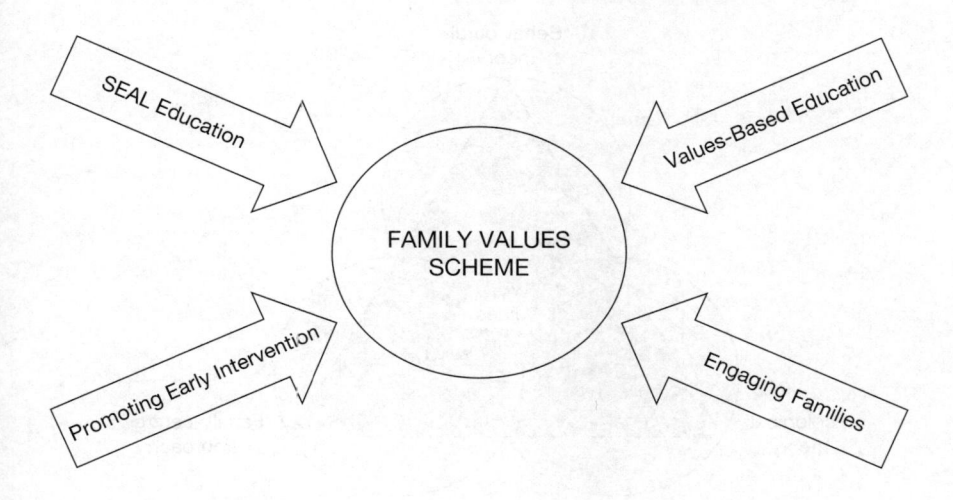

Figure 6.1 The family values approach.

[Diagram: Four arrows labeled "SEAL Education", "Values-Based Education", "Promoting Early Intervention", and "Engaging Families" pointing toward a central circle labeled "FAMILY VALUES SCHEME"]

love, share chores and decisions, and plan ahead. The Family Values Scheme is designed to promote these ideals, as Figure 6.1 illustrates.

Theoretical model partnerships

The Family Values Scheme is based on sound theoretical principles and models of effective partnerships. It was created to support schools and organisations in engaging families in a fun and interactive way but with maximum benefits.

Family values theoretical concepts

The Family Values Scheme is based on four theoretical concepts, as illustrated in Figure 6.2:

1. ecological theory;
2. behavioural theory;
3. family-centred approach; and
4. values.

Together, these four concepts formulate a partnership-centred approach. The Family Values Scheme believes that, by focusing more on a partnership concept, schools and families will achieve an equilibrium approach, one in which the family, school and organisation feel valued and recognised.

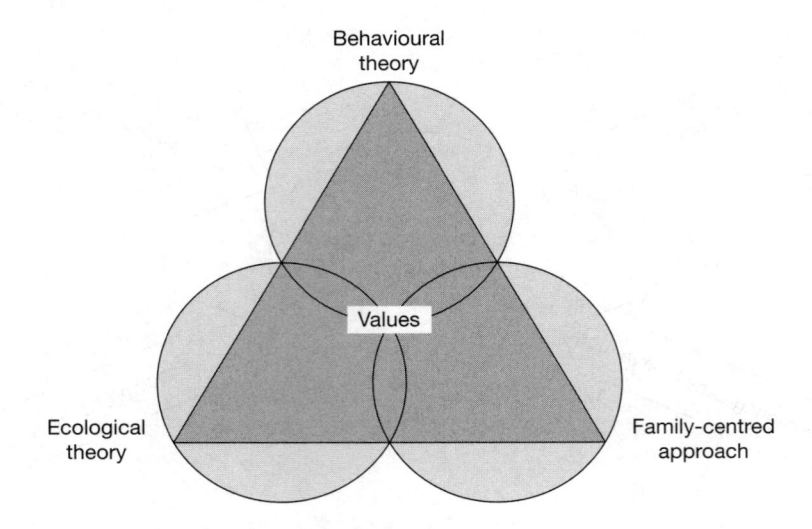

Figure 6.2 The family values approach model.

The ecological theory

The ecological theory is concerned with the multiple interdependable, inseparable systems or environments and contexts that surround children's development and education. This approach is well explained in Bronfenbrenner's (1979) *Ecological Theory of Development*. In that book, he identified that the environment surrounding children had major influences upon their development. He categorised his theory into five different environmental systems:

1. *Microsystem*: This refers to the immediate surroundings of the individual. This includes the child's family, peers, school and local community. The interaction between these parties enables children to engage fully with those around them, which allows them to be an integral part of their immediate environment.
2. *Mesosystem*: This environment is based on the relationship between the different microsystems (i.e. the immediate surroundings). The experiences that children receive may not always be positive, and this can have a detrimental effect on their development.
3. *Exosystem*: The level of involvement of parents/carers into the family home can be affected by external factors such as a break in the regular routines of family life (e.g. a parent commuting long distances to work, which in turn will have an effect on the level of interaction with the child).
4. *Macrosystem*: This is the setting in which members of the family live. The cultural context of the family would be an influencing factor, which would include their socio-economic status, including levels of poverty and ethnicity.

5   *Chronosystem*: The fifth environment is based on events over time as an influencing factor, such as transitions in the family unit. This could be a divorce, a death of a parent or moving the family home.

The key input taken from this theory is the importance of the mesosystem, the interaction of two most important microsystems in education (i.e. the link between the family home and schools and organisations).

The behavioural theory

The second important theoretical concept for the Family Values Scheme to consider was based upon behavioural theory, which focuses on the importance of learning as a contribution towards influencing the interaction between families, schools and organisations. The learner who is exposed to positive role modelling in the home and school environment will adopt these learned behaviours themselves. In practice, pupils in a values-based education setting will experience this from their own peers and staff in the school. This practice will then be transferred to the home.

The family-centred approach

Studies show that families spending quality time together can positively improve a child's learning by up to 60 per cent. To reiterate, it is the things that families actually do together that achieves the best environment for learning. This process is described by Sheridan and Kratochwill (2007) as the 'curriculum of the home'. This means that parents who are actively involved in their child's development are a major contributor in creating a positive learning environment. It is important that this is supported by interaction and continuity (i.e. 'closing the gap' between home, school and organisation). The integration of values and beliefs as a way of narrowing this gap is one that may have the greatest influence on a learner's achievement.

Values

The fourth theoretical concept on which the Family Values Scheme is based is the intrinsic way that values are integrated throughout the scheme. The work carried out by Professor Terry Lovat and his colleagues at Newcastle University, Australia, who have been monitoring and researching the effects of the Australian Government's Values Education Initiative, is important here. The university published its final report for the Australian Government, which looked at the evidence concerning the impact of introducing and developing values-based education in schools (Lovat *et al.*, 2009). Their research describes how values-based schools give increasing curriculum and teaching emphasis to values-based education. As a consequence, pupils become more academically diligent, the school assumes a calmer, more peaceful ambience, better pupil–teacher relationships are forged, pupil and teacher well-being improves, and parents are more engaged with the school.

The explicit teaching of values to children also provides a common ethical language for talking about interpersonal behaviour. In turn, this provides a mechanism for self-regulated behaviour. An important outcome is a more settled school that enhances quality teaching and enables teachers to raise expectations for pupil performance.

Links to SEAL

The Family Values Scheme enhances SEAL (social and emotional aspects of learning), with monthly and termly values being supported by the SEAL themes, as illustrated in Figure 6.3.

	Autumn	**Spring**	**Summer**
VALUES	Freedom Peace Co-operation Tolerance Responsibility Hope Honesty Friendship	Quality Simplicity Thoughtfulness Appreciation Humility Patience Happiness Trust	Caring Unity Courage Love Respect Understanding
SEAL	New beginnings Getting on and falling out (say no to bullying)	Going for goals Good to be me	Relationships Changes

Figure 6.3 Family Values Scheme and SEAL.

Aims of the scheme

By utilising the Family Values Scheme, teachers and their schools can significantly improve their relationships and communication with parents and carers, raise attendance, reduce bullying and help to nip potential or actual behavioural problems manifested by their pupils, either in the early or later stages, with the full knowledge, participation and cooperation of their parents. In order for effective partnerships to be established, the scheme aims for individual families and schools to:

- raise standards in the basic skills of reading and writing;
- strengthen relationships and increase interaction between the family, school and local community;
- use appropriate 'values' to inculcate appropriate standards as an intrinsic way of life both at home and at school;
- improve behaviour and attendance;
- complement and enhance existing personal and social education (PSE) and parental programmes (i.e. by using SEAL); and
- raise self-esteem.

We will now look at some of the key areas addressed throughout the Family Values Scheme:

- traditional family values;
- family learning; and
- understanding behaviour.

Traditional family values

Relationships

The Family Values Scheme is designed to enhance the effectiveness of key relationships between and among family members. Good, caring relationships are a key ingredient within the family unit as they encompass such skills as the ability to listen, communicate, recognise and respond to the needs and feelings of others, as well as helping to understand children's behaviour (Barlow, 1998).

This two-way communication is described by the Solihull Approach (Douglas, 2004) as reciprocity – '*the process whereby the parent is sensitive to the needs and feelings of the child and the child responds to the parent, in a two-way flow of communication.*' The term reciprocity was developed by Brazelton *et al.* (1974). It is the foundation for all present and future relationships and the development of language and communication, sleep, eating and drinking, as well as the ability to understand and manage one's own feelings and behaviour. The Family Values Scheme addresses these principles by encouraging families to:

- help their children to understand and deal with their feelings and emotions;
- problem-solve situations;
- understand the importance of active listening;
- positively reinforce good behaviour;
- negotiate differences;
- promote responsibility; and
- interact with their children.

Parents who work full-time spend just 19 minutes every day 'caring for [their] own children'. A further 16 minutes is spent looking after their children as a 'secondary activity', but this means that they are doing something else – such as the weekly supermarket shop – at the same time.

(Office for National Statistics, 2006)

Communication

Good communication is vital in helping family members to express their needs, feelings, concerns, love and appreciation for one another. This is why there are two main areas within the Family Values Scheme that are dedicated to effective communication; these are family gatherings and family essentials. A lack of communication skills can cause problems within the family and, in some cases, lead to behavioural difficulties in children, conflict, lack of intimacy and weak emotional bonding (Bray and Hetherington, 1993).

Therefore, in order to help with a child's physical, cognitive, social and emotional development, it is recommended that the parent and child start the communication process as soon as the child is born, if not before. Part of this process is also the parent's ability to listen and respond appropriately to the child's verbal and non-verbal cues. The parent's ability to listen, show interest, respond, demonstrate turn-taking and show patience all contribute to the development of the child.

Effective communication can take many forms (e.g. for young babies, using a 'sing-song' approach helps to stimulate the development of the brain). Below are some suggestions on effective communication and listening skills:

- Show interest by maintaining eye contact, giving the child full attention and ignoring any potential distractions.
- Be observant and listen to the non-verbal cues that the child gives you (e.g. facial expressions, change in tone, posture and patterns in behaviour), and then respond accordingly.
- Help children to start a conversation by asking about their day, and give them plenty of time to find the words to express how they are feeling. Do not put them under pressure, and respond as if you have all the time in the world.

- Use open-ended questions to encourage the child to respond and interact (e.g. ask him or her to describe and/or explain his or her thoughts, ideas, experiences, etc.).
- Help the child to bring a conversation to an end in a positive way. Look for signs that he or she is starting to disengage (e.g. a lack of eye contact).

Family meals

> *Family meals may be a useful mechanism for enhancing family togetherness, and for role modeling behaviors that parents would like their children to emulate.*
>
> (Fulkerson *et al.*, 2006)

Sitting down and having family meals not only bonds the family, but also promotes communication and creates a sense of belonging. The whole process allows the parent(s) to reconnect with their child/children and provides an excellent opportunity to find out about each other's day and help guide towards positive decision-making. The Family Essentials section of the scheme promotes these types of activities. Research has shown that, when parents take an active interest in their child's education, they achieve higher results. This is down to the opportunity given to children to talk about their day to their parent(s) and, as a consequence, they feel listened to and valued, which leads to fewer behavioural problems.

The whole process allows the parent(s) to model the desired behaviour while promoting good eating habits, nutrition, social skills, manners, interaction and problem-solving skills. Studies have shown that children who engage in family mealtimes are less likely to engage in habits such as tobacco, alcohol and other drugs (Meiselman, 2000).

Family mealtimes can generate many conversations on a variety of subjects. Below are a few suggestions:

- Think of something that made you smile today.
- Plan the forthcoming weekend, including food, fun activities, household tasks, etc.
- Talk about your child's favourite book.
- Discuss a recent film watched by the family.
- Ask what your child is currently learning about in school.
- Try to discuss foods from other cultures.

Scheduling a family walk after food allows the parent(s) to model the importance of exercise and togetherness and helps to improve communication within the family unit. Research carried out by the American College of Sports Science (2011) has shown that children who have been involved in exercise at an early age are more likely to continue into adulthood.

Family learning

> *Where child learning becomes family learning, and where educators understand that they cannot meet the needs of children and young people alone, true engagement and shared understanding are developed.*
>
> (National College for School Leadership, 2010)

Families are our first and most important teachers. Therefore, family learning in the home is just as important as the child's learning in school. This type of learning can take many forms, as not all families are the same and each have different learning interests and styles. Hence, within the Family Values Scheme, there are a variety of suggested activities to suit all different types of families. Family learning should therefore be based on positive caring relationships and good verbal and non-verbal communication. Potential academic outcomes should be secondary. Childhood is a time to experience and share through taking part in family-led activities such as learning through visiting a museum, Internet surfing, reading or tending to the garden.

Play and interaction

Throughout the Family Values Scheme, there are opportunities for members of the family to engage through play and fun activities, as emotional, physical and cognitive skills are developed through play, as well as through healthy brain development (Shonkoff and Phillips, 2000). Engaging in play enables children to discover more about themselves and the world. Play provides opportunities for children to learn through imitation, imagination and fun, and to learn about experiencing the consequences of their actions.

Play also has an effect on children's stress levels. Stress chemicals are lowered in the body when playing, which enables the child to deal with exciting or challenging situations more successfully by playing imaginatively and creatively. Gentle rough-and-tumble play and laughter are also known to have anti-stress effects, as this form of play activates the brain's emotion-regulating centres and causes the release of opioids, the natural brain chemicals that induce feelings of pleasure and well-being (Sunderland, 2006). Evidence has shown that children who engage in cooperative games (non-competitive games) are less likely to engage in aggressive behaviour (see Heck *et al.*, 2001).

Resolving conflict and building resilience are two important skills for children to learn and experience, as it enables them to successfully deal with future challenges. These can be learnt through unstructured play, as this is when children learn to develop their social skills, self-awareness, self-regulation and empathy in a 'real' context.

The basic skills

The Family Values Scheme aims to improve the basic skills of reading, writing and numeracy through its four elements: Family Gathering, Family Essentials, Family Activities and Family Reflections. In the Family Essentials part of the pack, there are lots of activities that reinforce the basics of everyday family life, including the basic skills of reading, writing and numeracy. The scheme supports the learning of the basic skills of reading, writing and numeracy through a range of related activities.

Reading

Supporting children at home with their reading is one of the best ways that parents can help their child. Schools and organisations support children with their reading at home through their home–school links policy. The scheme does not look to replace this support but seeks to enhance existing good practice, which is already available to the family.

Some of the benefits of reading are as follows:

- creates a bond between parent and child;
- helps to build a child's vocabulary and develop pronunciation;
- encourages the family to learn new things;
- improves communication skills;
- helps a child to acquire a greater knowledge;
- develops hand–eye coordination and motor skills; and
- improves ability and understanding of following a story from beginning to end.

FAMILY READING TIME

Families need to be encouraged to dedicate some quality reading time during the week or at the weekends. Creating the correct environment is essential if reading is going to be enjoyed by all the family.

READING ENVIRONMENT

Once a family reading session is planned, the following ideas can be just the thing for a comfortable, relaxing reading session:

- Get the whole family involved, including grandparents and younger brothers and sisters.
- Families can read together, in pairs or individually.
- Have a family DEAR (drop everything and read) time.

- Have a dictionary and simple thesaurus readily available for the reading time, and a picture dictionary for younger readers, to check the meaning of tricky words.
- Make visiting your local library a regular family essential.
- Reading is any material that stimulates or interests the reader; this can be jokes, riddles, poetry, facts, fiction or even plays.

Family reading strategies can be given to families to help them support their child with reading at home.

Writing

WRITING STRATEGIES

There are lots of opportunities in the Family Values Scheme packs that encourage writing. Here are some simple ways to encourage writing in the home through the scheme:

- Young children need to be encouraged to make marks, as this is the early stage of writing.
- Support younger children by writing a sentence and asking them to copy the words.
- Encourage children to keep a writing journal to write down daily events or record their moods.
- Contribute to writing the family and personal goal.
- Contribute to completing the 'stop, think and reflect' (STAR) evaluation at the end of the month.
- Create opportunities for writing from any of the activities (e.g. after a family walk or writing recipes).
- Create experiences that stimulate and encourage creative writing.

Developing confidence in number

Encouraging children to be confident in number work will make them confident in the basics (i.e. addition, subtraction, multiplication and division). Building number into day-to-day family living will reinforce mathematical concepts taught at school and will raise confidence and improve self-esteem.

Here are some ways we can support this in the home:

- Regularly measure heights of younger members of the family to see how much they have grown.
- Measure the height and record the progress of any Family Values Scheme activities that need to be grown (e.g. plants).
- Use a visit to the shops to practice the concept of money (e.g. weighing fruit and vegetables, budgeting for pocket money).

Understanding behaviour

As previously mentioned, the Family Values Scheme is an effective tool to help families manage their children's behaviour through positive interaction and by spending quality time together. Children display difficult behaviour (e.g. temper tantrums) as part of their developmental process, although some children can display more severe behavioural issues, which can impact on their ability to learn and develop (Richardson and Joughin, 2002). The most commonly reported reason for children's difficulties with social relationships and learning, according to Bone and Meltzer (1989), stems from behavioural difficulties. It is no surprise that, when families are experiencing behavioural difficulties at home, these become issues within the classroom.

According to Farrington (1995), the style of parenting is one of the major contributing factors to a child's behavioural problems. Types of parenting contributing to this include strict discipline, inconsistent practices, lack of supervision, persistent criticism, lack of involvement and low incidence of caring and love (Patterson *et al.*, 1993; Webster-Stratton, 1999).

There are numerous reasons why some families struggle to establish routines and manage behaviour within the home. These include, for example, the way that they were brought up as a child. According to Green *et al.* (2005), some of the possible causes of behavioural problems include the family having four or more children, poverty, having a relationship with mental health issues, especially among parents, and marital disharmony, as well as the family emanating from a low socio-economic background.

The incidence of behavioural difficulties in children not only impacts upon the family, school and community, but also has financial implications. Children displaying conduct disorders are likely to cost ten times more than children with no problems. In the UK, it has been estimated that these costs may reach £70,019 between the ages of 10 and 28 (Scott *et al.*, 2001). A Canadian study by Jenkins and Keating (1998) found that 50 per cent of children who experienced four or more of the following risks would significantly increase their incidence of behavioural problems:

- learning disability;
- low-income environment;
- parental alcohol abuse;
- large family size;
- having a teenage mother;
- hostility in the parent–child relationship; and/or
- parental divorce.

By contrast, this only applied to 10 per cent of other pupils with behavioral problems who did not manifest these symptoms.

Throughout the Family Values Scheme, consideration is given to the key areas of positive behaviour management, including setting clear age-appropriate rules, routines, boundaries and correctives, and positive reinforcements that are fair, consistent and a logical response to their children's conduct and teach the appropriate values and behaviour. But, more importantly, these encourage the family to understand their child's behaviour and why it is occurring.

Emotional literacy

It is important to help children understand why they have behaved in a certain way. More often than not, children are completely oblivious to why their behaviour is sometimes unacceptable. Engaging children in emotional literacy exercises such as SEAL (social and emotional aspects of learning) can help them to recognise the relationship between their thoughts, feelings and actions when responding to others. Sharp (2001) suggests four reasons why emotional literacy must be promoted in young children:

1. to recognise their emotions in order to identify them;
2. to understand their emotions in order to become effective learners;
3. to be able to handle and manage their emotions in order to sustain positive relationships; and
4. to be able to express their emotions so that they can develop and grow.

Morgan and Ellis (2012) describe emotional literacy as the ability to express feelings using words. The ability to show emotions, to show others how they are feeling, is a basic emotional need of all adults and children. If these emotional needs are not being met, children will express their emotions and feelings by displaying low-level to challenging behaviour. Some children find it hard to talk about their emotions and how they are feeling. If they identify their feelings, they can then be taught the skills to help manage and control those feelings. A good starting point is to ask the child to use 'I' statements:

- I feel sad.
- I feel unimportant.
- I feel hurt.
- I am unhappy.
- I am bored.

By identifying how they are feeling using these 'I' statements, they are becoming aware of their own feelings. Emotional literacy addresses this in balance by first identifying the following:

- the behaviour being displayed;
- the emotion (the way the child feels before, during and after the behaviour has occurred); and

- the skill and strategy needed to show the child how to regulate and motivate through planned activities.

The Solihull Approach (Douglas, 2004) identified three key questions to help parents understand and consequently manage their child's behaviour:

1. What is the exact age and developmental stage of your child? This may include 'What are they trying to do at the moment (e.g. learning to crawl, feeding self, overcoming difficulties getting to sleep, going out with their first girlfriend/boyfriend, etc.)?'.
2. What changes have taken place in your lives recently? Parents need to consider all recent changes, no matter how big or small (e.g. losing a child's favourite cuddly toy, a young person breaking up with their girlfriend/boyfriend).
3. How well can your child communicate his or her needs to you?

Sleep

A good night's sleep not only helps to reduce the incidence of hyperactivity and unwanted behaviour, but it is also necessary for optimal growth and development, as well as helping to set up a good routine for children. Family Essentials encourages bedtime routines. According to Ferber (1985), *'In our society the importance of sleep is vastly underestimated . . . for someone to be happy during the day, functioning . . . and learning efficiently, he or she has to have enough sleep on a regular basis'*.

The Sleep Council (2012) carried out a poll of 250 UK primary school teachers to establish the devastating effects of a lack of sleep among primary school children. The poll found:

> *nine out of 10 teachers (92 per cent) complaining that pupils are so tired they are unable to pay attention in class. More than a third (38 per cent) said lack of sleep among youngsters is a daily problem for them. Nearly nine out of 10 teachers (88 per cent) felt that too many distractions in the bedroom (games machines, TVs etc) were at the root of the sleep related problems along with the fact parents are simply not strict enough about enforcing bedtimes (82 per cent).*
>
> *For two thirds of teachers (65 per cent), the problem is so serious they consider that the long term progress of their pupils can be affected while nearly half (48 per cent) said lack of sleep made children unruly and badly behaved. And more than half (55 per cent) of those questioned agreed that the brightest children in the classroom are the best slept and most wide-awake.*

Bedtime routines create the feeling of a predictable, safe world. The Family Essentials section encourages the parent to create a relaxed, loving and predictable routine for bedtime, helping the child to go to bed feeling happy and safe. If a good sleep routine can be established, the child's behaviour will improve, and it is usually much easier to establish routines around behaviour management in school. Below are some tips to help parents develop a bedtime routine.

Tip 1: relax

It is important that your child is not over-stimulated before bedtime. Make sure that all activities such as homework, football training and computer games are finished at least 1 hour before bedtime to enable your child to have plenty of time to relax and unwind. Do not allow your child to fall asleep in front of the TV, as this could prevent them from having a good night's sleep.

Tip 2: the countdown

It is important to give your child time to finish what they are doing before asking them to get ready for bed. Let them know they have 10 minutes, then 5 minutes, before they need to get ready.

Tip 3: bedtime routine

Implement a good bedtime routine, as this will create a good sleeping habit for your child. At 7.30 p.m. ask your child to put on their pyjamas, brush their teeth, then get into bed and read a story with you. At 8.00 p.m. dim the lights and kiss your child goodnight. Try to keep the same activities as part of the routine every night so that your child knows what to expect.

Tip 4: no excuses

Once your child is in bed, it is important that they stay there. Your child may try to get you to engage with them by asking for a glass of water or some food. Therefore, make sure they are given the opportunity to ask for these before bedtime.

Tip 5: always be positive

Do not create an association between your child's unwanted behaviour and bedtime (e.g. '*If you don't put away your toys, you're going to bed*'). Going to bed and sleeping must be viewed as a positive, and it is important to tell your child why sleep is important. Say something such as '*Going to sleep helps you to grow big and strong so you can have lots of fun and it also helps your brain so you can do all your school work.*'

Summary

In this chapter, we have introduced some of the key principles behind the rationale for how the FVS works, as well as providing an insight into what the scheme is all about, including how it is based on sound theoretical principles. The development of the scheme was intended to bridge the gap between home and school using values as a concept within the scheme's three key guiding principles: helping with traditional families, family learning and understanding your child's behaviour. The key principle underpinning this chapter is how effective relationships can benefit all members of the family by using a traditional values approach. This is developed further in the next chapter, which looks at how the scheme operates in practice.

Chapter 7

How the Family Values Scheme operates in practice

In this chapter, we will now consider some of the practical issues involved in setting up the Family Values Scheme and its day-to-day running. The FVS is based around a set of 22 values. Each month, a different value, such as respect or cooperation, is chosen for endorsement. The 22 values are made up into monthly packs that encourage parents or families to participate in a series of fun tasks and challenges that they plan and carry out together within the flexibility of their own homes. Below is a list of the 22 values.

Freedom	Quality	Caring
Peace	Simplicity	Unity
Cooperation	Thoughtfulness	Courage
Tolerance	Appreciation	Love
Responsibility	Humility	Respect
Hope	Patience	Understanding
Honesty	Happiness	Friendship
		Trust

Figure 7.1 The 22 values.

There are four sections in the monthly values packs, with each section having a different number of points. Families are encouraged to complete all sections of the pack to achieve the maximum benefit. Below are the four different sections. These are described in more detail later in the chapter.

- *Family Gathering*: focus the family on the month ahead.
- *Family Essentials*: motivating the family to participate in everyday tasks.
- *Family Activities*: fun and exciting activities for the family.
- *Family Reflections*: focus the family on what they have achieved.

At the end of the month/half term, the family submits their evidence and are rewarded for their efforts. It is recommended that the Family Values Scheme operates on a monthly or half-termly basis to help families experience, implement and ingrain certain tasks and activities into their routines. The inculcation of good habits is useful, as they help families automatically do things such as getting to school on time, sitting around the table for a family meal and reading before bedtime. Lally *et al.* (2009) estimated that, for a new task to form into a habit, it can take up to 66 days. Aristotle said, 'We are what we repeatedly do. Excellence then, is not an act, but a habit.'

Target audience

The Family Values Scheme is aimed at families of children between the ages of 3 and 14 years as a way of encouraging families to spend more quality time together. It is particularly applicable for parents with young children and those in which the parents and their families may not have a disposition to valuing education highly. It is, however, extremely valuable as a compensatory scheme for those children who have fallen behind with their literacy and numeracy by the time they enter their secondary schooling, more especially for children being educated in deprived and low socio-economic areas.

The scheme works particularly well in universal services such as nurseries, schools, parenting programmes, children and family centres and residential settings, and for families identified at the Common Assessment Framework (CAF) Levels 1–3. Although it is important to understand that, for families who have complex needs such as for those families who have been identified on the CAF Level 4, where there are identifiable needs with statutory action and support needed to protect the child from, for example, drug and alcohol related issues, domestic violence problems and/or significant mental health problems, the Family Values Scheme may need to be supported by multi-agency involvement.

The scheme can be rolled out throughout the school/organisation or used solely with targeted groups, such as:

- specific school year groups (e.g. nursery/reception);
- identified families (e.g. to help improve school attendance);
- identified children (e.g. have an individual behaviour plan, or IBP); and
- support groups (e.g. adult learning).

Barriers to learning

Although the Family Values Scheme is designed to be easily accessible, flexible and fun, it is wise to remember that some family members may themselves have barriers to learning that may or may not be overtly apparent. These might include:

- impaired sight;
- impaired hearing;
- dyslexia;
- an inability to read and/or write;
- no confidence or interest;
- lack of time;
- problems with childcare;
- no transportation;
- work commitments; and/or
- lack of information about opportunities to learn.

These difficulties could therefore prove a barrier and restrict the family from taking part. In order to ensure appropriate participation in the scheme, it may sometimes be necessary to find ways to enhance parents' opportunities of enrolling and, when possible, of decreasing the barriers. Family members with a disability are normally pleased to discuss their needs, as well as to consider how schools can offer help and support.

For family members where English is not the first language, the tasks in the packs can be translated either professionally or through software packages. Identifying a family member who would be available to communicate with families in their first language, either face to face or by telephone, is a great resource.

Below are a few suggestions to help overcome the language barrier:

- Ask a member of the family who has good enough literacy skills to champion the scheme at home.
- Voice record on to a CD the tasks from the Family Values Scheme pack.
- Hold weekly evening and daytime Family Values Scheme sessions where the family can complete set tasks with the support of a member of staff.
- Use Google Translate, an online software, to help translate the packs.
- Provide childcare.

The Family Values Scheme champion

To successfully implement the scheme within schools/organisations, it is recommended that a champion is identified who attends a day's training programme that will provide essential information to help support and guide the implementation, as well as to ensure the success of the scheme. Course availability can be found by contacting info@behaviourstop.co.uk. Champions can be chosen from a variety of professional groups. These can include:

- education practitioners: head teachers, teachers, teaching assistants, pastoral support staff, learning mentors, family liaison officers, children centre workers; and
- health practitioners: school nurses, play therapists, health visitors, social workers.

Family Values Scheme evaluation

Families participating in the scheme will progress at different rates according to a number of factors:

- time and availability to participate in the scheme;
- the age and developmental stage of their child/children;
- the family's level of needs and intervention; and
- the child's level of needs and intervention.

Before implementing the scheme, establish a baseline from which the progress of the family can be assessed at different intervals through:

- a STAR evaluation form;
- questionnaires to parents/carers, staff and pupils;
- semi-structured interviews;
- literacy and numeracy data;
- behaviour and exclusion data;
- attendance data; and
- parent involvement within the school/organisation.

Launching the Family Values Scheme

There are many ways to launch the Family Values Scheme in schools/ organisations. Below are a few suggestions.

Whole school

1   The scheme can be launched as a whole-school approach to engage all families. This can be achieved by either holding a launch day within the school or by holding a Family Values Scheme presentation for families, informing them of the benefits of the scheme and how it works. Families can then join their child in class and take part in a Family Values Scheme activity. At the end of the activity, the families take the Family Values Scheme pack away to complete at home.

2   A letter with a request slip can be sent out to all parents requesting a pack and instructions.
3   Families can be invited to a presentation evening.

School year group

1   The scheme can be launched by identifying one, two or three year groups within the school. Families can be invited into class to be informed about the Family Values Scheme and take part in an activity with their child based on the monthly value. At the end of the activity, the families take a Family Values Scheme pack away to complete at home.
2   A letter with a request slip can be sent out to all parents requesting a pack and instructions.
3   Families can be invited to a presentation evening.

Identified children

The scheme can be used to help support children with problems such as behaviour, non-attendance, literacy and numeracy, self-esteem, transition, divorce, bereavement, etc. The scheme can also work alongside the child's individual learning plan (ILP) or individual behaviour plan (IBP).

An ILP is used when a pupil displays behaviour that causes some concern although the severity or the frequency of the conduct is not too great. The pupil's learning and behaviour targets can be incorporated on an ILP. Pupils whose behaviour is difficult to manage in school for a sustained period of time, despite the implementation of the ILP, or where a pupil's misbehaviour becomes more frequent, challenging and/or severe, will usually need to progress on to an IBP. The IBP is designed to record the strategies used to help the pupil to progress and it will set out the targets that the individual should be working towards. It provides more detailed planning and a greater level of differentiation than the ILP.

Identified families

The scheme can be used to help and support families implement positive behaviour management strategies within the home (e.g. setting routines), as well as helping to improve the adult-child relationship by spending quality time together. The scheme can also work alongside parenting groups, as well as multi-agency interventions.

Parenting programmes

The scheme can work alongside parenting programmes to help strengthen, support and reinforce the skills acquired by parents. On completion of the

To Mum and Dad

Will you come into school on Wednesday 25th May at 2.00pm and take part in an art and craft activity with me?

It will be lots of fun and I would really love you to be there. The activity is part of the Family Value Scheme, which is full of exciting activities we can do as a family, especially over half term. My teacher will tell you a little bit about the Family Values Scheme before we start the activity.

Lots of Love

Tim

High Street Primary School

Family Values Scheme

I will/will not be able to attend the Family Values Scheme activity on Wednesday 25th May at 2.30pm.

Child's name:_____

Parent(s)/carer(s) name(s): _____

Parent(s)/carer(s) signature(s): _____

Figure 7.2 Sample letter to invite families to the launch of the Family Values Scheme.

parenting programme, parents can continue using the Family Values Scheme as a long-term, flexible intervention to ensure the sustainability of good parenting skills.

Attendance and participation

In order to ensure good attendance and participation in the scheme, there are a few factors to take into account.

Timings

To ensure a good turnout, it is advisable to hold the launch time either 1 hour after the start of the school day or 1 hour before the end of the school day and/or evenings and weekends to help accommodate families' work schedules and other commitments.

Start date and end date

It is recommended that the Family Values Scheme packs are distributed on a monthly/half-termly basis to enable the families to focus on the values, as well as implement and ingrain certain tasks and activities into their routines. Families can then submit their completed packs at the end of the month/half term ready for the Family Values Scheme assembly.

Inviting families

There are a number of ways to invite families to join the Family Values Scheme and also to come along to the Family Values Scheme launch. Here are a few suggestions:

- Ask the children to personally invite a member of their family by writing a letter or designing an invitation (see Figure 7.2).
- Display posters around the school/organisation.
- Include information in newsletters and letters (see Figure 7.3).
- Announce information during assemblies.
- Include information in school brochures.
- Inform families during other scheduled activities (e.g. sports day).

Communication

It is important to ensure ongoing participation of families taking part in the scheme so that they can experience the full benefits. Here are a few suggestions on how to achieve this:

How the FVS operates in practice 91

- mega challenge;
- regular communication;
- Family Values Scheme assembly;
- trophy for the family of the month;
- social networking sites;
- text messaging service;
- school/organisation website; and
- email.

Family Values Scheme

Why not join us in MARCH?

Create some family time together by completing our monthly tasks and challenges, and have great FUN at the same time.

If you would like to join us for MARCH then please complete the slip below and return to school by Monday 1st March. New log files will be given out on Monday, which will tell you all you need to know for next month's exciting activities!

Each task and challenge achieves values points!

    Go for Bronze = 500 points

    Go for Silver = 1000 points

    Go for Gold = 1500 points

FAMILY VALUES SCHEME

We wish to take part/do not wish to take part in the Family Values Scheme this term.

My children's names are:_____

Class:_____

Parent(s)/carer(s) name(s):_____

Signed parent/carer: _____

Our email address is:_____

Figure 7.3 Sample letter to promote the Family Values Scheme.

Providing evidence

There are three ways a family can provide evidence that they have participated in the Family Values Scheme.

Log file

Evidence is gathered by the family during the month and placed in a log file. This can be a lever arch file or a simple scrapbook. There are several ways that families can gather their evidence. These might include:

- photographs of the event or activity;
- video clips;
- written evidence;
- by presenting participatory outcomes on the activity (e.g. through a painting or by making a friendship bracelet – whichever chosen outcome fits the theme best); and
- writing a book review.

At the end of each month, the parents or families are given a date to hand in their log files and/or the STAR evaluation sheets so that each family can be given their award for their efforts and achievements. The log files need to show evidence of the activities that they have completed. The log files can either be returned to the individual family or retained in school for display or self-evaluation purposes.

Submitting the Family Values Scheme pack

Families can tick the activities they have completed in the Family Values Scheme pack and submit, ensuring the child's full name is written on the pack.

STAR evaluation

Families can choose to complete the STAR sheets to evaluate how they have reinforced the value of the month and how they have achieved their individual and family goal. When we stop, think and reflect, we learn something about ourselves (see Figure 7.4).

Rewarding families

Celebrating families' achievements not only reinforces the scheme, but also raises their self-esteem and motivation. These achievements are celebrated and shared with the rest of the school/organisation. These celebrations and awards can involve a variety of prizes, which might range from stickers, rosettes or certificates,

STAR Family Evaluation
Stop, Think and Reflect

When you have completed the month's activities please self-evaluate and hand in the STAR family-evaluation form to your Family Values Scheme Co-ordinator.

Family name: ....

Registered email address:..

What did your family learn about this month's value?......................................
....
....
....

What was your family's favourite activity and why? ....
....
....

What activity did your family least like and why? ....
....
....

How has this month's value benefited your family? ....
....
....
....

Have you noticed any changes in your family since taking part in Family Values?............
....
....
....
....

Thank you for completing the STAR self-evaluation

Figure 7.4 An example of the STAR evaluation form.

to participation in a Family Values Assembly, or, for a lucky few, by winning a Family Values Cup.

There are two ways to reward and encourage family members to complete their tasks.

1. *Certificate of participation*: A certificate is awarded to a family who has completed one or more tasks from the pack.
2. *Point system*: Each task can have a set number of points and three levels of award:

   - bronze award: 500 points;
   - silver award: 1000 points; and
   - gold award: 1500 points.

Each family decides together at the beginning of the month what level of award they wish to achieve. This is entirely up to the family and is agreed upon by everyone. For example, if a family is particularly busy one month, they can choose a lower level of award or, if they really feel strongly about the value, and feel that it is one that they need to reinforce within their family, they can choose a higher level of award.

At the end of the month, the family total up the number of points they have achieved, and they are awarded with either a bronze, silver or gold certificate/rosette/badge.

Family Values Asssembly

Families are invited into an assembly to receive their end-of-month/half-termly award. The assembly can reinforce the value through song, prayer and/or story, as well as a 'show and tell' of children's work. Rewards such as rosettes, certificates or badges are given to each family, a different colour for each award level.

Family Values Cup

Each month/half term, a family who has worked the hardest to achieve their goal is nominated for the Family Values Cup. This is not necessarily the family who has achieved the gold award. The cup is presented during the Family Values Assembly, with the winning family holding the cup for a month. This achievement is then displayed on a 'Family Values Roll of Honour' chart, showing which family has won month by month.

The Family Values Scheme packs

The Family Values Scheme packs are divided into four sections to ensure families experience and take part in a variety of activities to promote interaction, problem-solving, communication, relationship and goal setting. The sections are:

- *Family Gathering:* focus the family on the month ahead.
- *Family Essentials:* motivate the family to participate in everyday tasks.
- *Family Activities:* fun and exciting activities for the family.
- *Family Reflections:* focus the family on what they have achieved.

Family Gathering

The Family Gathering section is the first part of each monthly pack and gives a step-by-step guide on how to start the tasks. The main aim of this section is for the family to begin the month by deciding on their family and personal goals and how to achieve them.

About the value

All the activities reinforce the selected monthly value, and every pack explains in detail to the family exactly what the value is and what it means, such as for the value of courage.

What is courage?

> *To have courage to try something which is different and that you are not familiar with is a real challenge in itself. Courage is not something that you are born with as it comes from within but it is very easy to care for. All you need to do is give it daily attention and it will grow big and strong! Having courage is persevering when things maybe don't turn out as they should or it could be having the confidence to stand up to someone or something you believe in.*
>
> (Ellis and Morgan, 2009)

Family goals

Setting goals as a family brings everyone together, enabling the family to keep their values, focus and motivation rather than getting sidetracked. The process is a collaborative one that encourages the family to discuss what they would like to achieve and to work together as a team by offering encouragement and support to achieve the goals.

Many parents, when asked, would like to spend more time with their family, but everyday obstacles such as work commitments and the day-to day running of the family home sometimes prevents this from happening. Setting goals to spend more time with the family must be planned out with a conscious effort towards that outcome. By planning an activity and completing it, one not only achieves the goal of more family time, but also of participating in something fun. Below are some examples of family goals:

- go for a family walk;
- have a family meal once a week;
- plan a holiday;
- organise a monthly family fun night; and
- grow a vegetable patch.

Personal goals

Learning to set personal goals is an important life skill that helps us to focus and achieve at school, work and home. Setting realistic goals that challenge us but are also attainable helps to improve our concentration, self-esteem and motivation, as well as helping us to overcome everyday challenges. Below are some examples of personal goals:

- learn to ride my bike;
- read my book every night;
- arrive at school on time; and
- spend more time with granddad.

> *To begin with the end in mind means to start with a clear understanding of your destination. It means to know where you're going so that you better understand where you are now so that the steps you take are always in the right direction.*
>
> (Covey *et al.*, 1994)

To kick-start the month, the family hold a meeting with as many family members as possible. This can include parents, carers, grandparents, extended family, aunts and uncles. They choose someone to chair the meeting and set a time and a date for the meeting to take place. Below are examples of discussion activities, which take place before the family start the tasks.

Family Gathering: the value of courage

Read together the 'What is courage?' section on the front page of the pack and discuss what this value means to you as a family. Using a large sheet of paper, write the word 'simplicity' in the centre and write down everyone's responses. Pair together any answers that are related to each other. Use a dictionary if necessary to make sure that everyone understands what the terms mean.

Together, discuss all the courageous things that each family member has done. Make a list. What does it mean to show courage? What qualities do you need to be a courageous person? Is it always easy to be courageous? Why? Discuss together.

Now you are ready to decide on what your family goals are for this month. Together, answer the following questions:

- What do you want to achieve on your own?
- What do you want to achieve as a family?

Complete the 'Family goals' page and put it where everyone can see it. Keep reminding yourselves throughout the month what you want to achieve, and be determined to find the time to do it! Think about how you will all feel when you have achieved what you set out to do.

Family Essentials

Routine family tasks are the core principles of Family Essentials – they are about how families organise themselves on a day-to-day basis. Family Essentials are designed to help family members set clear routines so that everyone knows what they need to do, by when and how often. Providing routines enables all family members to feel safe, secure and valued and, as a result, able to overcome daily challenges more successfully. When routines become consistent, they help to develop healthy habits such as going to bed on time and brushing your teeth.

It is through the completion of these everyday essentials that bonding is strengthened during the process, thereby enhancing family relationships. By families completing these tasks together, they are embedding essential requirements into their everyday lives so that, in due course, it starts to become routine. These Family Essentials change from month to month in order to encourage the family to achieve each of the basics.

> *In families, routines have been shown to increase health and psychological wellbeing, as well as improve social adjustment and academic achievement for children.*
>
> (Rawkins, 2010)

Routines help children to:

- develop healthy habits (e.g. brushing their teeth, going to bed on time);
- develop a sense of responsibility and a feeling of 'belonging';
- strengthen the bond between parent(s)/carer(s) and children through predictability and an element of fun; and
- spend quality time with their parent(s)/carer(s).

Routines help parent(s)/carer(s) to:

- feel more in control and more organised;
- complete daily tasks such as preparing a meal;

- share the responsibility of household tasks; and
- spend more quality time with the family.

Creating routines

Every family is different, and it is important that they understand what it is they want to achieve and design routines to help support. For routines to be effective, they need to be well planned, consistent and predictable. Routines also need to be fun, light hearted and adaptable to change to ensure that everyone is on board and motivated.

Below are some examples of Family Essentials routines:

- *Family meals:* Plan to eat a family meal together. Laying the table, serving and washing up are all part of having a family meal together. How many family meals can you do?
- *Time 4 school:* Can you get to school on time? How can you achieve this? Plan and prepare the night before to make your mornings go with a swing! If getting up is a struggle, set your clock forward by 10 minutes – this is a great trick that really works.
- *Family Values book club:* Plan time for a family reading session. Choose a book together that you will all enjoy! Sit down in a circle and take turns reading. Discuss characters, the plot and the illustrations (if any). At the end of the story, discuss your favourite parts and write a family book review.
- *Let's clean up:* Housework is never a chore if all the family gets in on the act. Make a list of all the housework to be done during the week and divide it up between all of your family. Dusting, washing, ironing and cleaning is essential for a clean home.
- *Turn the lights out:* Are all the lights on in everyone room, even if no one is in them? By turning the lights off when you leave an area, it will help reduce your electricity bill, but it is also very good for the environment.
- *Be organised:* This is the time to be organised. Sort through your belongings and anything you no longer need or use. This is your chance to donate them to charity or give them to someone else who could get a benefit from them.
- *Sleep! Sleep! Sleep!* Is it hard to get out of the bed in the morning? Are you yawning by lunchtime? Making sure you have enough sleep will not only make you feel more energetic, but is also an important part of looking after your body! So go to bed on time to make sure you have plenty of sleep!

Family Activities

Spending family quality time is important to help build strong relationships, as well as having fun and experiencing new and exciting things. The time spent together builds up an abundance of shared experiences and memories, which are a great source of conversation around the table.

Taking part in a variety of different activities helps to build up skills whether physical and/or mental that enable us to understand and develop what we are interested in and maybe have a talent for. This section of the pack is bursting with lots of hands-on activities suitable for all the family. All the activities in this section reinforce the monthly value, and family members can choose activities that interest them. For example, granddad may choose to grow a vegetable patch with his grandchild. Every month, the activities change to suit the value of the month. Below are some examples of Family Activities.

Try something new

Have the courage this month to try something new! Do something new as a family or individually. This could mean meeting up with an old friend, trying a new hobby, wearing a different colour or trying a new food.

Blindfolded obstacle course

Together, design an obstacle course in your back garden or local park. One family member plays the guide while the other is blindfolded. The one blindfolded must navigate the course by following the commands of the family member playing the guide. The guide yells commands such as, 'left', 'right' or 'straight', as well as warning the blindfolded partner about any obstacles. The aim is to complete the obstacle course successfully. Be creative, as the more interesting the course, the more courage one of you will have to complete it. Use paddling pools filled with water, blankets to climb under and objects to climb over.

Make a courage pennant

You will need cut out pennant shapes (triangle shapes) made out of card. Each family member will need three pennant shapes, crayons, markers and glitter glue.

Each family member will need to complete three tasks. The first task is to think of something that will make you feel powerful (e.g. 'I feel strong, I can do it!'). Write this on to your first pennant and decorate it using crayons, markers and glitter glue. The second task is to write your name on to the second pennant and be creative (e.g. if you have an 'O' in your name, you could turn it into a smiley face; or try making your name into a rainbow or a happy shape). On the third pennant, draw something that you enjoy doing, something that you are good at achieving. For example, select a favourite sporting event or animal to draw. Decorate this pennant with something that makes you smile.

Once you have completed your three pennants, be confident in what you can do and display them for everyone to see.

Make a family scarecrow

Design and make your own adorable scarecrow using recycled materials. Why not put your scarecrow in the garden and see if it frightens the birds away? If you need some ideas on how to make a scarecrow, look on the Internet or go to the library.

Family Reflections

The final part of the pack is designed to encourage the family to reflect on what they have learnt and achieved during the month. Families need time to understand what they have accomplished and also how to overcome problems that they have encountered along the way. This is brought about through reflection. Reflection is another word for learning, a learning that grows out of experiences – it is a process designed to promote cognitive learning. The reflective process helps the family to stop, think and reflect about the month by asking certain questions:

- What did your family learn about this month's value?
- What was your family's favourite activity and why?
- What activity did your family like least and why?
- How has this month's value benefited your family?
- Have you noticed any changes in your family since taking part in the Family Values Scheme?

This is achieved through a number of activities.

Family meeting

At the end of the month, it is time to hold a family meeting for everyone to reflect on how well they have achieved the following:

- demonstrated the value 'courage';
- communicated with each other;
- interacted with the school and the community;
- participated in individual goals; and
- achieved their family goals.

Time to evaluate

Evaluate using the checklist below:

- I/we have shown the value 'courage' this month by . . .
- I/we have communicated well with each other by . . .
- I/we have interacted with the school and the community by . . .

- I have achieved my individual goal this month by ...
- We have achieved our family goal this month by ...
- I/we feel that we could improve by ...

Family nominations

Together, decide who deserves your Family Values Cup. The nominations can be discussed around the table or written on a piece of paper and placed in a box. Pretend you are at the Oscars and present the winner with the trophy.

Families who are able to reflect and problem-solve are able to overcome a multitude of issues, which inevitably strengthens the family unit. Children develop resilience when they learn how to problem-solve through their parent(s)/carer(s).

> *Problem-solving is the family's ability to resolve problems on a level that maintains effective family functioning.*
> (Epstein *et al.*, 1993)

Problem-solving is a skill that can be learnt through the following stages:

- *Identify the problem*: This can be achieved through discussion and listening to other members of the family.
- *Generate options to deal with the problem*: Discuss and brainstorm a variety of options regarding the problem.
- *Agree on an option*.

The family collectively chooses an option that they all agree to work with and then:

- *Implement an action plan*: Decide what each member of the family is going to do and by when.
- *Monitor the action plan*: The monitoring process is very important, as it allows the family to keep track of their progress and achieve their goal.

Summary

This chapter focuses on the practical applications of the Family Values Scheme and how it uses the 22 values identified by Hawkes (2007) to engage families effectively. The four core elements of the scheme (Family Gathering, Family Essentials, Family Activities and Family Reflections) are referenced in detail in this chapter, with ideas on how to introduce it to families within a school setting, as well as sample letters to parents/carers. The final part of the chapter suggests ways to evaluate the scheme with families, with an emphasis on self-reflection,

102 How the FVS operates in practice

identifying and celebrating successes achieved during the month and how to improve and move things forward for the future. Chapter 8 takes us into another direction on how values are used in other educational settings, with an emphasis on the impact of values in these settings.

Chapter 8
Establishing the Family Values Scheme
The Coed Eva story

This chapter sets out through a detailed case study how the Family Values Scheme has been implemented in schools in different local authorities in England and Wales and the impact it has made from the perspectives of the staff, pupils and the families. The first case study, which is presented in the next two chapters, is based in Torfaen, south Wales, and will be followed by a primary school in Herefordshire, England. Herefordshire was the first local authority to adopt the Family Values Scheme in a number of its primary schools.

The school

The purpose of this case study is to examine the implementation of the Family Values Scheme in a primary school setting and to discuss its strengths and identify actions for future development. This case study is based on Coed Eva Primary School, Cwmbran, which is under the control of Torfaen Local Authority, situated in southeast Wales. It borders the county boroughs of Newport, the county of Monmouthshire and the county boroughs of Caerphilly and Blaenau Gwent. To put the school into context, the total population of Cwmbran is 47,254 (2001 census) compared to the total population of Torfaen, which is 90,720. In 2011, the percentage of pupils entitled to free school meals in Torfaen was lower than the Wales average, and some of its areas are in the 10 per cent most deprived areas in Wales.

There are a total of 40 state schools in Torfaen Authority, of which 8 are secondary and 32 primary. Coed Eva Primary is one of these primary schools, and was established in January 2009 following the amalgamation of Coed Eva Infant and Coed Eva Junior schools. The school is situated in a deprived residential area of the town that includes both privately owned and social housing. While the majority of pupils live within the immediate neighbourhood, a minority of learners are resident within an adjacent designated Communities First Area, which receives funding from the European Economic Union (EEC) as one of the most deprived regions within the UK.

The appointment of a new head teacher in January 2009 to amalgamate the two existing schools into the newly formed primary school was in line with the authority's strategic plan to reduce the number of separate infant and junior schools into larger, more cost-effective primary schools. The new primary school was a combination of the previous two existing schools. The number of children on free school meals (FSMs) is 20.9 per cent, well above the county norm. In addition, 18 per cent of pupils are designated as having special educational needs (SENs), also well above the local authority and Welsh norm. Therefore, Coed Eva Primary School, which is on the outskirts of Fairwater, is located on the edge of one of the most deprived parts of Wales and the UK, and this is reflected in the fact that its FSM children are double the national average.

One of the first tasks of the new head teacher was to reorganise the staffing into a new managerial structure that would benefit the amalgamation. This was carried out by the head teacher, the senior leadership team and the newly formed governing body. To this effect, the school has a roll number of 493 pupils aged 3 to 11 years, including a 52-place nursery. The school contains a number of pupils designated with serious kinds of either special or additional learning needs, as well as some with either mental health or behavioural problems, or both.

Classes are organised on a two-form entry basis, with no mixed year groups. The primary school has a senior leadership team, consisting of the head teacher, two deputy head teachers as part of a job-share and 2 teaching and learning responsibility (TLR2) post holders. The school has a teaching staff of 17, supported by 14 teaching assistants, of which one is a higher-level teaching assistant and one is a family liaison worker responsible for leading pastoral support throughout the school.

The primary reason that the scheme was implemented in the school was that the school's initial self-evaluation report (Coed Eva, 2009) identified the following areas for improvement:

- to raise standards in numeracy and literacy;
- to increase the level of parent involvement in the school;
- to improve attendance;
- to improve behaviour;
- to raise the self-esteem of pupils; and
- to improve the well-being of staff.

Prior to the scheme being implemented, the parents interacted with the school in the following ways: by attending parents' evenings to discuss pupil progress, by attending parent–teacher association (PTA) events, by receiving regular newsletters and by a minority of parents helping out on educational visits and in classrooms. The attainment of pupils in numeracy and literacy was below the local and national trends in both Key Stages.

Attendance levels

	2008/2009	2009/2010	2010/2011	2011/2012
Attendance figures (%)	93.00	92.25	93.4	94.6
Authorised absences (%)	5.28	5.2	1.4	0.8

The school comes under the jurisdiction of the Welsh Assembly Government, whose attendance target is 95 per cent. Official statistics show, particularly during the last 3 years, that the school had been below this target. Rigorous analysis of data showed the following reasons had contributed to this downward trend:

- holidays taken during term time;
- increased number of fixed-term exclusions;
- children absent for medical reasons; and
- poor attitudes towards learning.

Initially, the school had some serious behavioural issues, which began to have an impact on the well-being of staff, and this had to be overcome. Analysis of the school's behaviour policy showed the need for the implementation of a whole-school approach to behaviour that, in the first instance, was intended to reduce the number of incidents of challenging behaviour, such as refusal to work, running off site, and unacceptable acts of aggressive physical and violent behaviour displayed towards staff and other pupils.

The school identified six children on the infant site and twelve children on the junior site whose self-esteem was particularly low and whose behaviour was challenging and impeding the learning of others. There were three girls and fifteen boys in the group, of which three were on the autistic spectrum, two pupils suffered from attention deficit hyperactivity disorder (ADHD) and seven pupils had moderate learning difficulties (MLDs). The number of pupils on the FSM register in the group was 80 per cent, and 96 per cent of these pupils lived with one parent or with an extended family member who had little involvement in school life. Lateness and poor attendance at school, as well as poor attitudes towards learning, was a regular occurrence. One pupil had an attendance level well below 70 per cent.

It was therefore a priority to gain the trust of this group so that appropriate behavioural and other learning support strategies could be put in place and implemented, which included a highly effective reward system in the hope that these approaches would motivate them to make the right choices about their behaviour. To assist with this task, the school successfully employed the services of an independent behaviour consultant who specialised in supporting pupils in positive behaviour management. This intervention took approximately two terms to implement and for the school to begin to see a positive outcome from the investment. The implementation of values and the Family Values Scheme later on in the year became an integral part of this process.

The first priority for the school was to introduce a consistent approach towards behaviour on a whole-school level so that all staff members were singing from the same hymn sheet! This involved the training of staff at every level, communicating with parents, governors and pupils to ensure that there was an agreed understanding of school rules, an appropriate corrective list and, best of all, a reward scheme that benefited everyone!

The group of pupils originally identified for their challenging behaviour started to make the right choices and, over two terms, gradually started to improve and manage their own behaviour. Initially, the school's number of fixed-term exclusions increased, with the highest being in 2010/2011 with a total of 37 exclusions in a single year. This statistic meant the school was one of the highest excluding schools within the LA, although some of the reasons for these exclusions were extremely serious. These statistics prove that a consistent approach to behaviour worked! Within a short space of time, however, the combination of the new behaviour policy (Reid and Morgan, 2012) and the implementation of the FVS significantly changed this picture, as the school now has one of the lowest numbers of exclusions within the authority – a total of two fixed-term exclusions in 2012. Two other productive aspects of the new behaviour policy were to implement nurture groups and recruit a pastoral worker to support pupils, both of which have also been successful.

Nurture groups

The school's behaviour policy included the setting up of a breakfast and lunchtime nurture club to give extra support to those pupils who found it difficult to interact socially in the playground. Certain categories of children do sometimes find it difficult to interact with their peers, and this can often lead to confrontation, which may result in physical and aggressive behaviours being displayed.

During lunchtimes, two nurture clubs are in operation – one on each site – with the majority of pupils attending from the original designated specialist behaviour group. This policy means that any child can access either of the lunchtime clubs at any time. During these sessions, children are taught how to take turns, share with others and listen to one another. This is done through the playing of small group games, including circle-time sessions. Both the breakfast club and the nurture lunchtime clubs are supervised by qualified staff. These preventative measures very quickly had an impact on the well-being of pupils by improving their self-esteem and raising confidence, which has contributed to a reduction in exclusions, improved attendance and improved attitudes towards learning.

Pastoral support worker

The school appointed a level 3 teaching assistant primarily to support pupils with their behaviour and well-being. The role of the pastoral support worker also included a responsibility for the close monitoring of the school's behaviour policy. In practice, this has involved carrying out daily checks with individual children to ensure their well-being and to offer behaviour support. It has also led to a daily drop-in session for parents, as well as the school liaising with designated families and external agencies.

Values-based education

Six months on from the amalgamation, the school was ready to commit itself to becoming a values-based school. The vision was to create a school that was caring, respectful and positive, and yet one that encouraged learners to be challenged in a creative and stimulating environment. The school wanted to adopt a holistic approach in which it could build on the good relationships that already existed and develop them. Staff wished to be seen as people who not only talked about values superficially, but put these values into effect and for them to become central to the culture, ethos and philosophy of the school's daily life.

The insight into values-based education originated from preliminary visits to Ledbury Primary School in Herefordshire as part of the school's self-evaluation process into improving its own practices. The head teacher was an inspiration, and staff were keen to look at how they could recreate Ledbury Primary School at Coed Eva. It was from this firm foundation that values-based education was born and the ideas of Hawkes and Lovat (see Chapter 5) on values-based education developed and grew. Three years later, the school has seen the considerable benefit that has resulted from making values-based education intrinsic to school life and is made manifest in practice through its effective behaviour policy, good positive relationships with all stakeholders and the calm, reflective environment, as well as the pupils' good attitudes towards learning and teaching and the good links with outside agencies.

Values and SEAL (social and emotional aspects of learning)

As part of the school's targets for improvement and a local authority initiative, the school implemented SEAL (social and emotional aspects of learning) to compliment the personal and social education programme that already existed and to enhance the values-based approach. The school identified the social and emotional aspects of learning as a key focus for their work with the children. This included a group of children whose learning was being held back due to a lack of understanding in being able to manage their feelings and an inability to work cooperatively in groups, to motivate themselves and to show resilience when faced with setbacks.

SEAL (2005, 2006) is a curriculum resource that aims to develop the underpinning qualities and skills that help to promote positive behaviour and effective learning. It focuses on five social and emotional aspects of learning: self-awareness, managing feelings, motivation, empathy and social skills.

The materials help children to develop skills such as understanding one another's point of view, working in a group, sticking at things when they get difficult, resolving conflict and managing worries. They build on effective work already in place in the many primary schools who pay systematic attention to the social and emotional aspects of learning through whole-school ethos, initiatives such as circle time or buddy schemes, and the taught personal, social and health education (PSHE) and citizenship curriculum.

The materials are organised into seven themes: 'New beginnings', 'Getting on and falling out', 'Say no to bullying', 'Going for goals', 'Good to be me', 'Relationships' and 'Changes'. Each theme is designed for a whole-school approach and includes a whole-school assembly and suggested follow-up activities in all areas of the curriculum. The colour-coded resources are organised at four levels: Foundation Stage, Years 1 and 2, Years 3 and 4, and Years 5 and 6. Pupil reference material and photocopiable teacher reference materials accompany each theme.

A SEAL coordinator was appointed within the school to lead and monitor the programme. Time was allowed for staff training and the purchase of resources, and the scheme was successfully implemented throughout the whole school.

The establishment of a PSE programme that gave progression and continuity year on year was effective and benefited all pupils. The school decided to link the SEAL themes to the 22 values so that they could enhance the programme and make the values more meaningful and purposeful for the children. In Figure 8.1, we show how the school achieved this and linked it to our values.

	Autumn	**Spring**	**Summer**
VALUES	Freedom	Quality	Caring
	Peace	Simplicity	Unity
	Co-operation	Thoughtfulness	Courage
	Tolerance	Appreciation	Love
	Responsibility	Humility	Respect
	Hope	Patience	Understanding
	Honesty	Happiness	
	Friendship	Trust	
SEAL	New beginnings	Going for goals	Relationships
	Getting on and falling out (say no to bullying)	Good to be me	Changes

Figure 8.1 Linking SEAL to values.

The genesis of the scheme

Within the first few months of introducing values into the school, parents started to ask questions and wanted to know how they could replicate the use of values at home. One family came into the school and asked to see the head teacher to share with her what had happened at home. They had a 6-year-old daughter in a Year 1 class and she had asked for extra time at bedtime. They promptly said 'No!' and that she really needed to go to bed. She turned and asked them if they could please show her some respect and cooperation as she wanted to finish drawing her picture for her teacher. This is a lovely example of how values-based education was beginning to have an impact at home in an innocent and sensitive way.

One of the areas identified for improvement from the school's self-evaluation report (Coed Eva, 2009) was to improve its relationship with its parents. The journey of amalgamation, the successful implementation of a whole-school approach to behaviour and values-based education meant that the school had grown from strength to strength. However, the drive to improve relationships with its parents still needed to be overcome. The school needed to engage parents in a more interactive and meaningful way. Values was having an impact and being promoted within the school but it was not having the same impact in the home.

The head teacher and a work colleague realised that there was a gap with what the children were being taught in school with values and what was happening in the home. There also appeared to be an inconsistency between the two! The aim, therefore, was to narrow the gap between the home and the school using values. It was recognised that, if this happened, it would benefit not just the school, but also improve the school's relationships with its own families. We needed values-based education to empower not only staff and pupils, but also the parents and the quality of their family life! It was during this process that the Family Values Scheme was born.

One of the first tasks was to write down the aims of the scheme, which would not only benefit Coed Eva Primary School, but also any school that wanted to create better and more effective partnerships with its parents. Therefore, it was decided to:

- strengthen relationships between family, school and community;
- use 'values' as an intrinsic way of life, both at home and at school;
- engage parents to create effective partnerships between the home, school and community;
- compliment and enhance existing PSE and parent programmes (e.g. SEAL);
- improve behaviour and attendance; and
- raise standards in the basic skills of reading and writing.

The primary aim was to engage parents in a more effective way, using values as a tool to bridge the gap between the home and school. A consistent approach between home and school was important in order to improve behaviour, attendance and the basic skills. The strategies adopted in school could be shared and used at home to support parents. It was also important to use existing personal and social programmes such as SEAL into the scheme so that one could compliment the other.

It must be said from the onset that the Family Values Scheme was designed to operate differently from a typical parent programme. Parent programmes have their place in supporting parents with family issues and are often extremely successful. However, the programmes usually only last for a number of weeks and the support is only as good as the commitment of the parents or family members who attend those sessions. These are often held during the daytime, which makes commitment to the programmes more difficult for some families.

Therefore, one of the main differences between the Family Values Scheme and a typical parental programme is its sustainability. The scheme puts the ownership of responsibility on to the family members. It is because of this flexibility that the scheme is far more sustainable. There is no start and end point, as families can join and finish whenever they wish (i.e. they can opt in and out as family commitments allow). Activities are fun and stimulating for the whole family, and everyone from the youngest member to the oldest member benefits.

Previously, the school had formed a positive parents, positive pupils group, with the aim to meet weekly to problem solve behavioural issues and to support the parents with the same strategies that were being used in school. The number in the group varied from week to week from four to ten parents and, although at first discussion was stimulating, it soon became apparent over the following weeks that, often due to poor or irregular attendance, the original intentions were not being met, and so the school decided to disband it. It was then reorganised, reintroduced and re-launched, and it was the parents within this group who became the starting inspiration for the Family Values Scheme.

It was as a result of the feedback from the parenting group that we decided to create something unique for all family members. Therefore, the term 'family' includes any family member, including grandparents, aunts, uncles, cousins, etc. This way, the scheme could be inclusive as well as not being exclusive.

The scheme uses the same values being used every month in school. Time is planned at the beginning of each month by each family, and it is up to individual families to determine how much time they can dedicate to the scheme. This will vary from month to month depending on family commitments.

Once the 22 monthly packs were written, a decision had to be made as to which families needed to be involved in the scheme first. The scheme was targeted for a group of families that the school had identified previously in the positive parents, positive pupils group as needing extra support in terms of improving their children's behaviour and attendance. Engagement of this group into school life was limited and relationships had historically been poor. If relationships could be improved with this group of parents, then this would be a good way of measuring the impact of the scheme.

Commencing the scheme

Once this had been agreed, the next step was to decide how to empower the group of parents into the scheme. The launch had to be something special that would really stimulate them into wanting to be involved, as attendance from the previous parent sessions had been inconsistence. For this to work, it needed all the family members engaged all of the time. Lots of ideas were discussed but in the end it was decided to do something completely different and out of the ordinary. A camping weekend in the Forest of Dean was arranged. This was not too far away in case of an emergency and yet far enough to offer a complete contrast to their home roots. A small grant was obtained that meant the weekend was offered to all the families for free! This was a real incentive, as all the families were on low incomes and would have found it difficult to fund the weekend themselves, which would have been an obstacle for their attendance.

The primary aim of the weekend was to provide a role model to all the families about how Family Values could be utilised into their home as part of their everyday lives. This was done in the following ways:

- by teaching respect using positive strategies for behaviour;
- by cooperation and teamwork to develop tolerance and patience;
- by communicating with each other;
- by relationship-building using quality as the value;
- by increasing self-esteem; and
- by learning new skills.

The role of the adult helper

The weekend was meticulously planned. It was decided that parents and their children needed to spend some quality time on their own in order to network with other parents and reflect. A sample of the itinerary is presented in Figure 8.2.

Part of the pre-planning exercise was to carry out a comprehensive risk assessment for the visit. This included a visit to the site to ensure that it met safeguarding requirements, collation of medical information, including dietary requirements, and personal details of all family members, including contact numbers. Regard was also given to the relevant number of qualified staff and adult helpers needed for supervision of the individual and family activities. It was important that we had an appropriate number of staff who were also first aid trained so that they would be on hand if any accidents occurred. Activities organised by the centre such as raft-building and the adventure walk activity were fully supervised by qualified instructors from the centre, so this was well catered for, and copies of the centre's risk assessments were also kept on file. This information was vital to ensure that everyone was safe!

To notify the families, a letter explaining the reasons for the weekend was sent out and a meeting was held to share the itinerary, set out the expectations

Saturday	
9am	Depart from school
10.15am	Arrive at Viney Hill Outdoor Pursuits Centre
10.20am	Welcome and introduction by staff of facilities on site
10.30am	Families given time to set up their living arrangements in tents
11.00am	Group talk re health and safety issues such as fire arrangements, medical
11.15am	First activity – familiarisation – face painting
12.00am	Lunch (packed lunches)
12.45pm	Second activity – parents raft building with qualified instructors. Games arranged for children included rounders, bouncy hopper games, climbing frames. Stickers and praise for rewards.
4.00pm	Free family time
5.00pm	Tea time for everyone!
7.00pm	Log circle fire – toasting marshmallows and singalong
8.00pm	Family quiz time
	Reflection time!
Sunday	
8am	Family breakfast together
9.00am	Family free time 'relationship building'
9.30am	Forest adventure walk including survival activities and den building
12.00pm	Lunch break
1.00pm	Family 'kempo ru' by qualified instructor (a form of martial arts)
2.00pm	Outdoor climbing activities
	Celebration and achievement time
	Reflection time!
3.00pm	Home time!

Figure 8.2 The programme for the weekend camping bonding event.

and answer any questions that the families needed. This information was also conveyed to staff and the governing body and was received well. Fortunately, the chair of governors offered to join in for the weekend, which was also a fantastic result!

The date for the weekend arrived and, armed with suitcases, games equipment, packed lunches and a sense of excitement, all our families, including children, arrived on time. In total, there were 10 families, composed of 14 parents and 15 children – a total of 29 people. To supervise and support these 10 families, we had 10 suitably qualified staff, including the head teacher, the chair of governors and a behaviour consultant. All of the children selected had previously shown inappropriate behaviour in school, with adverse conduct ranging from aggressive to violent behaviour, which had even resulted in some of the children having a history of fixed-term exclusions.

The families were supported by staff working alongside them in order to help reinforce a similar and consistent approach to behaviour that was being adopted in the school while away on the field trip . To this effect, one tool that was used was a concise pattern of language when a child would not follow instructions. This script was typed up, laminated and placed on a key ring for each of the parents, which they clipped on to themselves. This strategy was invaluable and was used time and time again! Here is an example of the script and the behaviour strategies that we used to support parents when their children refused to do the following.

Not following direction

If the child refused to follow a simple direction, such as not going to the designated timeout area, the following process was utilised. After each time of using the script, the parent had to walk away from his or her child to allow them enough time and space to think about making the right choice.

Asking their child to follow direction when they are calm

1   *I'm asking you for the first time to . . .*

    Walk away from your child and return within 5 minutes.

2   *I'm asking you for the second time to . . . Remember, if you do not follow my direction, you will be making the wrong choice and this will have a consequence to it.*

    Walk away from your child and return within 5 minutes.

3   *I'm asking you for the third time to . . .*

    If your child follows direction, praise them for doing so.

    If your child does not follow direction, attach a consequence for making the wrong choice. It is important that this is carried through and supported by all family members.

Asking your child to follow direction when they are not calm

1. *I'm going to give you 5 minutes to calm down and think about making the right choice, then I'm going to ask you to follow my direction. Remember, if you don't follow my direction when I ask you for the third time, you could have a consequence, which will mean taking away something that you like and enjoy doing.*

   Walk away from your child and return within 10 minutes.

2. *I'm asking you for the first time to . . .*

   Walk away from your child and return within 5 minutes.

3. *I'm asking you for the second time to . . . Remember, if you do not follow my direction when I ask you the third time, you could have a consequence.*

   Walk away from your child and return within 5 minutes.

4. *I'm asking you for the third time to . . .*

   If your child follows direction, praise them for doing so.

   If your child does not follow direction, implement a consequence, which again needs to be supported by all members of the family.

The use of a positive reinforcement such as this gives parents a practical tool to strengthen the expectations of behaviour in a positive, assertive way. Using the choice method, children quickly get to understand the consequences of their behaviour and the effect that it can have on their peers and other adults. A consistent approach is vital if this method is to become embedded successfully.

Children enjoy routine, as it gives them confidence and familiarity of what is expected of them. It cannot be emphasised enough that the same message about expectations of behaviour must be practiced by all members of the family for the best results. A change in this consistency can disrupt what you are trying to achieve. Therefore, good planning and clear communication with everyone will ensure success!

One of the ways that we can use positive reinforcement is to reward children immediately if they display or respond with a behaviour that we wish to see. This could be by saying something such as a simple 'thank you' to inviting them to participate in a group activity, which will also reinforce the values that we want them to learn. All children love being praised. Hence, we should never underestimate the power of using words of praise or rewarding them with tokens or stickers. The more energy we put into reinforcing positive behaviour, the more of this type of behaviour we will see adopted in the classroom. All praise must be well deserved and given genuinely by a member of staff for children to continue to show this behaviour again and again. Children who have low self-esteem or shy tendencies can be praised individually rather than in front of whole class. Negative responses are non-productive, and a classroom that focuses on these types of response will often incur inappropriate behaviour.

Teaching and role modelling to the parents on how to praise their children was an important part of the weekend, as was training them to focus always on the positive rather than upon the negative in their use of speech! If children listen to their parents using praise towards them, they will soon start to praise each other and to also identify with the value they have been using. Simple strategies such as saying 'well done!' or clapping and smiling does not cost anything. If the message is delivered consistently, it does work.

Also, the majority of children understand the consequences of their actions if they step outside the boundaries of what is expected of them. Children are more likely to accept these consequences if they believe that the situation has been dealt with fairly by their parents and by their school. Once children see that the school and the home are working together, they are likely to start very quickly to repeat the same positive behaviour on a regular basis. The end result must always be praise. Sometimes that can mean spending quality time together as a family and just completing the designated Family Values activities. It was this consistent style and approach that we wanted to use with the parents and the children for the weekend.

Nestling between the River Severn and River Wye in the beautiful Royal Forest of Dean, it was the ideal venue for families to relax and to discover the great outdoors through adventurous and challenging activities, albeit in a supportive environment. The centre is staffed by professional instructors whose ultimate aim is to give everyone an excellent adventure experience. They are all qualified to appropriate National Governing Body standards and are fully CRB checked and well trained in outdoor first aid.

The layout of the centre was perfect, as it consisted of a former vicarage, which was the main house. Adjacent to this was a campsite that was fully self-contained. The campsite section was set within 5 acres and included a small self-catering block, toilet and washing facilities and ready-erected tents, as well as an outdoor play area and log circle for group discussions and campfire sessions. On arrival, each family was allocated a tent that contained their basic needs, including camp beds, seating and a changing area. Families were asked to bring a list of suitable equipment, which included such things as pillows, sleeping bags, outdoor clothing, suitable footwear and a waterproof coat in case of inclement weather.

The itinerary, as shown in Figure 8.2, initially included an ice-breaker activity followed by joint and separate activities for both parents and children. This was to enable parents to network with each other and discover new skills. During these sessions, it gave school staff an opportunity to reinforce behaviour strategies and teach and model the designated values for them to follow, including the use of appropriate language.

We will now outline below some of the detail of what took place in the actual activity sessions.

Raft-building for parents

The aim of this activity was to have fun and to work on team-building skills. The instructor from the centre provided the group with enough hints and equipment with which to build their own raft and to get them to a destination across placid water. Team games took place once the raft was on the water. Parents were transported by minibus to Mallards Pike, ideal for this type of activity. The values that were targeted for this activity were cooperation, patience, trust and courage.

Family bush craft

The aim of this activity was to teach parents and children basic bush craft skills: what to eat, how to find water, how to build a shelter and how to make a fire. It was a fantastic way to discover more about our natural environment and to understand how we can interact with it and sustain it. The values that were targeted for this activity were appreciation, understanding and respect.

Family forest walk

This was a guided walk through the Forest of Dean with the intention of exploring the forest and discovering some of its history. Some of the families had never walked in a forest, and this was a popular activity. At the beginning of the activity, all family members were encouraged to adopt camouflage as a bit of fun (e.g. daubing their faces with mud and making a hat from leaves and twigs lying on the ground). This proved to be an excellent ice-breaker as it enabled everyone to have fun and it soon broke down any of their concerns that they had about the activity. The walk was along small forest tracks and involved showing everyone how to respect the environment by walking only on the designated paths and areas. One of the highlights was to create a den that would be large enough to fit in all of their family. Time was given to start and finish the task, and a winning family was chosen for their final product, as well as indicating how their creative skills had met their designated values. The values targeted for this activity were respect, cooperation and unity.

Face painting

The weekend was introduced via an ice-breaker activity that involved all the family. The idea was for everyone to have their faces painted of an animal character that they wanted to be! The twist was that all members of the family had to face paint each other. The idea behind this was that it prompted talk! The values targeted were respect, trust and cooperation.

Team building

This was a variety of short games and activities situated within the grounds of the centre, with the activities involving families to use skills such as communication, planning, problem-solving and teamwork. The values targeted for this activity were cooperation, trust and honesty.

Campfire singalong

In the centre of the campsite was a log circle that was used for group sessions, but also for a singalong session during the early evening. The campfire was used to toast marshmallows, much to the delight of the children. Song sheets helped with the singalong session, with everyone joining in. The values for this activity were happiness and friendship.

Final activity: the listening game

One of the closing activities was a listening game to see if children would follow instructions from their parents positively. Within the campsite, there was a play area that consisted of a large wooden assault course. All of the children were asked to go and play on the course with their parents' support. Parents were then asked to call their children individually using the language script that had been practiced earlier. One by one, the children returned to their parents and were rewarded for their promptness and listening skills. The value targeted for this activity was respect.

Celebration and achievement time!

Notes were taken during the weekend of achievements that had been made either from the parents, individual children or as a family. This could be something as simple as eating a meal together or working together on one of the team games. This was a time of celebration, and certificates were given to show this success! It was important that everyone had a certificate and had been praised for something that they had achieved. The values reflected here were happiness and hope.

Reflection times

Throughout the weekend, school staff felt it was important to build in quality time to enable everyone to reflect on what had been happening and to highlight the strengths of the programme, as well as to problem-solve those areas that some family units had found more difficult. A collective approach was used to ensure unity within the group. These sessions demonstrated the value of peace.

Family mealtimes

Meals were a family affair, with tasks delegated to individual families to encourage cooperation and relationship building. The self-catering block allowed for the seating of every group member, which made mealtimes fun and inclusive. Packed lunches were made in the morning, helped by the children, and this system worked well. Evening meals were easily prepared using the well-equipped kitchens in the self-catering block.

Outcomes of the weekend

The weekend was a huge success, and a debriefing with the group came up with the following ways in which everyone felt that they had benefited:

- New skills had been learnt, particularly the behaviour strategies that had been applied. All of the parents felt confident in continuing to use the same strategies in the home.
- Self-esteem and confidence had increased for both children and adults.
- New friends had been made, and it was the intention of the group to network more with each other for support.
- Daily values had been reinforced and awareness raised of values in practice, such as the teaching of respect, honesty, trust, etc.
- Relationships had been repaired and strengthened between adults and children, and also staff at the school.
- A video of the weekend enabled the school to disseminate good practice with other schools This is available from www.behaviourstop.co.uk.

Testimonials from families

Family participants made some of the following comments during the formal evaluation of the event:

> *'For the first time in 7 years, my son has listened to and done what I have asked him. I can't wait to practise this at home.'*

> *'We have never sat and eaten together as a family before. It was great for us to have our meals together in one big group.'*

> *'I feel far more confident now with dealing with any challenging behaviour that my boys might show.'*

> *'I feel that I have found new friends and I have not stopped smiling. What a great weekend.'*

> *'One of the best things for me was the raft-building. I learnt new skills and developed new confidences that I didn't think I had.'*

'It is good to know that we can come into school and someone will listen to us.'

'We all loved the values and we will be practising them at home every day. It has made such a difference.'

The next step!

Back at school, all of the families were very motivated and keen to carry on with the good work that we had started on the weekend. Every family was given a Family Values pack to start off the month and encouraged to pop into school whenever they needed any help or support. Feedback from the weekend was given to school staff and a presentation given to governors. Family Values had been launched and was ready for off!

By popular demand, it was decided to introduce the scheme 2 months later to all our families. One of the ways that this was done was to target a particular year group, and we asked the children to invite their parents in for a family activity afternoon. This approach was very successful and enabled other families to see and hear how the scheme had impacted on their family life. The Family Values membership was growing and, from an original group of 20 members, it had soon grown to a huge database of 132 families. We now find that families opt in an out each month as they choose and new families are invited along every month. It is this flexibility that makes the scheme so sustainable.

At the beginning of each month, a date is set for a Family Values challenge night. This activity is not necessary to the scheme, but it was something that the school felt it wanted to put on for parents so that they could network with one other. The challenge nights ran for just 1 hour and were held after school.

Attendance was high, with all family members becoming involved. This included grandparents, aunts, uncles and cousins. Each challenge night coincided with the monthly value, whatever it might be. The popular ones involved arts and crafts resources such as paint, glitter, collage, etc. Below are some of the challenge nights that have been held at the school.

Value: freedom

This challenge night, families were given the task and supported in making kites out of canes, paper and string. Each family was allowed to choose a design to build that they felt confident with (e.g. box kites, triangular kites).

Value: trust

Families enjoyed working together in teams to complete a blindfold obstacle course and mini circuit session.

Value: friendship

Families created a poster about friendship using hands and feet to paint. This was a fun way of getting everyone involved. The families also wrote a poem together and proudly read them out at the end of the session.

Value: honesty

Armed with large cardboard boxes, families very quickly turned them into colourful, vibrant, attractive 'honesty boxes'. During the month, if any family member showed the value of honesty, they put their name on a slip of paper and popped it into the box. There was a reward for the family member with the most slips.

Value: appreciation

A fashion with a difference was the objective of this challenge! Using junk material brought from home, families had to create an exciting, innovative designer outfit. This was a great way to demonstrate an appreciation of the environment using recycled materials. Family members strutted their creations down the catwalk to end the session.

Value: cooperation

The 'Great Egg Challenge' was the title of their next mega challenge. Families worked together to create a container in which a real egg could be placed and, when dropped from a great height, would stay intact. The only materials they were allowed to use were a newspaper, Sellotape and twelve art straws. Families loved working together to solve this problem and, at the end of the given time, each family was invited to drop their egg from a height. A countdown was given by everyone before each family dropped their egg! Those that stayed intact got themselves a prize. Real eggs always work best!

Log files

A great source of evidence for the scheme is the log files that are handed in at the end of each month. Every log file is unique, as it is personalised by the family and demonstrates how they have shown the monthly value through their combined activities. This is shown through their use of photographs, pictures, story writing, collection of theatre tickets or restaurant receipts, etc. Log files are kept for display and to demonstrate to others, and are normally returned in due course to the individual family. Families love to keep the files as a living memory of family involvement over the months. It is a great talking point for families to share their favourite moments with each other.

Family Values assemblies

In order to monitor progress within the family groups the school holds a Family Values assembly at the end of each month. This is also a great opportunity to invite all family members into school. Log files identify the level of work each family has carried out and certificates and rosettes are awarded appropriately. Each month, a family is chosen for the Family Values Cup. This is awarded to the family whom the school feels have demonstrated the evidence best for the monthly designated value. The winning family keep the cup for a month and then it is returned and passed on to the next winning family.

Displays

There was plenty of evidence collected from the Family Values activities, and so it was not long before there was sufficient to create a Family Values display to show how the effective partnership worked and to provide the evidence, including pictures of all the smiling faces. Coed Eva Primary hosts this in the entrance of the school for visitors to browse through and admire. A roll of honour, showing month by month which families have won the Family Values Cup, takes pride of place!

Involving external agencies

The scheme has been effective in its use as a tool for involving a range of external agencies, both in school activities and to support families. Examples of this include:

- Child Protection and Child in Need Meetings as a strategy for repairing relationships within families. Social services have found this effective to aid communication when there has been a breakdown through social and domestic violence and drug and alcohol abuse.
- Family liaison services such as CAFCASS that support young children when parents seek access through the court.
- Family learning services to support families in the basic skills of reading and writing.

The school perspective

Coed Eva Primary has benefited from the implementation of the scheme in lots of different ways. The biggest impact has been the noticeable improvement of the relationship with its parents and the improved behaviour within the school. The scheme has been partially instrumental in achieving these goals. The scheme has also supported the drive for change since the school's amalgamation and opened doors for parents to embrace other aspects of school life. The school was inspected in 2010 under ESTYN criteria, and the following judgement was made regarding the school's partnership with its parents and local community:

> 'The recent focus on "values" is beginning to have a positive impact on learners' attitudes, behaviour and relationships both in and around the school.'
>
> 'The high quality personal and education programme permeates the life of the school and provides learners with many rich, varied learning experiences. This is an outstanding feature. The school ensures that effective procedures are in place and shared with learners to support them during times of stress. Furthermore, a particularly successful feature is a nurture club for vulnerable pupils. This promotes successful inclusion and improved confidence and self-esteem.'
>
> 'The school has some very effective procedures in place to guide children in the areas of personal, social and health education (e.g. the values-based education programme, healthy eating workshops and the "walking bus"). The school makes effective use of specialist services, including health professionals, to help deliver these aspects of the programme.'
>
> 'The monitoring of behaviour, attendance and punctuality is excellent. The school's policies and procedures to promote good behaviour work exceptionally well and are consistently and fairly applied by staff. The appropriate procedures were implemented in line with national guidance.'
>
> 'Parents and friends make a good contribution to the life and work of the school, supporting school activities, helping out in the classroom and fund-raising through the newly established Parents and Friends Association. Parents support initiatives very well, such as the Family Values Scheme.'

Here is a list of some of the benefits that the scheme has given to the school:

- a contribution to the overall vision and ethos of the school as a happy, caring, welcoming school;
- an increase in the number of adult helpers in school;
- an increase in the number of parents completing school placements for further qualifications, such as NVQ and teaching assistant courses;
- an increase in the number of applications for the role of parent and community governors;
- a reduction in the number of fixed-term exclusions;
- an increase in attendance levels;
- a reduction in the number of parental complaints;
- communication between school and home is now much better and a strength of the school;
- an increase in the number of grandparents involved in school events (e.g. as a school governor, adult helper or leading an after school chess club for the more able and talented); and
- an increase in the number of PTA members.

Summary

This chapter has described how the Family Values Scheme was created, implemented, developed and sustained. We will now consider some further evidence on these issues in the next chapter before showing how the FVS is beginning to be rolled out in other parts of the country.

Chapter 9

Case studies

In this chapter, we will be evaluating two short case studies of two families who have been members of the Family Values Scheme. The studies will give a step-by-step approach of how the scheme was utilised from the perspective of each family member, followed by a short paragraph on how the scheme has impacted on each individual in order to give a real insight into how it is viewed from different family perspectives. We will then present the head teacher's own perspective.

Haralambos and Holborn (1995) define a case study as the involvement and examination of a single example of something. Nisbet and Watt (1984) describe it as *'the study of an instance in action'*. The single instance here means the individual parents, pupils and head teacher. A major drawback of using case studies, according to Bassey (2000), is that it is not possible to generalise on the findings using one case study. This is why, in order to give an honest account, we are using two longer case studies supported by several exemplars.

Semi-structured interviews were undertaken with each participant, as this type of interview allows for flexibility within the questioning (Cohen and Manion, 2011). It also allows for the interviewee to develop his or her own thoughts and ideas. For the purposes of our case studies, the interviewees will not be identified by name, as they are real parents, children and families. So, in accord with normal good practice, fictitious names have been used.

The format of the interviews was considered important, and so a considerable amount of pre-planning and preliminary thinking took place. Time was given to plan the nature of the interview and the line of questioning. The pace of the interview was also taken into account, given the nature of the family backgrounds. It was considered essential to include relevant introductory opening and closing questions at the end of the interviews. The use and types of questions chosen were also important factors (Marjoribanks, 1979; Simon, 1982; Lewis and Wray, 1997; Reid *et al.*, 2010a, 2010b).

Adelman (1980), Nisbet and Watt (1984) and Hitchcock and Hughes (1985) have expressed concern about how issues are used and introduced into case studies and how subjects are initially selected and identified. However, the choice of questions used in our case studies was directly pertinent and relevant to the ongoing work and activities within the FVS.

It was also equally important that the interviewees were supported throughout the session, which included clarification of any of their questions and/or answers as necessary in order to ensure that their own ideas and thoughts were explored. Silverman (1993) believes that this type of interview offers a rich source of data that particularly lends itself to finding out how people feel. Haralambos and Holborn (1995) reinforce Silverman's view that it offers flexibility and can be used to ask people about their attitudes, behaviour, motives and feelings. They also highlight that the interviewer bias cannot be totally eliminated because there is always some degree of unintended or unexpected interaction between the interviewer and interviewees.

Cohen and Manion (2011) are also supporters of this type of questioning as they say that it allows participants to raise issues that might not have been previously planned. Carspecken (1996) describes the use of paraphrasing in association with semi-structured interviews. He suggests that care needs to be taken to guard against prompting or making inferences when carrying out the interviews.

Silverman (1993: 92–3), a supporter of the use of semi-structured interviews for qualitative data, states that, '*Interviews in qualitative research are useful in gathering facts, accessing beliefs about facts, identifying feelings and motives which may be behaviour-related.*' This is consistent with the choice of methodology chosen for the case studies presented in this chapter.

The family perspective

The two families chosen for the short case studies are the Smith and Webster families. Both sets of families emanated from different backgrounds and shared a wide range of differing experiences, apart from being members of the Family Values Scheme. We will now begin to consider each individual family, sharing their family settings, how the scheme was implemented within each family, the development of the FVS over time and an evaluation from the different family members.

The FVS provides families with two options of involvement. The first one is a reward scheme approach and the second one is a more flexible approach. The reward scheme offers families a choice of choosing whether they want to achieve points for each of the activities in which they participate. These choices are at three levels: bronze, silver and gold. At the beginning of each month, families choose which level they wish to achieve, adding up the points as they go along. To achieve the bronze level, a family needs 500 points; for the silver level, 1000 points are needed; and for the gold level, 1500 points.

The second option is more flexible and allows families to take part in the scheme without the restriction of achieving a level through a values points system. Families who like this approach have more time constraints placed upon them as a family and often prefer to do the activities without the added competition of competing for an award level. Both of these options are available to all families who become members of the scheme.

In respect of the short case studies, the Smith family chose to take part in the scheme using the flexible option and the Webster family chose the award level approach. By choosing both options in the studies, we hope that it provides a good overview of how both systems work within the scheme.

Case study 1

Family background

The Smith family consists of two parents and two children. The children are both boys and are aged 6 and 10 years. For the purpose of this study, we will call the younger boy Mark and the older boy David, and the parents will be referred to as Mr and Mrs Smith. Neither name has any form of association with their designated family titles. The Smith family live within the catchment area of the school.

Mr and Mrs Smith are a one-income family and both children are eligible for free school meals. Both parents were born within a 3-mile radius of where they currently live and have family close by who give their support. The family live in social housing adjacent to the school and Mrs Smith receives disability benefit that prevents her from working. Mr Smith left school at 16 and trained as a mechanical engineer but is currently unemployed. The family own one car but do not go on regular holidays or have family days out due to budget restrictions. Mr Smith's parents are currently unemployed and live locally. Mr Smith's father has a history of mental illness and is supported at home by his wife, who is his carer. Mrs Smith's mother works in the local grocery shop 15 hours a week and her husband works full time as a delivery driver for a local supermarket.

Both children have special educational needs, Mark having moderate learning difficulties while David is autistic and in receipt of a formal SEN statement as outlined in the code of practice. The family found difficulty in interacting and socialising with other families due to the high level of intervention needed for David on the autistic spectrum. A timetable of regular routines was therefore initially established, with effective strategies put in place to support the family as and when necessary. However, the most routine tasks such as going shopping or visiting a restaurant had to be planned well in advance. This made family life difficult, with David often becoming frustrated and displaying behaviour that was challenging. As a result, during their participation in the FVS, the family unit stayed on familiar territory, which was mostly the family home and school. Attendance of both children in school was very good, 98 per cent for Mark and 97 per cent for David. Academically, Mark has special needs in the basic skills and received 2 hours per day additional one-to-one support and was targeted to raise his academic standards in both reading and writing. David spectrum received 100 per cent additional one-to-one support and 5 hours per day special tuition. A teaching assistant employed by the school provided this support. Strategies such as a visual timetable, time given during the school day to express feelings and emotions and attendance at a breakfast and nurture club have proved effective with him.

Academically, David was targeted to achieve the expected attainment levels at the end of Key Stage 2. Occasionally, outbreaks of challenging behaviour impeded his learning, which was manifest in the following ways: running off site, refusing to work, not listening to instructions and, on occasions, becoming violent and aggressive towards his peers and other members of staff.

The family became members of the FVS because the school was well aware of the difficulties that they faced at home and it provided a potential opportunity for them to spend some quality time together. After the scheme's initial success in the school with other parents, they approached the school to see if they could become allowed to take part in the scheme. It was explained that involvement in the scheme should hopefully improve their family relationships, the children's behaviour and interest in learning. After several preliminary meetings to discuss and explain their potential involvement in the scheme and in order to raise their expectations and knowledge of the scheme, the Smith family members joined and took home the 'tolerance' pack.

The family was excited about taking part in the scheme, and they commenced enthusiastically after first taking the pack home to read. The first thing that they did was to get an overview of what the pack was all about. They found that there are four sections to the scheme: Family Gatherings, Family Essentials, Family Activities and Family Reflections. They found the instructions clear and simple to read and suitable for all ages.

The first section on the family gatherings involved holding a meeting around the kitchen table, not something that they would normally do, and Mrs Smith was nominated to chair it. They all read out the 'tolerance' section at the front of the pack and then wrote down all their responses to it that they managed to think about.

Mr Smith considered that it meant compromising with one other even if you did not agree with the other person. Mark said, '*Being tolerant is putting up with someone or something that you don't like.*' From these responses, the family created a list of how they could be more tolerant towards one another on a daily basis. Mrs Smith suggested that they try and listen to one another's points of view '*instead of charging in without thinking sometimes*', while David felt that it was '*all well and good doing that but he wasn't sure how it would all work*'.

The scheme suggests that each family set goals at the beginning of each month to provide themselves with a focus point. At the same time, they also set themselves with individual goals that they felt were achievable with a little bit of effort. Finally, they decided that they would give a small prize to the person who demonstrated the best effort over the course of every month. The box overleaf shows the Smith family goals for the value of 'tolerance'.

The second section of the scheme is the Family Essentials section. From this section of the pack, the family decided to choose just two of the activities to do over the month. The first one was 'Time 4 school' and the second one was 'Family

> **Smith family goals**
>
> *'To listen to each other when asked about something before charging in with an answer.'*
>
> Mrs Smith
>
> *'I want to work on being more patient with everyone.'*
>
> Mr Smith
>
> *'I know that I don't show how I feel enough so I want to practice saying how I feel more often. If I feel sad because someone has done something I don't like, I am going to say it. Also, if someone has made me happy, to say "why?"'*
>
> Mark Smith
>
> *'I just want to argue less with my brother and to not make mum cross.'*
>
> David Smith
>
> *'I think that I can try to not to get so angry with everyone.'*

meal'. The reason these were chosen above the others was because Mrs Smith found it difficult to get the boys to school on time, despite an established bedtime routine. This resulted in the boys being late approximately twice a week to school. Mrs Smith discussed this with the boys and asked them if they would like to go to breakfast club, which started at 8.15 a.m. so that they could have breakfast with their friends. The boys agreed this.

Due to work and school commitments, family mealtimes were irregular and meals often taken at different times. They all decided that they would eat together as a family once a week, and this was planned for the weekends. Mrs Smith was surprised by how enthusiastic the boys were about the planned formal meal, particularly David.

In the main part of the pack, the Family Activities section outlines all the possible activities that reinforce the value of 'tolerance'. The Smith family subsequently identified four activities from within the Family Activities section of the pack. They planned to do one activity a week, and this was carried out at the weekends. The first activity, which became the family favourite, was making papier mâché masks. The aim of this activity was to identify the emotional differences they displayed between each other by making a facial expression on the mask. The activity took quite a long time, but they all managed to complete the task. During the first stages of the activity, David did not like getting his fingers wet and found this part really difficult. Very often with children on the autistic spectrum, this is common. However, with support from the other family members, he did manage to do it, although it took a lot of encouragement, and several initial attempts were abandoned before the task was eventually completed.

At the end of the activity, they displayed the masks in the family kitchen for all their friends to see. Mr Smith had a mask with a frown because Mark said he always frowned when he was cross. Mrs Smith had made David look frightened as he had his mouth open and his eyes were large. This was when he was unsure of situations because of his autism and his facial expression completely changed. Mr Smith said that he did not like this perception of himself and it had been a real shock to the system to be viewed in this way.

The second activity the family participated in was called 'leaf painting'. Mark reported that he loved the leaf painting activity. The family planned an outdoor visit and decided to travel to the Forest of Dean to collect the leaves they needed in order to complete the activity. David and Mark both reported that they really enjoyed collecting the different coloured leaves for their painting. Mr and Mrs Smith both said that they could not remember the last time that they had all gone out for a family walk. When asked about how they showed tolerance throughout the activity, they said that they had to take turns with the paint as they only had one pot of different colours. The end result was they said they had achieved something of which they were all proud and they even took photographs of the finished masterpieces to add to their creation of a family gallery in the kitchen.

'Every time I look at mine, I think of how nice it looks with all the different shapes and colours. It seems strange that we are the same but different in the way we say and do things, just like my picture', said David.

At the end of the month, a family meeting was held and they completed the STAR (stop, think and reflect) evaluation at the end of the pack. When they returned to their original goals they had made at the beginning of the month, they said that they had all demonstrated the value of tolerance, although they admitted that they had managed it for only about 70 per cent of the time. When asked about whether they had achieved the family goal, Mrs Smith said that they had certainly talked more and argued less over the month. Mrs Smith, David and Mark all nominated Mr Smith for their Family Values trophy, as they felt that he had told everyone when they had done something well and he had not shouted or become as angry. The one thing that they all wanted was to continue with the scheme, as they all said that it had given them a focus and something to do at the weekends. '*It has also helped us to get on better!*' said both boys.

Each family is expected to complete a log file over the month to record the evidence of their family activities. The Smith family reported:

> *The log files are great fun and the boys just love showing everyone who comes to the house what we have done month to month. After each activity there are always suggestions of how we can record the evidence. We all enjoyed taking photographs, saving memorabilia in places we visited and writing about*

what had happened. Every one of us contributed to the log file over the month. We did find that we did run out of time the first month but over the following months we improved. The boys couldn't wait to take theirs into school to show everyone and it was always a great talking point when people came to the house. We have kept them all and put them in a box.

Impact of the scheme

We now present a short summary of the difference that the scheme has made to the Smith family. The study timescale for these responses was 4 months. We hope that this list gives an indication of the questions and issues raised throughout by the family taking part in the study.

- All the family members felt that the scheme was easy to understand and they loved the flexibility of it fitting in with their daily family life. They felt that they were able to choose what time they could dedicate to the scheme month by month.
- They said that they felt more in tune with things that were happening in school.
- Lateness at school is now a thing of the past, as the boys love attending the breakfast club.
- 'We feel that because we are now spending quality family time together we are more relaxed around the boys.'
- 'We have noticed a huge difference in the behaviour of the older boy who is autistic. He loved the monthly mega challenge on the value of caring. We had to design a poster to promote caring using our hands and feet. Our older boy really surprised us on the night when he wanted his hands and feet painted as he never would have this done before. Autistic children generally do not like having their hands and feet touched in this way. Our younger boy really enjoyed taking part and for the first time we worked together as a family and we were very proud of what we achieved that night. It was more than completing the activity we felt it was a real step forward in strengthening family relationships.'
- 'We used to have days when the boys did not want to go to school but since we joined the scheme our boys really look forward to going to school.'
- Since becoming members of the scheme, both children have become more aware of cooperating with each other and respecting each family member. Both parents have said that tolerance has been the one value that they have all benefited from on a daily basis.
- The success of the scheme has been the family planning the activities during the month. However, on two occasions during the month they found that, despite rigorous planning, family illness and other unexpected events had meant that they had to rearrange what they had originally planned. They found, though, that they were able to catch up the following weekend.

- Mr and Mrs Smith said that they thought they had always used the scheme's values in their everyday lives previously but the scheme had really highlighted each value differently to them and made them more conscious of how these concepts were used. '*Now*', Mrs Smith said '*we talk openly about values!*'
- '*Collecting evidence for the log files was time consuming at first and we did not want the collating of the evidence to overshadow the carrying out of each of the activities. We found therefore, that one of the easiest ways of recording the evidence was by taking photographs with our mobile phones.*'

Case study 2

Family background

The Webster family also consisted of two parents and two children. For the purpose of this short case study, the parents will be known as Mr and Mrs Webster, the children will be referred to as Chloe and Molly and the grandparents as Grandma Webster and Granddad Webster. This again is solely for the protection of the family. Mr and Mrs Webster both came from working-class backgrounds and both parents attended local primary and secondary schools. Mr Webster left school after attending sixth form to attend the local college to study accountancy. He now works as a company accountant full time in Bristol and travels to and from the family home. Mrs Webster went on to further education after leaving school, attending university and gaining a second class honours degree in business studies, and is now employed in the role of business manager for a local recruitment company. The children do not qualify for free school meal status as both parents earn a good joint income. The family live in the leafy suburbs on the outskirts of the local town in an area of residential private housing . They have lived in the four-bedroom family home for 9 years. The family own two cars and take regular family holidays twice a year. The children, both girls, attend the same school. One of the girls is in Year 3 and the other is in Year 1. Both girls are academically able and are expected to achieve their attainment levels in literacy, numeracy and other target areas by the end of Key Stage 2. Their attendance is very good at 97 per cent and neither of the girls has been excluded or is on the special educational needs register. Both parents are in full-time employment and find it difficult being competent parents due to time and work constraints, and they have also found it hard to dedicate quality time together. Support from other family members is limited but they do have one set of grandparents who live in the vicinity of their family home. Neither the parents, nor the grandparents, attended school events, and they appeared to perceive school as a place that the girls attended that had little to do with their own lives. Both girls attended the school breakfast club and also the after school club until they were collected either by their parents or their grandparents. The parents' involvement in the school was principally limited due to their work commitments, but fortunately a lot of the childcare was shared with the grandparents.

The school identified the family as one that would benefit from being members of the scheme. The school approached the grandparents and asked them if they would like to consider being part of the scheme, and their response was positive. They were then invited into school for a discussion, during which the role of the grandparents and other family members was shared and they were asked if they would like the flexible or the award-level option. After much consideration, they decided to opt for the award-level option as they thought it would give the family a real goal to aim for over the month. Also, attending the end-of-the-month Family Values assembly to which members are invited and individual families are praised appealed to them.

The Family Values pack of 'caring' was sent home via email and the first people to view the pack were the girls and the grandparents. Grandma Webster said that it would give them something worthwhile to do when they looked after the girls instead of them watching television all of the time. All the family members were keen to be part of the scheme but felt that they needed to identify the reasons why they wanted to take part.

The first section of the pack set out clearly how the family could set goals for the month and also advised them how the different award levels function. The family gathered together and decided after a family vote to go for the bronze award because they felt that they were new to the scheme and wanted to test the water so to speak! A family goal of achieving the bronze level meant completing activities worth 500 values points. One of the Family Gathering activities is to understand the monthly value, and the family sailed through this by listening to each other and making a comprehensive list of how they could be more caring towards one another during the month. Chloe and Molly said that they wanted to make sure that they made Grandma and Granddad feel special during the month. '*I want to show them that I really do care about them*', said Chloe.

With the three stars coloured in the appropriate section of the pack, the family were ready to choose activities from the Family Essentials section. The activity that the family took forward for the month was 'Let's clean up'. The aim of the activity was to show everyone in the family that they cared by helping with the everyday household chores such as washing up, tidying, hoovering, dusting and shopping. Granddad Webster volunteered to create a 'Let's clean up' chart that showed a list of chores, the person responsible and the time they had to be completed. Figure 9.1 is the chart that the Webster family created:

They used a coloured chart system to show when family members had completed their chores and this was displayed in the kitchen at the height level of the children so that they could take an active part. In the first week, everyone was enthusiastic and keen to help each other. Chloe said that she thought it was fun and loved helping everyone. By the end of the month, the chart had become very tatty from constant use. Everyone said that it was a simple idea but it worked, even though there were occasions that some of the chores had not been completed because of other family engagements. Mrs Webster recalled one occasion when

Family member	Dusting	Hoovering	Washing up	Tidying	Taking the dog for a walk
Mr Webster	Saturdays		Daily (Evenings)		
Mrs Webster		Saturdays	Daily (Evenings)		
Chloe Webster				Saturdays Bedroom	Daily
Molly Webster				Saturdays Bedroom	Daily
Grandma Webster		Wednesdays			
Grandad Webster			Daily (Mornings)		Daily

Figure 9.1 The Webster family chores.

she was supposed to hoover the house, but due to a birthday party the girls had been invited to attend, and with her husband at work, this was not carried out. Overall, they all felt that they had helped each other more during the month.

In the Family Activities section, the activity that was the family favourite was making the caring cupcakes and cherry vanilla smoothies. Mr Webster recalled that it was the girls' idea to do the cooking because they wanted to give their grandparents afternoon tea to show they are really special. The cakes were well received and washed down by homemade smoothies. Granddad Webster laughed when he recalled the icing on the cake was not perfect and the cakes were a bit flat, but it did not matter as it was a lovely thought. Towards the end of the month, the family began to add up their values points from completing the activities. They were surprised to find that they had a total of 650 points. The Webster log file included photographs of the cake and smoothie making and the 'Let's clean up' chart with its coloured squares, pictures and writing from the girls. The school invited the family to join them in their end-of-month Family

Values assembly. Both grandparents attended and proudly received the family bronze rosette for gaining in excess of 500 values points.

When questioned about the impact of the scheme, the family gave the following responses:

- *'The main reason for taking part in the scheme was to spend some quality time together due to work and family commitments, and we all feel that we have certainly seen a lot more of each other.'*
- Both grandparents have taken part each month and attended the Family Values assemblies and the end-of-month mega challenges. One example of how the scheme has particularly impacted on their family life was at the end of the summer holidays when they asked if the scheme was going to run during the school holidays. At this request, a summer bumper special was written based on the value of 'caring'. One of the summer assignments was to think about caring for the environment. This involved each family member growing a sunflower seed and planting it in a pot with the family member's name on it. Upon our return to school in September, the family came into school and proudly announced that the activities had been great and they had grown one of the sunflowers to a height of 9 feet, 9 inches. This was a great talking point on the school playground with other parents and the focus of the first weekly newsletter for the new term.
- Both grandparents are now members of the school's parent–teacher association (PTA) and contribute to school life.
- *'We have a limited amount of time to spend together but the Scheme has focused us so that what time we do spend together is used effectively'*, said Mr Webster.
- Granddad has now become a school governor, a role for which he would never have considered or been involved in prior to the family taking part in the scheme.
- Granddad also now runs an after school club and feels that he would never have had the confidence to have approached school to take an after school club before he took part in the scheme. He said, *'The scheme has opened doors for me and I enjoy taking part in school life in ways that I didn't do before.'*
- One of the ways in which the scheme has particularly impacted is in the change to the family routine. Both parents said that they now make an effort to sit down and have a family meal together, and this has encouraged the family to communicate and discuss each other's thoughts and feelings.
- Both girls said that they enjoyed practising the values at home and enjoyed showing other family members the values that they were doing in school. They also said they loved completing the log files that they collected month on month.

Chapter 10

The head teacher's perspective

This chapter focuses on how the Family Values Scheme is used in school from the head teacher's perspective. It sets out to explain, from a leadership and management point of view, the thought processes behind introducing the scheme into school and the implications that this decision-making brings with it at a school, staff and parent level. This chapter also explains in detail both the strengths and shortcomings of the scheme from these perspectives, starting from its infancy through to its final mature state.

The school chosen for this short case study is one that this book has already showcased in Chapters 8 and 9 for its excellent work involving values-based education. Coed Eva Primary, one of the largest primary schools in Torfaen, sits on the edge of a Community First area in the Fairwater area of Cwmbran. The 493 pupils who attend the school live within the catchment area. A large majority of the pupils who attend the school live in social housing, although a small percentage of the pupils do live on the outskirts of Coed Eva in owner-occupied housing. This statistic is reinforced by the fact that the school has 20.9 per cent of its pupils on free school meals (FSMs).

It is from this point that the story of how the Family Values Scheme was implemented at Coed Eva will begin. Throughout this case study, I will be providing you with my thoughts of how things have taken place and why. To start this process, I feel that I need to give you some information about myself to give a true insight into the journey that I have undertaken. Previous to my appointment as head teacher in January 2009, I was head teacher at Bishop Child's Church in Wales School, VA, in St Mellons, which is under the jurisdiction of Cardiff Local Authority. This was my first headship after being promoted from Deputy Head Teacher at Archbishop Rowan Williams VA School in Portskewett, Monmouthshire. Both of these schools were group 2 schools, having approximately 210 pupils on roll. Archbishop Rowan Williams is situated in a picturesque village on the outskirts of Chepstow, Monmouthshire and Bishop Childs VA is located in the village of St Mellons on the eastern side of the city of Cardiff. Neither school had high percentages of pupils on free school meals. The majority of pupils could be classified as emanating from low-middle-class backgrounds. The children could not be generally classified as either being disadvantaged or advantaged and the majority of parents were homeowners, with only a small percentage of pupils living in social housing. The contrast between the settings of the schools in which I have worked is therefore extremely varied both in terms of their geographical and socio-economic settings. However, I thoroughly enjoyed my time spent at Bishop Childs VA School and, after an excellent ESTYN Inspection (the Welsh School Inspection Service) in my third year in post, I felt well equipped after 5 years to address the challenges that now faced me at Coed Eva Primary.

I was appointed as head teacher in January 2009 after the two previous head teachers of the infant and junior schools had both retired in the previous December. My main role at the newly created school was to amalgamate them into one large primary. I can well remember my first day at the school, feeling excited and yet completely overwhelmed with the task that confronted me. I had previously gone through a similar amalgamation as a deputy head teacher that was extremely successful. However, the sheer size of this new school at Coed Eva, together with the much larger staff and the diverse needs of the children, made it a much more daunting task.

I have, however, always enjoyed a challenge and I felt sure that, together with my natural enthusiasm, previous experience and the capable support from the staff, the transition into one school could be achieved effectively. It is probably best to give you a picture of the scale of the task by describing it to you in greater detail. The school consists of an infant and junior site with 15 classes, which include a 52-place nursery, a sessional day care facility that offers a wraparound care scheme, a large information technology (IT) and music centre, and two large halls.

The school was originally built in the 1970s on a single level apart from the junior site, which is a two-storey building. The school building is in good order and encompasses large grounds, with good facilities and a school car park. On site, there are also two large playgrounds, a forest school site, a conservation area and a large outdoor sports area, which is both for school and local community use. The school itself is nestled in a housing estate at the end of a small road, with the backdrop of the Welsh Mountains behind it.

I felt that a school of this size needed an effective senior leadership team with a clear vision and strategic direction. Therefore, the creation of this new team was one of my first tasks in the new school. Fortunately, the newly formed governing body had a very experienced chairman and vice chairman, and this proved a lifesaver to me in the early stages of the school's amalgamation. It was a great relief for me to be able to talk first hand to two governors whom I could fully rely upon and whom I knew supported me in my decisions. Together, we analysed the school's delegated budget and, in the first year, I was able to appoint four new members to the senior leadership team (SLT).

The team comprised of a job-share between two deputy head teachers and two other team members who were both awarded a teaching and learning responsibility (TLR2). This gave the school a team of five senior leaders, with me as the fifth team member. All members of the team, apart from me, had a full-time teaching commitment.

The second priority for me was to work with the governors and senior leaders on restructuring the school. We decided to split the school into four distinct phases, with each phase having two-year groups. However, as Coed Eva is a two-form entry school, this meant that each phase in effect had four classes. Here are the four different phases that were created for the new school:

- Phase 1 includes nursery and reception classes (pupils aged 3 to 5).
- Phase 2 includes Year 1 and Year 2 classes (pupils aged 5 to 7).
- Phase 3 includes Year 3 and Year 4 classes (pupils aged 7 to 9).
- Phase 4 includes Year 4 and Year 5 classes (pupils aged 9 to 11).

Each member of the senior leadership team has clear roles and responsibilities and leads a phase team within the school. The phase teams include all teaching staff, teaching assistants and non-teaching adults, and they meet on a regular basis to discuss individual pupils' progress and curriculum issues. Leadership and management time is dedicated to one day a week for the two deputy head teachers and me. During this time, we work diligently on the actions of the school improvement plan and quality assure standards within the school.

The first few months were a blur of coming to understand the school's strengths and weaknesses, and also the changes that the school needed to make in order to move it forward. The importance of accurate self-evaluation was always at the forefront of my mind, and in this task I was keen to involve staff, governors, parents and pupils in producing an honest and open account so that the school could build on its existing strengths and yet accurately identify its future needs and challenges. In the early days of its amalgamation, the school brought with it many challenges. These included the reorganisation and re-training of the staff, including making a number of new and key appointments, the remodelling of the building, and the reviewing of school policies and existing policy documents, as well as creating a new governing body with appropriate terms of reference.

The school staff were understandably nervous about the amalgamation but were also up for the challenge! It took approximately two terms for me to carry out a rigorous self-evaluation with my senior leaders and for me to be able to fully understand the logistics of the school. Enough has been said in earlier chapters of this book about the review of the school's behaviour policy and the challenges that went along with this task, so I will avoid writing any more on this and instead go straight ahead to the school's situation regarding its partnership arrangements.

The self-evaluation process had identified that the school had always had good partnerships with its parents, and this was confirmed in previous ESTYN inspection reports carried out in 2003 and 2005. However, like most good schools, its communication with its parents was through the normal channels of regular newsletters, holding parental meetings and parent–teacher association

(PTA) events, as well as through accessing the school website. I felt that this was all well and good, but we needed to think of some other and better ways in which parents could actively be more involved in school life!

This was quite a challenge, as not all staff are always keen on engaging in more and easier parental access and involvement. Similarly, not all parents wish to have more to do with their children's school!

We had already worked hard at creating a positive culture, and part of this was to improve on the educational, learning and caring provision for all of our pupils. In practice, this involved a well-attended breakfast club, two walking bus services at the start and end of the school day, the installation of two lunchtime nurture clubs, a newly implemented stay-and-play after school club and a daily drop-in session for parents. The breakfast club and one of the walking bus services were already in existence prior to my appointment and were very effective, but the additional services were new additions to the school.

The senior leadership team and staff felt that these services had started to make an impact on the well-being of all the pupils and they had also started to improve the school's relationships with its parents. This was evident from the high percentage of pupils who used the breakfast club every day. We currently have 147 pupils on the register of the breakfast club and a regular 120 pupils who attend on a daily basis. This early-morning provision was therefore opened up to our nursery pupils after we received lots of requests from parents who had older siblings attending the club and yet still had to find childcare for their younger children. Also, the implementation of a second walking bus service was becoming very popular, with 24 pupils regularly using this service.

The after school club was an opportunity for us to offer another service to parents that was very attractive. The setting up of this was not without its difficulties, as we had to comply with the criteria of the Care and Social Services Inspectorate Wales (CSSIW) who have overall responsibility for giving the club the acknowledgement and consent that it was appropriate and needed to open. Also, the CSSIW service inspects all sessional day and after school care facilities to ensure that relevant standards are met on an annual basis. Thus, it was imperative that we ensured these criteria were being met.

Despite these early teething problems, the new stay-and-play club opened in September 2010 and was immediately successful in increasing the numbers of children who attended on a weekly basis. The club has already been in existence for over 12 months, and the number of children attending has made it a viable and worthwhile provision. The school now therefore provides both before and after school care, as well as a summer play scheme facility for all of its pupils that is run and organised by Cwmbran Community Council. The uptake for the attendance on the play scheme is high, and places are limited on a first-come, first-served basis. The high percentage of attendance on all these services showed us that there was a genuine need for the provision. Thus, the more instances in which the school could help and support its parents in this way could only help to create even better home–school relationships.

The main reason that I decided to introduce the school into the Family Values Scheme was because I felt that it would build on our previous values work (see Chapter 5), which was already having a huge impact within the school. Attendance, behaviour and attitudes towards learning were improving fast, and in order to capsulate this I thought it would be a brilliant idea if we could go one step further and really get the parents actively involved by taking part in the scheme. Therefore, I came up with the following thought process and checklist:

- How do we introduce it to parents?
- Which families would benefit the most from the scheme?
- What implications would the scheme have on the school budget?
- How do I inform the governing body and get them onside?
- What staff training would I need to provide?
- What resources would be needed?
- Which members of staff should be involved and at what level?
- How would we monitor the scheme?
- How would we notify parents?
- Would it be sustainable?
- What evidence could I gather?
- What time of year would it be best to introduce the scheme?
- How could we involve pupils best in the scheme?
- Should it be a whole-school priority?
- How would I organise the Family Values assemblies?
- How could I disseminate it to other parties involved in school life and within the local community?
- How would I know that it had made a difference?
- Would it provide value for money?
- Would it improve personal and interpersonal relationships?
- Would it compliment existing personal and social education programmes?

The positives and the pitfalls!

The above list and my thought processes seemed endless and more than a little daunting! Introducing any major new scheme into a school is never easy and provides more than a few challenges, especially for the staff.

The first thing that I did, therefore, was to identify a clear link between the school's self-evaluation report and the school's own improvement action plan. This analysis suggested that the school needed to further improve its own partnerships with its own parents by fully engaging them more and better in school life. It was hoped that this would not only impact better with our pupils, but also help to forge stronger links between the parents and the school. Once this action and new policy was agreed by the senior leaders, the next step and challenge was to think about which families we should introduce first to the scheme, as there was no shortage of potential candidates and need.

The decision to target a set of parents who were vulnerable seemed an ideal place to start. If the scheme could make a difference to the daily lives of these families, then it was clear that the school would certainly see an immediate impact. The reason why this group was chosen above all the other families was because lots of the children from these families were displaying challenging behaviour that had resulted in an extremely high number of fixed-term exclusions. Prior to my appointment and the reorganisation, and in the early stages of my headship, it was obvious that the school had a high and disproportionate number of pupils with serious behavioural problems. This behaviour impacted negatively on levels of school attendance and helped to promote and foster a real breakdown in family relationships and between some parents/carers and the school. Communication between some parents and the school was also poor. Hence, there was a real lack of common understanding between all parties. It was an easy decision, therefore, to target this group of families for the scheme. The whole idea behind my introduction of the FVS into Coed Eva was to:

1 improve basic communication and support between the home and the school, especially among certain designated challenging families and their difficult, often non-compliant, children;
2 improve both the behaviour and attendance of the children who, prior to the introduction of the FVS, were of considerable concern to the local authority;
3 reduce the number of fixed-term and permanent exclusions, as well as the number of recorded and serious behavioural incidents; and
4 provide a focus for all the staff within the school, irrespective of their specific responsibilities, and, in so doing, facilitate better home–school relationships, especially with the parents.

However, I knew that the Scheme could work well for all parents and, after its initial trial period, the FVS was opened up to all parents, and this proved to be a popular decision (see Chapter 8). What happens now is that all new families attending the school automatically become members of the scheme. This process has enabled the school to build up a very large database, as well as providing an appropriate and interesting focus for both new and existing parents to mutually engage with us.

Initially, the monthly packs and log files (see Chapters 11 and 12) would be photocopied and given out to families by pupil post, but it soon became apparent that this was neither cost- nor time-effective. Now, all packs are sent out by email to all family members. The scheme is sustained easily by regular reports in the weekly newsletter, the *Coed Eva Chronicle*, which is sent to parents. The Family Values assemblies are held at the end of the month. The mega challenge events are also held at this time, while the data provided on the school website is then changed and updated.

The support of the chair of governors and the governing body has certainly been most helpful. A written evaluation in the regular head teacher's report presented at the governor's meetings helps to keep all members of the governing body fully informed.

The lead person in the school with responsibility for the scheme to be implemented effectively was myself, as one of my roles is to lead effective partnerships within the community. I did delegate some of the organisational work to a teaching assistant within the school who regularly reported upon progress to my senior leadership team. This works well, and over time has become embedded into the daily practices of the school.

The training of all the staff was carried out in-house during designated staff meeting time. This training was planned in two staff meetings at the beginning of September when we started. The school was inspected in May 2010 by ESTYN and the scheme came out well in their report as supporting the school in its partnerships with parents (ESTYN, 2010). The log files and photographic displays (see Chapter 11) also gave the inspection team first-hand evidence of the impact that the scheme had made in the school. Later, ESTYN included the work of the FVS at the school in a report on good practice in Welsh schools that they produced (ESTYN, 2011: 8).

From a head teacher's point of view, the log files really showed the positive impact that the scheme was making on the lives of ordinary people at home. They also allowed me to create a Family Values display in school. A selection of the log files are always on display for visitors and other parents to see. The use and maintenance of the log files is one of the best and most important parts of the scheme. In the next chapter, we will see how the log files are used in a practical way. The use of these files is explained in far more detail, with practical examples being provided on how they have been used effectively by families within the scheme.

My views

I feel that the scheme has made a great contribution to the progress that the new school has made over the last few years, especially with improving the school's effective partnership with its parents. The values are shared between all the staff, parents and children, and the communication gap that existed between the home and the school has significantly decreased. I have also had a marked increase in the number of adult volunteers in the school. Some of these students came from local college placements either for teaching assistant or initial teacher training courses, or from higher education. The number of visitors from other schools, local authorities and even officials from the Welsh government is increasing all the time as the good messages spread.

Of course, this aspect of the scheme was not catered for, but I feel that it has really opened other doors and that parents now see their school as a place of learning not only for their children, but also for themselves. The parents, like the staff and myself, take a great pride in being part of the FVS.

As a head teacher, I am always looking for new ways to help other schools fund projects such as the Family Values Scheme to ensure that good practice becomes embedded within schools. There are, of course, some grants available for these purposes if you are lucky. These can be used to implement and measure the impact of the scheme, including its evaluation. In Wales, for example, all schools have recently benefited from the introduction of a new pupil deprivation grant (PDG). The Welsh government has allocated a total of £32.4 million to all Welsh local authorities in an effort to reduce the link between deprivation and educational attainment. How the money is to be used is up to individual schools, but the emphasis is on collaborating with other schools in order to make a real difference to those children on free school meals (FSMs). The grant is to be used to target disadvantaged children to give them the same opportunities as those children who are not on free school meals. The Family Values Scheme meets the criteria for this new grant and can be used to target vulnerable families within schools.

Summary

In this chapter, we have taken the Family Values Scheme on to a different level by examining it from the perspective of a senior leader and manager of a school, the head teacher within its founding school. The story of how the senior leadership team has been involved during its implementation and evaluation and the success and pitfalls is one that we hope can be useful for everyone. The next chapter focuses upon the practical usage of the Family Values Scheme log files. These files provide first-hand evidence to show how the scheme has impacted in the children's homes and in their learning at school.

Chapter 11
Log files

In this chapter, we will go into detail about how schools, parents, staff and any other people or organisations can evidence the FVS. This evidence is presented in the scheme's log files. These are individual record documents that the families produce during each month to show the detailed evidence on what they have achieved. The files can make great displays to show to visitors. More importantly, they can also provide first-hand evidence for schools to show to inspection teams and local authorities about how the scheme has impacted on the school. For this chapter, we have selected a variety of extracts from a number of individual families' log files to demonstrate the different types of evidence that can be produced in order to give a flavour of how different families have organised and personalised their files to make them relevant and meaningful for themselves.

As described in earlier chapters, the purpose of the FVS is primarily to bring the families of the pupils in our schools into closer partnerships with their schools to improve home–school relationships. These good and positive relationships between the two stakeholders should then maximise the support both parties can give to every child to help them to achieve their potential. We have already provided evidence throughout the book (especially in Chapters 8, 9 and 10) of various examples, including short case studies, on how the FVS uses traditional family values as a tool to enable this to happen. Therefore, the log files are used to provide the day-to-day and monthly record-keeping on the families' participation in the scheme by theme and each individual value. We hope that, by providing some examples of this evidence in this chapter, it will help to provide an even richer source of evidence for you about the FVS.

The log files, therefore, are created and used to provide rich evidence to show that the partnerships between home and school are not only effective between the family members themselves, but also between the home and the school. Let us not forget that, although each family completes the various activities under the different sections during the month, the reason for doing them is to improve family and school relationships, improve attendance and behaviour and raise everyone's self-esteem.

In lay terms, the log files are like scrapbooks, in which the participants collect memorabilia such as photographs, examples of their practical activities, writing, drawings and paintings. Families purchase or make their own files themselves and then decorate them with the value of the month on the front covers. Inside each log file is a lot of blank pages. These blank pages are then completed and filled in, or added to, over the month by any participating member of the family. The instruction packs for the scheme clearly specify what evidence is needed for each activity. However, how the families interpret this evidence is entirely up to each individual family.

As we have also already explained in previous chapters, there are 22 FVS packs on the various values, with each pack being split into four sections. These are: Family Gathering, Family Essentials, Family Activities and Family Reflections.

Each section of the pack specifically identifies the type of evidence needed for each activity. You may question why we need to ask families to produce evidence at all. Feedback from schools and organisations has shown that families actually enjoy creating the log files during the month as it provides them with a family-friendly focus that, over time, enables them to build up their own record of happy memories, which, in due course, they will look back upon with a sense of pride! In fact, lots of families really enjoy participating in the log file activities every month and some have gathered quite a collection!

The log files that we have chosen to present as examples in this chapter are used to promote the following values:

- understanding;
- thoughtfulness;
- friendship;
- freedom;
- unity; and
- courage.

Under each of these headings, we will now provide some practical examples of how each family has completed the activities and how they have each provided their evidence. One of the beauties of the scheme is that each log file is unique to every family. This will be made even clearer when the specific examples are presented.

In the 'courage' and 'friendship' packs, we have also included evidence on how different families have completed the same value to give a slightly different dimension. We will develop this theme even further in the next chapter by presenting one of the sample packs on 'courage'.

In order to give a real insight into how the log files have been used, we will present them in the form of a family diary. Thus, we will provide real quotes of the thoughts and feelings of some of the participating families involved from one school. We have changed the real names of the participating family members involved in accordance with conventional good practice.

Log file: understanding

The Goode family

The family comprises Mr and Mrs Goode, their three children and two sets of grandparents. Mr Goode is the prime carer for his wife, who suffers from acute anxiety and is disabled. Mrs Goode, after a history of depression, does not like to leave the house and is totally reliant on her husband to support her with the day-to-day running of the family home. Mr and Mrs Goode receive income support and both children receive free school meals. The family live in social housing in a deprived area of their home town. Both sets of grandparents live within close proximity of the Goode family home and help out whenever they can by collecting the children from school and by taking them to their various after school activities. One of the children is currently in the reception class and the other is in the juniors in Year 4. Both children are poor attendees, below 90 per cent on the school register for attendance. The children have limited social skills and find it hard to sustain friendships. However, both children are well behaved in school and the older child receives 1 hour of support a day to assist with his poor literacy skills. The assessment baseline conducted at the end of Key Stage attainment in Year 2 showed that the boy has made slow progress upon entry into school. Mr Goode also has a daughter from a previous partnership whom he sees on alternate weekends.

The school approached the family to become members of the scheme in order to improve relationships between the family and the school, and to improve the self-esteem of the children and to improve their attendance. The first FVS pack the family was involved in was on the value of understanding. They opted to earn Family Values points for each section that they completed in order for them to achieve an award at the end of the month. We will now describe and show how the family got on in the first section of the FVS pack on Family Gathering.

Family Gathering

In this section of the pack, the family completed the three discussion activities, which then enabled them to shade in the three stars in this section. One of the activities for this section is to complete the family goals section, whereby each family member has to write their name and either draw or take a photograph of themselves before writing their own personal goal for the month. Once this was completed, the Goode family set themselves a family goal, which is something concrete that they can all work on together. Here is the Goode family's family goal for the FVS on 'understanding':

> *We want to make sure that everyone has a point of view and that we all listen to each other more. We want to make decisions together!*

Each Family Gathering activity is worth 150 points within the scheme, and the Goode family completed three activities, which gave them a total of 450 points. When asked about whether they had found any difficulties in completing this section, they said that it took a while to understand what was required of them but they were really pleased that they completed the tasks.

Family Essentials

In this section, the family chose the activity, 'Be organised', which meant that they had to sort through all their clothes, toys and household items that they no longer needed. Both sets of grandparents helped out as well, and the whole family together decided that they would give the clothes they no longer wanted to the local charity shop and sell the toys, games and bric-a-brac at a car boot sale! The two children said:

> We just loved selling on the stall with mum and dad, and I sold lots of my old games and I even sold my cuddly elephant.

Mr and Mrs Goode also wanted to make a big effort and have more family meals together, which is one of the Family Essentials activities. They decided at the beginning of the month that they would eat a minimum of four family meals together over the month, and this also included their grandparents. Granddad said:

> I have really enjoyed sitting down and eating meals together; it's something we used to do years ago.

The family earned themselves 100 points for the completion of two activities in this section.

Family Activities

All the activities in this section of the pack reinforce the value of understanding. The family successfully completed four activities over the month from this section: charades, a listening walk, 'guess the animal' and the balloon marathon. In the charades activity, everyone takes turns to act out the title of a television programme, a film or a book. The person carrying out the charades had to make sure that everyone understood the actions. Mrs Goode said about the activity:

> We had lots of fun playing this. Everybody joined in taking turns and acting out a film or book and guessing what we were trying to act out. Even granddad had a go!

The family took photographs of family members carrying out the activity and put it in their log file with their family quotes.

The second activity the family chose was the listening walk activity, which meant that they had to stop and listen very carefully to understand the different kinds of noise that they might come across on a family walk:

> *When we went on our listening walk we heard the following:*
> - *birds chirping*
> - *wind whistling*
> - *thunder*
> - *people talking*
> - *the roar of a motorbike*
> - *cars on the road*
> - *pigeon cooing*
> - *a rooster's cock-a-doodle-doo and hens*
> - *tree's rustling*
> - *an aeroplane whizzing.*

The evidence for this activity was a list of the noises that they had all heard and a photograph of the walk. The photograph and list was included in the log file under the Family Activities section.

The next activity the family completed was 'guess the animal'. This was a family game with each member of the family taking it in turns to describe a different animal without using any words:

> *Playing 'guess the animal' was a lot of fun. We all took part acting out different animals and trying to understand what each other was being. It was very funny too!*
>
> *Examples of animals that we did for the activity were a:*
> - *ostrich*
> - *rabbit*
> - *rhinoceros*
> - *frog*
> - *mole*
> - *cow*
> - *horse*
> - *snake*
> - *chimpanzee*
> - *lion*
> - *chicken*
> - *fox*
> - *kitten*

The family included the list of animals in their log file as evidence that they had completed the activity. The final activity for this section completed by the family was the balloon marathon. The aim of the activity was to use a large balloon to try to keep the balloon from falling on to the floor. Everyone must fully understand the instructions in order to make sure that everyone in the family can join in with the game while making sure that the balloon does not land on the floor. It is a team effort!

Grandma said about the activity:

> *This game was a very good exercise making us stretch and jump around to try and keep the balloon from touching the floor. We had two balloons on the go at the same time, and found that sometimes we were trying to keep both balloons from touching the ground. It was lots of fun and everyone enjoyed playing this.*

The family took two photographs of themselves playing the activity together and they cut and pasted these into their log file as evidence that they had completed the activity. They earned themselves 400 points, as each activity completed is worth 100 points each.

Family Reflections

This is the final section of the FVS pack. It is crucial that this section is completed at the end of the month to give the family an opportunity to find out what they did best and in what way the family has benefited from the activities. The Goode family completed the STAR (stop, think and reflect) family evaluation form.

Here are the family's responses to the questions:

What did your family learn about this month's value?

> *How to understand one another's feelings and that everyone needs some help and if we work together better we will have more time for play.*

What was your family's favourite activity and why?

> *We really liked the 'guess the animal' game because we had so much fun. We ran out of animals in the end. We laughed until our sides ached.*

What activity did your family like the least and why?

> *The balloon game because some of us were not very understanding when we dropped the balloon on to the floor.*

How has this month's value benefited your family?

> *Frances has understood that if she helps out around the house, we have more time to play and she can also be rewarded for her help. We all agreed that we have learnt to understand each other's feelings a lot more.*

Have you noticed any changes in your family since taking part in the FVS?

> *The values are worked into our family life all of the time. It is good to have the values to remind each other of how important we are as a family.*

The Goode family earned a total of 1050 points from completion of the activities, which qualified them for a silver award. The family's log file of evidence contained photographs, drawings and other materials, while their written evidence demonstrated an ongoing record of the activities that confirmed their achievement. The family subsequently received a blue rosette!

Log file: thoughtfulness

The French family

The French family consists of Ms French, who is in early twenties, her partner David and her two children aged 7 and 9 years from a previous relationship. The two children have access to their real father one day a week and on alternate weekends. Relationships between mum and dad are strained due to past involvement with the courts over parental responsibility. Ms French is unemployed and she receives income support, while the children are eligible for free school meals. The family lives in social housing but they are currently on the house swap register as they would like to live closer to her parents, who live approximately 10 miles away. Both Ms French and her partner do not drive or own a car and therefore visiting the grandparents and their wider family is difficult.

Her partner David is a relatively new relationship for her and he is also unemployed. They met through an Internet dating website. David has previous criminal convictions for burglary and some of his previous relationships have ended in domestic violence, which has resulted in involvement with social services. Currently, there have been no police reports of domestic violence in this new relationship but, because of his previous history, the children have been placed on the at-risk register. Thus, the family is being carefully monitored by social services staff. Both Ms French and David do not hold any formal educational nor professional qualifications as they both left school at 16 without any. Ms French is on the jobseeker's register but as yet has not been successful in gaining any employment.

The family was introduced to the scheme by social services as a tool for nurturing positive relationships within the family home and also with the children's real father. Initially, new partner David was resistant to being involved in the scheme but, after several one-to-one sessions conducted by individual social workers, they were persuaded that the scheme would help to show that he was making a valid contribution to the family home. Hence, he agreed to take part.

Below we present the families log file of evidence.

Family Gathering

The family completed the three discussion activities, which meant that they could colour in the three stars in their pack. The family goal that they set themselves was:

> *A month spent being thoughtful to each other and thinking about how our actions will affect others. We are going to set ourselves the challenge of achieving the bronze award level.*

Family Essentials

The family completed only one activity in this section due to family illness during the month. The activity they completed was family reading, and this is the evidence the two children provided, which earned them 50 points:

> *Our bedtime story book is about a butterfly fairy called Twinkle. It follows her adventures with her friends Dazzle and Skipper. Twinkle gets into trouble by falling in the pond when she is showing off her beautiful wings. Dazzle and Skipper have to rescue her before the pond skaters come. We loved the story!*

Family Activities

The family completed the following activities with, each completed activity earning the family 100 points:

- making a thoughtful cake (see Figure 11.1);
- helping a friend;

Figure 11.1 Thoughtful cake.

Figure 11.2 Thoughtful box.

- making a thought box (see Figure 11.2);
- being thoughtful to other family members; and
- visiting a family member.

Here is the list of evidence that the family provided for their log file on thoughtfulness:

- A picture of the thoughtful cake: '*I made a thoughtful cake for my sister helped by my mum. I made it because my sister makes me laugh. I love her and I know she likes cake although she didn't eat it all, we all had some.*'
- A drawing of one of the children helping a friend down a slide in the park.
- A decorated thought box that the children made for one of their teachers. Inside the box were little thank you notes and a dried flower that they thought the teacher would like. The outside of the box was decorated in pink tissue paper decorated with coloured sequins and stars.
- A report on how they had been thoughtful to each other: '*Mummy and David have said "I love you" to each other every day. We both said it at school in the morning, during the day and we said it every day at bedtime. This was an easy task because we always make sure we tell each other all the time. It always makes us happy to hear these words.*'
- A photograph of their visit to their great grandmother. They wrote: '*She is 84 years old and she is in hospital with a broken leg.*'

Family Reflections

The family completed the STAR form at the end of the pack. Here are their original answers to the questions:

What did your family learn about this month's value?

> *We all learnt not to take each other for granted and to really think about each other's feelings.*

What was your family's favourite activity and why?

> *I loved making the thoughtful cake for my sister and decorating it with sweets because it made her smile.*

What activity did your family like the least and why?

> *We didn't like visiting great nan in hospital because there were lots of ill people there.*

How has this month's value benefited your family?

> *We feel that we have achieved our family goal and we have been surprised how easy and fun it has been. It's made us really think about what we say and do!*

Have you noticed any changes in your family since taking part in the FVS?

> *We now enjoy having bedtime reading every night after our bath.*

The French family earned a total of 1000 points from completion of the activities, which qualified them for a silver award. The family's log file of evidence confirmed their achievement. The family received a blue rosette!

Log file: friendship

The Carter family

Mr and Mrs Carter and their two children Emma and Miranda brought their log file on friendship into school to be verified. Mr and Mrs Carter are both active members of the school's parent–teacher association and enjoy getting fully involved in the education of their children. Both parents live on the outskirts of a residential estate and are homeowners. Mr Carter is employed full time as an information technology consultant and is their sole source of income. Total family income is approximately £35,000 per annum. The family also owns a family car, which Mr Carter uses during the week to get himself back and forth to work. The Carter family does not meet the criteria for family income support and neither children receive free school meals.

Mrs Carter heard about the scheme from a school newsletter and was keen to involve the whole family. The family approached the FVS pack of friendship with enthusiasm and, at the end of the month, produced the following log file as evidence that they had completed their activities.

The log file was presented very simply in a white plastic two-ring binder with the evidence displayed inside 'polly' pockets. Here is an outline of the activities that the family involved themselves in during the month and the supporting evidence that they provided. The family chose not to compete for the points levels, as they preferred to take the competitive nature out of their participation.

Family Gathering

The family completed two of the discussion activities, which they self-assessed by colouring in two of the three stars. The family comments on their personal and family goals are listed below:

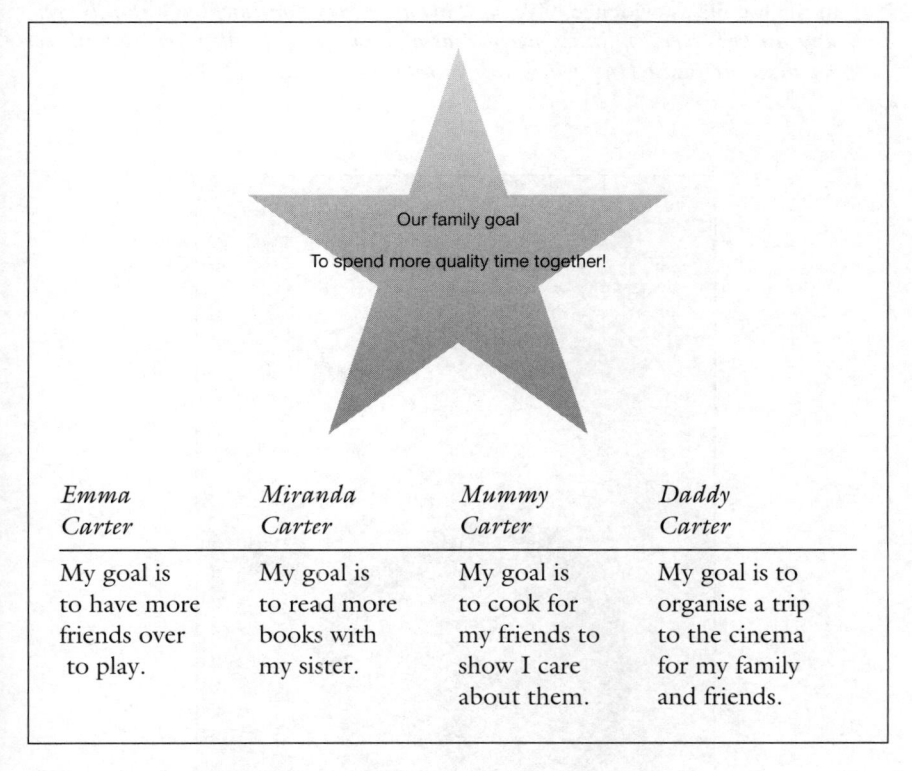

Our family goal
To spend more quality time together!

Emma Carter	*Miranda Carter*	*Mummy Carter*	*Daddy Carter*
My goal is to have more friends over to play.	My goal is to read more books with my sister.	My goal is to cook for my friends to show I care about them.	My goal is to organise a trip to the cinema for my family and friends.

Family Essentials

The family completed four activities in this section, which they self-assessed by ticking the sections and providing the following evidence. They chose the following activities because they wanted a better routine for getting to school and to encourage the girls to spend more time reading at home:

- time 4 school;
- family mealtime;
- family reading time; and
- recycling.

The supporting evidence provided by each member of the Carter family for their Family Essentials activities were:

- The girls received an attendance certificate from school for being on time to school every day. This certificate was included in the family's log file for the month.
- The family meal was taken at Pizza Hut and a copy of the receipt was included in the log file as evidence. '*We tried to have at least one meal as a family every day. In half term, mummy decided as a treat we could all meet up with her for pizza at Pizza Hut, which was yummy*' (see Figure 11.3).

Figure 11.3 **Eating together.**

Figure 11.4 Recycling truck.

- '*I have been reading my book called 'Clever Toe' and it is really good*', said Emily.
- A painting of the local recycling truck with plastic bottles and paper on the front (see Figure 11.4).

Family Activities

The Carter family completed the following activities and provided the following evidence:

- making a friendship bracelet;
- making friends special;
- Valentine's Day friendship card;
- blindfold obstacle course;
- cooking friendship biscuits; and
- the detective game.

Supporting evidence from the family activities section included the following:

- Friendship bracelets made out of wool (see Figure 11.5).
- A photograph of the family and friends sleepover.

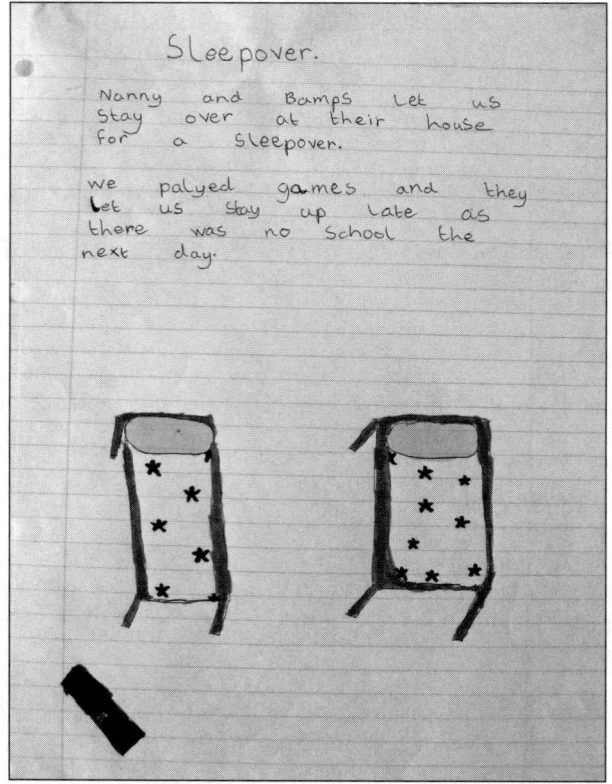

Figure 11.5 Friendship bracelets and sleepover.

'*Nanny and Bamps let us stay over at their house with two of our friends for a sleepover. We played games together and they let us stay up late because there was no school the next day*' (see Figure 11.5).
- Decorated Valentine's Day cards for all family members (see Figure 11.6).
- A drawing of the course of the blindfold obstacle game.
- Cooked and iced friendship biscuits (see Figure 11.6).
- A hot seat interview asking individual members to identify an occasion in which they felt left out and how they handled the situation. Here are two extracts when the two children were put in the hot seat. Emily Carter: '*I felt left out yesterday because my friends wouldn't play with me and I had to play on my own. I didn't tell a teacher but I should have done. I think the buddy base should be the sad spot!*' Miranda Carter: '*I felt left out at school and went to the buddy base on the playground but I think it should be called the lonely space. Someone picked me up from the spot and I was OK, but it didn't feel very nice.*' Mrs Carter said about the activity: '*The girls liked this activity as it helped them to talk about different situations that they did not want to be in and didn't like. I think that this sort of conversation should be part of a weekly routine as it made the girls feel much better once they had talked things through.*'

Figure 11.6 Valentine's Day card and friendship cakes.

Family Reflections

What did your family learn about this month's value?

We learnt to spend more time with our friends.

What was your family's favourite activity and why?

I really enjoyed making the friendship bracelets in everyone's favourite colours.

What activity did your family like the least and why?

We didn't enjoy getting up earlier to get to school on time.

How has this month's value benefited your family?

We made lots of new friends and had lots of fun.

Have you noticed any changes in your family since taking part in the FVS?

Things that were extras have now become part of our family routine, like getting up earlier and eating together as a family. We now talk more!

Log file: unity

The Ahmed family

The Ahmed family consists of Mr and Mrs Ahmed and their three daughters. Two of the daughters attend a local primary school and the eldest daughter, Chloe, is in Year 8 at a local high school. Mr Ahmed works full time for a well-known pharmaceutical sales company as area sales manager for the southwest of England. This means that Mr Ahmed commutes to work and staying overnight for 2 or 3 days a week is not unusual. Mrs Ahmed is a qualified primary school teacher but does not hold a permanent teaching post. However, she does have regular supply work at local schools. She usually works as a supply teacher for an average of 3 days per week during term time. This allows Mrs Ahmed to be available during school holidays for her three daughters.

  The youngest daughter is Molly who is on the school's special educational needs register for poor attainment in literacy. Sophie is the middle daughter and is currently in Year 3 and on target to achieve the expected attainment levels by the end of Year 6. Both girls attend their after school club when their mother is supply teaching. Both girls have a good circle of friends and behave well in school. The family's eldest daughter, Chloe, is currently in Year 8 and has found it difficult to make new friends, despite good transition arrangements being in place when she moved to the school in Year 7. However, nearly 2 years on, she is currently enjoying life at school. Academically, she is a more able child in maths and enjoys problem-solving activities.

The family are homeowners and they live in a residential area in a four-bedroom house, which has a double garage that accommodates the family's two cars. Due to their financial earnings, they do not qualify for any income benefits as they have a joint income in the region of £60,000. The family became members of the Family Values Scheme because they wanted to spend more quality time together at the weekends and they thought that this would help them to facilitate this arrangement.

Family Gathering

Each member of the family set themselves a monthly goal and here are some of the words they used: to be more thoughtful, to support one another more, to help each other and to show kindness. The family goal for the Ahmed family was to show the value of unity by working together during the month, and the reason that they wanted to do this was to bring the family closer together.

Family Essentials

The family chose the activities 'Time 4 school' and 'Let's clean up!' and produced two timetables, which they displayed in their kitchen. The box overleaf shows the timetables that they created.

Family Activities

The family completed the following activities from the Family Activities section of the pack:

- all stand together;
- balloon throw;
- human machine;
- community scrapbook;
- family learning;
- circle lion (see Figure 11.7); and
- mega paper chain (see Figure 11.8).

We will now select examples of the evidence that the family produced for the circle lion, mega paper chain and community scrapbook activities.

For the circle lion activity, the family used CDs to cut out lots of circles and then they put them all together to create a cuddly friendly lion (see Figure 11.7).

> **Time 4 school**
>
> <u>Before going to bed, do the following:</u>
>
> Uniforms ready
> Lunch boxes ready
> Alarm set for 6.15 a.m.
>
> <u>In the morning:</u>
>
> Up at 6.15 a.m.
> Breakfast at 6.30 a.m.
> Brush teeth at 6.45 a.m.
> Get dressed at 7.00 a.m.
> Hair done at 7.20 a.m.
> Shoes on at 7.30 a.m.
> School bags ready at 7.45 a.m.
> Lunch boxes done at 8.00 a.m.
> Coats on at 8.10 a.m.
>
> <u>We are now ready for school!</u>
>
> **Let's clean up!**
>
> *Mummy:* Hoover/Washing
> *Daddy:* Kitchen/Bathroom
> *Chloe:* Polishing/Living room
> *Molly:* Mop/Fold washing
> *Sophie:* Sweeping/Dining room
>
> **ALL KEEP OUR ROOMS TIDY!**

For the mega paper chain, the activity involved all family members working together to create a large paper chain out of coloured paper. They counted the number of weeks to their annual family holiday and the total number of links on the chain corresponded to the number of weeks to their vacation. Each week, they all took turns in tearing off one of the chains.

'*It was so simple yet great fun, a real motivator for us all to work together and gave us something to look to*', said Mr Ahmed.

The family created a community scrapbook, which included researching the history of their local area. They also included a 'what's on' section on all the local events in their area. Mrs Ahmed helped the girls on this activity, as she said it gave her something to do during the week when her husband was away.

Figure 11.7 Circle lion.

Figure 11.8 Mega paper chain.

Family Reflections

What did your family learn about this month's value?

We learnt that working together can be helpful and rewarding.

What was your family's favourite activity and why?

Doing the circle lion activity and paper chain, as we like doing crafts.

What activity did your family like the least and why?

Nothing. We all enjoyed everything.

How has this month's value benefited your family?

We have shown the value of unity this month by working as a team and feel we have achieved our family goal. We have communicated well with each other by showing each other love and we feel that we have communicated more with our daughters' schools by looking up information about what is going on.

Have you noticed any changes in your family since taking part in the FVS?

Chloe likes keeping busy and is a very thoughtful child anyway, but this month's challenge has changed Chloe into her helping her younger sisters even more.

Log file: freedom

The Green family

The log file that we will now present extracts from comes from a single-parent family. This consists of Mr Green and his two daughters, Samantha and Jocelyn, aged 4 and 7 respectively, and his 14-year-old son, Ben. Nan Green helps and supports the family, and took part in the scheme for the month of 'freedom'.

Mr Green has a history of mental illness and suffers from depression. He is a single parent after his partner left him when the children were very young. Since her departure, Mr Green has found it very difficult to manage without the support of his mother, Nan Green. Mr Green lives in social housing and is on income support, with all three children receiving free school meals. Mr Green became a member of the Family Values Scheme after the school felt that it would help to improve his children's attendance (87 per cent) and improve the behaviour of his son, Ben, currently attending the local high school, as well as improving relationships within the family.

Ben, the eldest child, has been in receipt of a 5-day fixed-term exclusion for displaying violent and aggressive behaviour against a member of staff after she confronted him about vandalism of the school toilets. The family decided to see if they could achieve the bronze award as a family. Below are some selected extracts from the family's log file on 'freedom'.

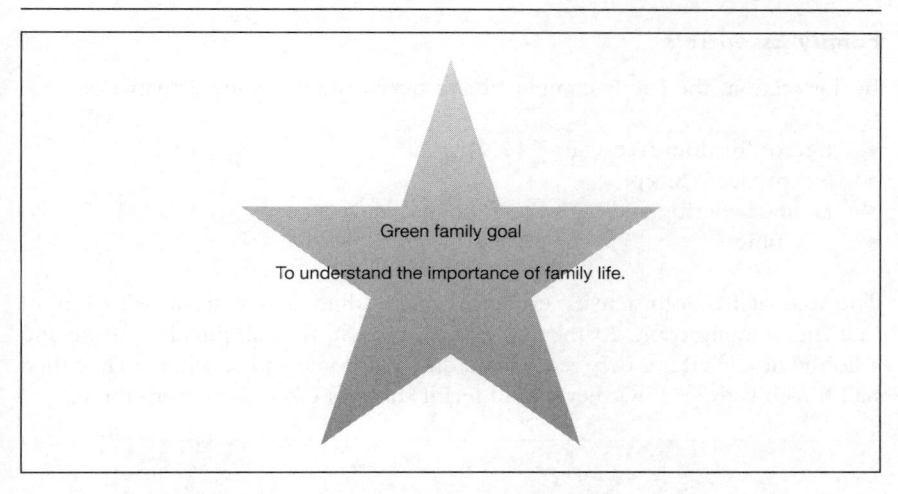

> Green family goal
> To understand the importance of family life.

Family Gathering

Mr Green gave the following personal account after one of the discussion activities:

> Today we discussed the importance of rules and boundaries and why we have them. We talked abut how life runs better and happier if we have rules that are set in place. For example; rules about cleaning, personal hygiene, bedtimes, watching television. If these rules are not put in place, we as a family would not have any structure and we would not be happy so its good to have rules. Ben has different rules to Sam and Jocelyn as he is fourteen and is expected to do things differently and is given more freedom than Sam who is four. However, he is expected to respect his family and home and when needed help out in the house.
>
> Sam is at an age where she is still learning about rules and we all had a really good conversation about the value of freedom and talked about why it is that people lose their freedom when they have done something wrong and have to go to prison because of their actions.
>
> We talked about the couple Paul and Rachel Chandler who were taken by Somali Pirates off the Seychelles and held for over a year against their will until they were recently freed and how they must have felt when it happened. We all agreed that they must have felt terrified with what was happening to them. Thankfully, they are free today and are now much happier. We also discussed about the Chile miners that had their freedom taken away from them accidentally when they were trapped underground for sixty-nine days. How difficult it must have been for them knowing they were trapped underground with their families above them. Again, a happy ending when the miners were brought up a few weeks later and how happy they must have felt to have their freedom again.

Family Essentials

In this section, the family completed and ticked the following activities:

- tree of freedom (see Figure 11.9);
- Sleep! Sleep! Sleep!;
- family favourite; and
- tidy time.

The tree of freedom activity evidence was to draw a tree trunk with lots of branches coming off it. At the end of each branch, they all put their name and a hobby or something they really liked doing at home and at school. They then had to think about how they would feel if this was taken away from them.

Figure 11.9 Tree of freedom.

Below are some of the ideas that the family came up with for their tree of freedom:

- Sam loves swimming and colouring.
- Jocelyn enjoys going to parties – '*I would hate not being able to go to parties and dress up*'.
- Jocelyn likes to dress up and have her nails painted.
- Ben likes playing and listening to music with his friends – '*Music is my life and without it I am lost*'.
- Nan Green likes to cook and bake for the family.
- Dad enjoys reading and being quiet.

Sleep! Sleep! Sleep!

Going to bed on time is essential for a good night's sleep. Mr Green said this about the activity:

> *After half term, we noticed that it was a little harder getting up early in the morning. So, we consciously went to bed 15 minutes earlier, which definitely gave us more energy in the morning.*

Tidy time!

Nan Green commented on this activity:

> *We all had a good sort out of our bedrooms. We were surprised how much stuff we have but haven't touched in a very long time. Jocelyn went through her bedroom and sorted out a lot of toys she doesn't play with anymore. I sorted out her wardrobe and filled two black bags full of clothes that I am going to give to charity. Ben tidied up his bedroom and filled a black bag that was just rubbish and clutter. We all have so much room now and feel much better for doing it!*

Family Activities

The family took part in the following activities:

- hide and seek;
- picture perfect;
- flying discs (see Figure 11.10); and
- mind and body.

Figure 11.10 Flying discs.

Mind and body

Going for a family walk to de-stress the day to somewhere you have never been before.

> *On the weekend, we went for a lovely walk around our local town. We talked about the leaves we could see and the nice scenery around us. We decided to walk into town and had a really wonderful surprise when we saw Santa and his friends. Sam was lucky enough to have her picture taken with Santa inside his grotto. It was a lovely family afternoon that ended happily!*

Family favourite

> *On the weekend we all sat down to watch a wonderful brand new film we hadn't seen before called, My Neighbour Totoro. It was about the story of two sisters, Suski and little Mei, who moved to the countryside and befriended a giant spirit that lived in the forest. We all really enjoyed just being together and watching the film, even Ben!*

Family Reflections

What did your family learn about this month's value?

All the different ways we can have our freedom and lose it too.

What was your family's favourite activity and why?

Hide and seek because it was very funny when we found each other.

What activity did your family like the least and why?

We liked all the activities.

How has this month's value benefited your family?

As a family, we are all grateful that we enjoy our freedom and Sam just loves everything in this month's pack.

Have you noticed any changes in your family since taking part in the FVS?

It has helped give me more confidence and we have done more fun activities together and we have enjoyed discussing the different topics about people who have lost their freedom.

FVS courage pack

In this section, we give examples of two different families using the same pack to show how different families organised and presented their evidence. Throughout the accounts, we will be making direct comparisons as to how the two families chose the activities for the various sections and the issues that they raised.

The Hayes family

Mr and Mrs Hayes are a professional couple and are homeowners living in a sought-after area of their local town. They are company directors for their own cleaning and home improvement business, which employs approximately 25 people. The business is profitable, with an annual turnover of around £750,000. Mr and Mrs Hayes have twin sons, Harvey and Liam, who are both in Year 2 class at their local primary school. Both parents have little time to attend school events and, apart from reading the occasional newsletter and attending the annual parents' evening, neither parent is involved in school life.

Mr Hayes was privately educated and attended Oxford University, where he read English. Mrs Hayes, while state educated, also went on to higher education where she obtained a 2:1 degree in History. They got involved in the Family

Values Scheme when they received an invitation from their children inviting them into a Family Values afternoon. Mr Hayes was unable to attend due to other business commitments but Mrs Hayes did. She was impressed with how the scheme encouraged people to use traditional family values at home and also how it helped to foster and promote links to their children's school. The FVS pack that they decided to complete was about promoting the value of courage (see Chapter 12).

The Webster family

Scarlet and Thomas are both looked-after children with the local authority and are currently in foster care. They were placed on the child protection register for their parent's neglect after previously living with their mother who, at the time, suffered from alcohol abuse.

The children are aged 6 and 8 years and they have been placed with a foster family in close proximity to the school with whom they have been living with for 6 months while mum Webster is going through a rehabilitation programme supported by social services. Dad Webster left the family home when both children were very young and they have since had no contact. Scarlet has a speech impediment and receives support from the speech and language service. She also has low self-esteem and lacks confidence. She is on the school's special educational needs register for poor literacy skills, and receives 2 hours a day of learning support with a teaching assistant.

Thomas is academically able and makes good progress in the core subjects, achieving the expected level at the end of Key Stage 1. Both children receive supervised access to mum once a week but are happy with their foster placement. The school invited the foster carers to take part in the scheme to help the children to raise their levels of self-esteem and to improve the quality of their 'family relationships'. This was especially helpful for their mother, as the activities would provide them with a focus during supervised access times organised through social services. Courage was the first FVS pack that the children and their foster parents took part in.

Family Gathering

The Hayes family

The first thing the family had to do was to find out the meaning of the value of courage. Harvey and Liam with their mother researched on the Internet and came up with this definition of the word 'courage': 'The state or quality of mind or spirit that enables one to face danger, fear with confidence, to feel fear and still be able to face danger, pain or trouble'. The family discussed what this meant between them so that they all understood it. They then came up with answers to the following questions:

What's the first thing you think of when you hear the word 'courage'?

Being brave like the lion from Wizard of Oz.

Think of some examples of courage from a book you have read, a film you have seen or something that has happened in school.

In The Lion King, Simba shows courage by coming back to Pride Rock and challenging Scar so he can be the rightful king.

Nemo shows courage when he helps a school of fish caught in a fisherman's net. He gets in and tells everyone to swim down so they can break the net and escape. This is the first situation where Marlin lets Nemo do something dangerous and doesn't hold him back or overprotect him.

Do you think that being courageous involves taking risks? Why or why not?

Yes, because to be courageous you have to face your fears.

What can you do to today to show courage?

The twins showed courage today when confronted with a big spider while helping mum set up the paddling pool.

The Webster family

The Webster children and their foster carers chose to complete the 'Courage is' activity, where they had to draw and write two pictures of how they would show courage (see Figure 11.11). '*I have drawn two pictures: when I walk upstairs by myself and when I try to swim 10 metres*', said Scarlet. The writing activity was supported by foster mum but the drawing was completed independently. '*My two examples of courage are: removing a spider from the bath as I am really scared of spiders and going in the attic as it is really dark and I don't like ladders*' (completed by foster mum). '*When I walked into the police station I was a bit scared and when I try to eat carrots that I don't like*', said Thomas. '*Diving from a height into a swimming pool as it seems a long way to jump and being able to climb a tree in order to get a ball or kite as I fear falling*', said foster dad.

170 Log files

Figure 11.11 Courage paintings.

Both Scarlet and Thomas also completed the 'Courage is' activity and together they came up with the following statements:

Courage is being brave around insects.

Courage is not being afraid of spiders.

Family essentials

In this section, the Hayes family chose to complete the sporting activity and provided a swimming and locker receipt in the log file to prove this. '*I went swimming with my mummy and daddy and my sister to the leisure centre. We had lots of fun jumping in the water and playing in waves when the wave machine came on*', said the twins.

The Webster family completed the following in this section:

- having a meal together;
- family walk;
- reading a book;
- tidying up the garden;
- attending a school event; and
- playing a board game together.

Evidence for the above activities for the Webster family came from the following:

- menu from Pizza Express;
- visit to the boating lake and a leaflet of the park;
- six reading books and book reviews;
- sports day stickers and medals; and
- Connect 4 photograph.

Family activities

Both the Webster family and the Hayes family completed the 'make a family scarecrow using recycled materials' activity. Both families took photographs of the event and pasted them into their log files to prove that they had completed the activity.

Here is the evidence from the Hayes family:

> *Together as a family we all made a scarecrow and we used newspaper and straw to stuff his trousers and jumper.*

Here is the evidence from the Webster family:

> *Making a family scarecrow was great and we took photographs stuffing the trousers, stuffing the shirt and we finished him off by placing a plant pot on his head and calling him Mr S Crow.*

The Webster family also completed the following activities and provided the following evidence:

- Making a family rainbow poster (see Figure 11.12).

Figure 11.12 Making a family rainbow poster.

Figure 11.13 Courage pennant.

- Making a courage pennant (see Figure 11.13).
- Bubble-blowing activities. '*To make bubbles we used:*
  - *straws;*
  - *pastry cutters;*
  - *forks;*
  - *potato masher;*
  - *toilet rolls;*
  - *pipe cleaners; and*
  - *cut up pop plastic bottles.*

  We found out that straws make lots of little bubbles and the cut up plastic pop bottles made the largest bubbles.'
- Wizard of Oz cartoon strip. The family included the theatre tickets in their log files as evidence (see Figure 11.14). '*We all went to see the Wizard of Oz and we were lucky enough to meet Dorothy afterwards.*'

Figure 11.14 Wizard of Oz cartoon strip.

- Blindfold challenge. In this activity, the family had to find and cover four boxes and label them 'touch me', 'hear me', 'taste me' and 'smell me'. The objective of the game is to find foods that fit the above criteria. The foods are placed in the boxes and the family member is blindfolded and has to chose a box to identify what the food is. The Webster family put the following foods into the boxes (see Figure 11.15):
  - 'Touch me' was a jelly.
  - 'Hear me' was pasta.
  - 'Taste me' was raw carrots.
  - 'Smell me' was an onion.

  '*This challenge gave us the most laughs.*'

- Is it strong enough? Can a piece of paper hold up a book? Do you have the courage to persist and find the answer? The Webster family wrote in their log file that they first of all tried with the paper folded in half standing up. Next, they tried again with the paper folded in half but the other way around and again it did not work. Foster dad then had a clever idea to roll the paper in a cylinder shape and use a smaller hardback book to balance on the top, and it finally worked (see Figure 11.16).

Figure 11.15 Blindfold challenge.

Figure 11.16 Is it strong enough?

Family Reflections

Both the Webster and the Hayes family completed this section of their log files.

Hayes family reflections

What did your family learn about this month's family value?

Not to be afraid when confronted with things that make us scared and to try and be brave.

What was your family's favourite activity and why?

We enjoyed painting what courage is on big bits of paper. Mummy, daddy and grampy all enjoyed making the scarecrow as they said it took them back to their younger days.

Which activity did your family like the least and why?

We enjoyed everything!

How has this month's family value benefited your family?

It has been really enjoyable and again showed how well we all work together especially when we built the scarecrow.

Webster family reflections

What did your family learn about this month's family value?

Not to be afraid when confronted with things that make us scared and to try to be brave.

What was your family's favourite activity and why?

We loved making the scarecrow and the rainbow painting activity.

Which activity did your family like the least and why?

Admitting that we were scared of things.

How has this month's family value benefited your family?

I have laughed a lot more and the visits with mum have been better as she has been able to do some of the activities with us and we put her in the log file.

Summary

In this chapter, we have tried to demonstrate through selected examples and extracts taken from participating families' log files how the Family Values Scheme can be evidenced. The log files are autonomous and unique to each family. Therefore, different families provide a variety of their own first-hand evidence for each of the varying activities. The Family Reflections section is an honest account of how the family feels that they have benefited from using the pack related to each of the activities for the individual value that they have been undertaking during the month. This provides evidence of the strong links between the assessment process achieved during the compilation of the log files and the overall impact of the scheme on family life. We will now demonstrate this evidence and one of the themes explored in this chapter even more by taking the value of 'courage' a stage further by presenting one of the packs used in the process in the FVS in Chapter 12.

Chapter 12

Courage

In this chapter, we present evidence from one of our values-based packs for the Family Values Scheme. The one we have chosen is on the value of 'courage'. The pack and materials are largely self-explanatory. You should soon discover how and why the children, parents and extended family members enjoy working their way through them and have lots of enjoyment undertaking all the practical activities. The whole idea behind the style and content of the packs is to make them as user-friendly as possible for everyone, including teachers and professional support staff.

178 Courage

FAMILY VALUES SCHEME

Inside

Family Gathering

Family Essentials

Family Activities

Family Reflections

Instructions

Resources

COURAGE

WHAT IS COURAGE?

To have the courage to try something that is different and that you are not familiar with is a real challenge in itself. Courage is not something that you are born with, as it comes from within, but it is very easy to care for. All you need to do is give it daily attention and it will grow big and strong! Having courage is persevering when things maybe do not turn out as they should or it could be having the confidence to stand up to someone or for something you believe in.

REMEMBER:

1. Read the safety guidelines in the 'Instructions' section.
2. Tick the tasks you complete and collect evidence.
3. Complete the STAR family evaluation to qualify.
4. Share your successes on the forum at www.behaviourstop.co.uk.

Better Behaviour through Home–School Relations, Routledge © Gill Ellis, Nicola S. Morgan and Ken Reid 2012, adapted from the Family Values Scheme, Gill Ellis And Nicola S. Morgan, 2012

FAMILY GATHERING

Get started this month by holding a family meeting with as many family members that you can. You can meet around a table in the house or be creative and make use of the outdoors. Set a date and time to hold the meeting, select a family leader to chair it and then follow the steps below to get yourself started on this month's family value. There are three discussion activities and against each one there is a yellow star. Together, aim to colour in all the stars before you start this month's Family Values tasks.

★ Read together the 'What is courage?' section on the front page of the pack and discuss what this value means to you as a family. Using a large sheet of paper, write the value 'courage' in the centre and write down everyone's responses. Pair together any answers that are related to each other. Use a dictionary if necessary to make sure that everyone understands what it means.

★ Together, discuss all the courageous things that each family member has done. Make a list! What does it mean to show courage? What qualities do you need to be a courageous person? Is it always easy to be courageous? Why? Discuss together.

> 'The greatest barrier to success is the fear of failure.'
>
> Sven Goran Eriksson

REMEMBER: The value!

Better Behaviour through Home–School Relations, Routledge © Gill Ellis, Nicola S. Morgan and Ken Reid 2012, adapted from the Family Values Scheme, Gill Ellis And Nicola S. Morgan, 2012

FAMILY GATHERING

Now you are ready to decide on what your family goals are for this month. Together, answer the following questions:

- What do you want to achieve on your own?

- What do you want to achieve as a family?

Complete the 'Family Goals' page (at the back of the pack) and put it where everyone can see it. Keep reminding yourselves throughout the month what you want to achieve and be determined to find the time to do it! Think about how you will all feel when you have achieved what you set out to do!

When you have completed the 'Family Gathering' activities, colour in the stars and get ready to have some family fun!

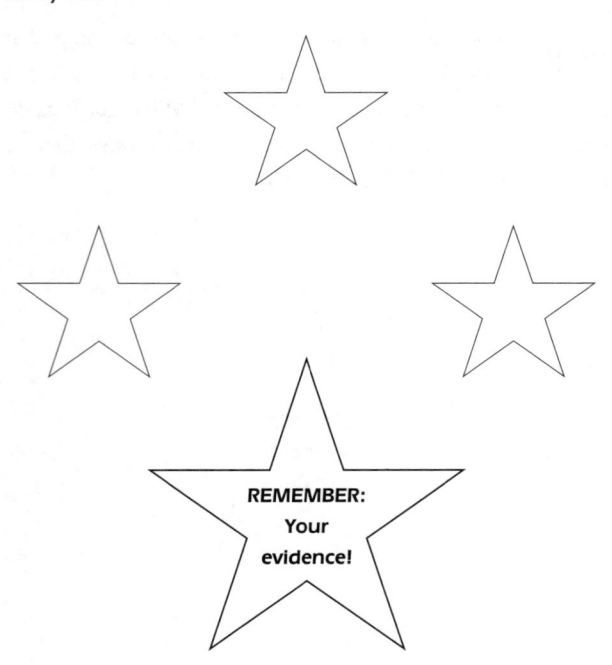

'Having the courage to admit one's errors not only clears up the air of guilt and defensiveness, but often helps solve the problem created by the error.'

Dale Carnegie

REMEMBER: Your evidence!

Better Behaviour through Home–School Relations, Routledge © Gill Ellis, Nicola S. Morgan and Ken Reid 2012, adapted from the Family Values Scheme, Gill Ellis And Nicola S. Morgan, 2012

FAMILY ESSENTIALS

Routine family tasks are the core principles of Family Essentials. It is these basic essentials that will help to strengthen family relationships! Family Essentials is a really easy way to achieve points for your Family Values award. The more tasks you complete, the more award points you earn as a family.

Family Values book club ☆

Plan time for a family reading session. Choose a book together that you will all enjoy! Sit down in a circle and take turns reading. Discuss characters, the plot and the illustrations (if any). At the end of the story, discuss your favourite parts and write a family book review. See www.childrensbooks.about.com for some of the UK's top children's books.

Time 4 school ☆

Can you get to school on time? How can you achieve this? Plan and prepare the night before to make your mornings go with a swing! If getting up is a struggle, set your clock forward by 10 minutes. This is a great trick that really works.

> 'You gain strength, courage, and confidence by every experience in which you really stop to look fear in the face. You must do the thing which you think you cannot do.'
>
> Eleanor Roosevelt

REMEMBER: To help out!

Better Behaviour through Home–School Relations, Routledge © Gill Ellis, Nicola S. Morgan and Ken Reid 2012, adapted from the Family Values Scheme, Gill Ellis And Nicola S. Morgan, 2012

FAMILY ESSENTIALS

Family meals ☆

Plan to eat a family meal together. Laying the table, serving and washing up are all part of having a family meal together. How many family meals can you do?

Let's clean up ☆

Housework is never a chore if all the family gets in on the act. Make a list of all the housework to be done during the week and divide them up between all your family. Dusting, hoovering, washing, ironing and cleaning are essential for a clean home!

Family learning ☆

Is completing homework a chore? Why not work together to find out something new? Visiting the local library or researching on the Internet are great ways of doing this. Completing homework can be fun! Encourage each other to learn something new.

> 'Courage doesn't always roar. Sometimes courage is the quiet voice at the end of the day saying, "I will try again tomorrow".'
>
> Mary Anne Radmacher

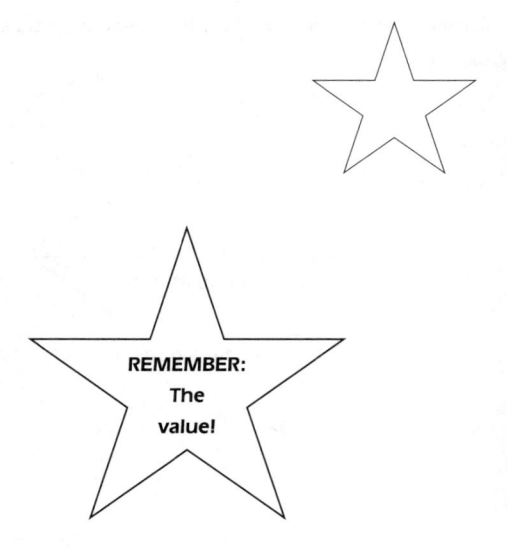

REMEMBER: The value!

Better Behaviour through Home–School Relations, Routledge © Gill Ellis, Nicola S. Morgan and Ken Reid 2012, adapted from the Family Values Scheme, Gill Ellis And Nicola S. Morgan, 2012

FAMILY ACTIVITIES

Tin man treats ☆

Find the part in the story of *The Wizard of Oz* (by Frank L. Baum) where Dorothy and the scarecrow are fighting with the apple trees and they discover the tin man. As you know, the tin man wanted to go with Dorothy as he did not feel he had a heart. Have a go at making tin man treats by cutting out small hearts from pieces of apple and banana and any other fruit you can think of. Melt some chocolate and cover the fruit in the chocolate and leave to set in the fridge. You will need a small heart cutter to make the hearts. Place in an airtight container.

Over the rainbow ☆

Make a rainbow cake using a Victoria sandwich recipe. Once cooked, fill the sponges with jam and buttercream and place on top of each other. Decorate the cake with buttercream icing and, to make the rainbow, use coloured Smarties. Do not forget to put in the yellow brick road!

REMEMBER: Involve everyone!

COURAGE TIPS

Do the right thing even if you find it difficult.

Try something different whether it is food or a new activity.

Never give up! Even if you are finding something difficult, stick with it and never give up!

Better Behaviour through Home–School Relations, Routledge © Gill Ellis, Nicola S. Morgan and Ken Reid 2012, adapted from the Family Values Scheme, Gill Ellis And Nicola S. Morgan, 2012

FAMILY ACTIVITIES

Try something new ☆

Have the courage this month to try something new! Do something new as a family or individually. This could mean meeting up with an old friend, trying a new hobby, wearing a different colour or trying a new food. For inspirational stories to give you the courage to try out new things, be inspired by checking out the following website: www.dailymail.co.uk/.../National-Bravery-Awards-2012.

Wicked witch's hat ☆

Make yourself a wicked witch's hat using black paper and card. Decorate the hat to make it look as spooky and scary as possible. Paint on spiders, cobwebs and creepy crawlies in dark colours. Roll the paper into a cone shape and measure to fit your head. Secure it tightly with Sellotape or glue. Once finished, wear the hat and try to think of what it would feel like to scare someone and what would they feel like.

Courage is . . . ☆

Together, draw a picture showing courage in action, then complete the sentence 'Courage is . . .' and write it on the top of your piece of paper. Display the pictures around the home to remind everyone of this month's value.

> 'Courage is what it takes to stand up and speak; courage is also what it takes to sit down and listen.'
>
> Winston Churchill

REMEMBER: Have fun!

Better Behaviour through Home–School Relations, Routledge © Gill Ellis, Nicola S. Morgan and Ken Reid 2012, adapted from the Family Values Scheme, Gill Ellis And Nicola S. Morgan, 2012

FAMILY ACTIVITIES

Blindfolded obstacle course ☆

Together, design an obstacle course in your back garden or local park. One family member plays the guide while the other is blindfolded. The blindfolded family member must navigate the course by following the commands of the guide. The guide yells commands such as 'left', 'right' or 'straight', as well as warning the blindfolded partner about obstacles. The aim is to complete the obstacle course successfully. Be creative, as the more interesting the course, the more courage one of you will have to complete it. Use paddling pools filled with water, blankets to climb under and objects to climb over.

Make a family scarecrow ☆

Design and make your own adorable scarecrow using recycled materials. Why not put your scarecrow in the garden to see if it frightens the birds away? If you need some ideas on how to make a scarecrow, look on the Internet or go to the library.

Is it strong enough? ☆

Can a piece of paper hold up a book? Together, find ways for a piece of paper (and nothing else) to hold up a hardback book. Do you have the courage to persist and find the answer?

> 'Each person has inside a basic decency and goodness. If he listens to it and acts on it, he is giving a great deal of what it is the world needs most. It is not complicated but it takes courage.'
>
> Pablo Casals

REMEMBER: Your goals!

Better Behaviour through Home–School Relations, Routledge © Gill Ellis, Nicola S. Morgan and Ken Reid 2012, adapted from the Family Values Scheme, Gill Ellis And Nicola S. Morgan, 2012

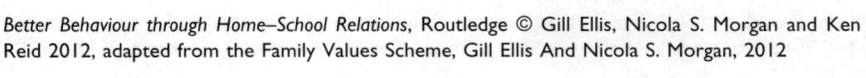

FAMILY ACTIVITIES

Make a family rainbow poster ☆

Get messy this month and get the paints and brushes out! Create a family rainbow. Each member of the family paints their hand with a lovely bright colour then places their painted hand on to a large sheet of paper, repeating the hand print across the paper into a semi circle shape. The end result will be a colourful rainbow. Do not forget to paint in the pot of gold!

Wizard of Oz cartoon strip ☆

What might you say if you were Dorothy on the yellow brick road and you suddenly met the cowardly lion? What advice would you give to him?

Divide the following characters between your family: Dorothy, the cowardly lion, tin man and Toto. Imagine you are all going on a journey to a magical place and on the way you bump into someone who needs a bit of courage to set them on their way. Write a cartoon strip using speech bubbles to put in what each of the characters say.

> 'Courage is the discovery that you may not win, and trying when you know you can lose.'
>
> Tom Krause

REMEMBER: The value!

Better Behaviour through Home–School Relations, Routledge © Gill Ellis, Nicola S. Morgan and Ken Reid 2012, adapted from the Family Values Scheme, Gill Ellis And Nicola S. Morgan, 2012

FAMILY ACTIVITIES

Make a courage pennant ☆

You will need cut out pennant shapes (triangle shapes) made out of card. Each family member will need three pennant shapes, crayons, markers and glitter glue.

Each family member will need to complete three tasks. The first task is to think of a something that will make you feel powerful (e.g. 'I feel strong', 'I can do it!').

Write this on to your first pennant and decorate it using crayons, markers and glitter glue. The second task is to write your name on to the second pennant and be creative (e.g. if you have an 'O' in your name, you could turn it into a smiley face). Why not make your name into a rainbow or a happy shape? On the third pennant, draw something that you enjoy doing, something that you are good at (e.g. a favourite sport or a favourite animal). Decorate this pennant with something that makes you smile!

Once you have completed your three pennants, be confident in what you can do and display them for everyone to see.

'If we're growing, we're always going to be out of our comfort zone.'

John Maxwell

REMEMBER: Involve everyone!

Better Behaviour through Home–School Relations, Routledge © Gill Ellis, Nicola S. Morgan and Ken Reid 2012, adapted from the Family Values Scheme, Gill Ellis And Nicola S. Morgan, 2012

FAMILY ACTIVITIES

Blindfold challenge ☆

How well can you use your sense of hearing, taste, touch and smell? Set up four stations, one for each of your senses, and place objects or food in each one. Cover the stations so no one can see the objects or food. Take it in turns to blindfold each family member and then let them try to guess what each of the objects or food is by using their senses.

Going fishing ☆

You will need some paper, hole punch, paper clips, wooden dowel, string, magnet and a can. Give everyone a small piece of paper. Fold it in half. On the upper half, write down something you are, or were, afraid of. On the lower half, write what you did or can do to get over this fear. You don't not need to put your names on the paper. Punch a hole through the top of both pieces of paper near the fold, then attach a paper clip. Place the pieces of paper in a can. Give everyone a 'fishing pole', a wooden dowel with string and a magnet attached to the end. Together, take turns dropping the end of the pole into the can. The magnet will attach to the paper clip. Then 'reel in' the clip of paper and read what is on the paper. Discuss how it takes courage to overcome our fears.

> *'If you wait to do everything until you're sure it's right, you'll probably never do much of anything.'*
>
> Win Borden

REMEMBER: Have fun!

Better Behaviour through Home–School Relations, Routledge © Gill Ellis, Nicola S. Morgan and Ken Reid 2012, adapted from the Family Values Scheme, Gill Ellis And Nicola S. Morgan, 2012

FAMILY REFLECTIONS

Family meeting

At the end of the month, it is time to hold a family meeting for everyone to reflect on how well the family has done the following:

- demonstrated the value 'courage';
- communicated with each other;
- interacted with the school and the community;
- achieved individual goals; and
- achieved family goals.

Time to evaluate

Evaluate using the checklist below:

- I/we have shown the value 'courage' this month by . . .
- I/we have communicated well with each other by . . .
- I/we have interacted with school and the community by . . .
- I have achieved my individual goal this month by . . .
- We have achieved our family goal this month by . . .
- I/we feel that we could improve . . .

'A great leader's courage to fulfil his vision comes from passion, not position.'

John Maxwell

REMEMBER: The value!

Better Behaviour through Home–School Relations, Routledge © Gill Ellis, Nicola S. Morgan and Ken Reid 2012, adapted from the Family Values Scheme, Gill Ellis And Nicola S. Morgan, 2012

FAMILY REFLECTIONS

Family nominations

Together, decide who deserves your Family Values trophy. The nominations can be discussed around the table or written on a piece of paper and placed in a box. Pretend you are at the Oscars and present the winner with the trophy.

The Family Values trophy can be purchased from www.behaviourstop.co.uk.

Family Values STAR

For your family to qualify for this month's Family Values award, please complete the STAR family evaluation form at the back of this month's pack. Together, calculate how many Family Values points you have achieved and send the evidence and form into your school's Family Values Scheme coordinator.

Family Values motivator

Remember to keep showing the value 'courage' within your family today and every day!

> 'Promise me you'll always remember: You're braver than you believe, and stronger than you seem, and smarter than you think.'
>
> Christopher Robin to Pooh (A. A. Milne)

REMEMBER: Your family STAR!

Better Behaviour through Home–School Relations, Routledge © Gill Ellis, Nicola S. Morgan and Ken Reid 2012, adapted from the Family Values Scheme, Gill Ellis And Nicola S. Morgan, 2012

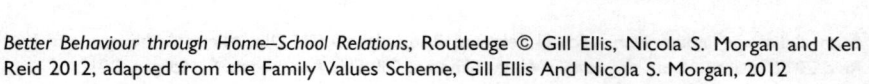

INSTRUCTIONS

Getting started

Step 1
Please read the 'Safety guidelines' on the next page before getting started on the activities.

Step 2
Together as a family, set your goals. A family can consist of any number, so invite mum(s) and dad(s), brothers and sisters, grandparents, uncles, aunts, cousins, godparents, close family friends, support workers.

Step 3
Gather your evidence for each activities and display it in your Family Values logbook. Your evidence can include, for example, photos, videos, tickets, pictures, written accounts, etc.

Step 4
Complete the STAR family evaluation form to qualify and hand it in to the Family Values Scheme coordinator at your school/organisation/children's centre.

Step 5
Tell us about your success stories on the forum at www.behaviourstop.co.uk or email us on info@behaviourstop.co.uk.

> 'In family life, love is the oil that eases friction, the cement that binds closer together, and the music that brings harmony.'
>
> Eva Burrows

REMEMBER: Your evidence!

Better Behaviour through Home–School Relations, Routledge © Gill Ellis, Nicola S. Morgan and Ken Reid 2012, adapted from the Family Values Scheme, Gill Ellis And Nicola S. Morgan, 2012

INSTRUCTIONS

Safety guidelines

Please read the safety guidelines before getting started.

Web safe code for children

1. Do not give out your home address or phone number without permission. Ask first!
2. Do not give out the name and address of your school/organisation/children's centre without permission. Ask first!
3. Do not meet anyone who you contact on the Internet unless your parent/carer says it is OK to do so and they go with you.

General safety

1. Always ensure activities take place in a safe environment.
2. Keep sharp implements and potentially dangerous substances (e.g. glue) away from your child/children.
3. Ensure that your children are supervised by a responsible adult at all times.
4. Stop immediately if you or another member of your family feels unwell when taking part in an activity, and seek medical advice.

Disclaimer

Behaviour Stop Ltd is not responsible or liable directly or indirectly for any damages made by any organisation, staff, children and/or family member(s) resulting from the use or misuse of information/tasks contained in the Family Values Scheme packs.

'Families are the compass that guide us. They are the inspiration to reach great heights, and our comfort when we occasionally falter.'

Brad Henry

REMEMBER: Stay safe!

Better Behaviour through Home–School Relations, Routledge © Gill Ellis, Nicola S. Morgan and Ken Reid 2012, adapted from the Family Values Scheme, Gill Ellis And Nicola S. Morgan, 2012

Courage 193

FAMILY GOALS

Draw or photograph each family member and write their goal, then decide on your family goal.

Name:
Goal:

Name:
Goal:

Name:
Goal:

Name:
Goal:

Our Family Goal

Name:
Goal:

Name:
Goal:

Name:
Goal:

Name:
Goal:

Name:
Goal:

Name:
Goal:

Better Behaviour through Home–School Relations, Routledge © Gill Ellis, Nicola S. Morgan and Ken Reid 2012, adapted from the Family Values Scheme, Gill Ellis And Nicola S. Morgan, 2012

STAR FAMILY EVALUATION

Stop, think and reflect

When you have completed the month's activities, please self-evaluate and hand in the STAR family evaluation form to your Family Values Scheme coordinator.

Family name: ....

Registered email address: ....

What did your family learn about this month's value? ....
....
....

What was your family's favourite activity and why? ....
....
....

What activity did your family least like and why? ....
....
....

How has this month's value benefited your family? ....
....
....
....
....

Have you noticed any changes in your family since taking part in 'Family Values'? ....
....
....
....
....
....
....

Thank you for completing the STAR self-evaluation

Better Behaviour through Home–School Relations, Routledge © Gill Ellis, Nicola S. Morgan and Ken Reid 2012, adapted from the Family Values Scheme, Gill Ellis And Nicola S. Morgan, 2012

> 'The only rock I know that stays steady, the only institution I know that works is the family.'
>
> Lee Iacocca

WELL DONE!

We hope you have enjoyed this month's Family Values pack. Remember to tell us about your thoughts and success stories on the forum at www.behaviourstop.co.uk. We are always looking for ways to improve the Family Values Scheme, so let us know if you have any suggestions for:

- Family Gathering;
- Family Essentials;
- Family Activities; and/or
- Family Reflections

For trophies, rosettes, logbooks, etc., log on to www.behaviourstop.co.uk and go to our online shop. *Remember to get next month's Family Values pack!*

REMEMBER to complete the STAR family evaluation form to qualify and hand it in to the Family Values Scheme coordinator at your school/ children's centre/ organisation.

Better Behaviour through Home–School Relations, Routledge © Gill Ellis, Nicola S. Morgan and Ken Reid 2012, adapted from the Family Values Scheme, Gill Ellis And Nicola S. Morgan, 2012

Summary

In this chapter, we have presented one of our 22 Family Values packs based on each of the values in the scheme. In addition, in the FVS, some other packs have been prepared and are used on key issues such as implementing the scheme, evaluation and the use of the Family Values themes and ideals to enable pupils with their literacy, behaviour and attendance, and this will be the theme of our second follow-up book. In the next chapter, we will look at the implementation and evaluation of the FVS to date in Herefordshire.

Chapter 13

Even more evaluation

This chapter provides two further short case studies of how the Family Values Scheme has made an impact. We will do so, first, at a local authority level and, second, through using a contrasting type of primary school in a very different location. Whereas in Chapters 8, 9 and 10, the case data was based on a very large primary school located in a deprived area, the one used in this chapter is quite small.

The first case study used in this chapter is based on Herefordshire Local Authority, who pride themselves on being a values-based education authority. The other short study is based on Clehonger Primary School, a small rural primary school situated just outside Hereford, to illustrate what using the FVS means to a different school and one based in England. In earlier chapters, we have focused on providing case studies from a Welsh dimension. However, the case studies in this chapter give a perspective from schools located in England.

Following on from the case studies is a concluding paragraph that draws on all the evidence of the case studies throughout the book. This provides a balanced view of how the FVS has impacted on behaviour, attendance and, above all, improved partnerships with parents. In turn, this will be followed by the concluding chapter for the book, which reinforces some of the main themes and critical aspects of the FVS.

Herefordshire local authority short case study

Before we start exploring the reasons why Herefordshire Local Authority took on board the Family Values Scheme, it is important to describe what the county of Herefordshire is like. Afterwards, we will move on to consider how schools are organised within the authority.

Herefordshire tourist information centre describes Herefordshire as a *'gloriously rural county at the heart of England'*. Hereford is an ancient cathedral city and important market centre for livestock. If you ask anyone about what they know about Herefordshire, they might perhaps mention the Mappa Mundi, a unique map of the world drawn around AD 1300. The Cathedral itself is situated in the centre of the city and dates from the eleventh century. It is a big tourist attraction, with visitors coming from all over the world. Herefordshire is also well known for its farming communities, village fetes and white cattle. The River Wye meanders through the unspoilt countryside amid the many historic market towns and the beautiful Symonds Yat, which is famous for its outdoor wildlife centre and river activities.

Education in Herefordshire

Herefordshire LA has 100 schools within its remit of which 81 are primary schools, 15 are secondary schools and 4 are special schools, including 3 pupil referral units. Many of the schools in Herefordshire are mirroring other English schools during the coalition era by switching to academy status, which are publicly-funded independent schools. This status gives a school greater freedom and more of a chance to innovate and raise standards. Academies are free from local authority control, have the ability to set their own pay and conditions for staff, a free rein on delivering the curriculum and can even change the length of terms and school days if they wish. Academy schools receive the same level of funding that other authority schools receive but they have greater flexibility on how to delegate their budgets to ensure that all pupils benefit the most.

Herefordshire and values-based education

Herefordshire primary schools took on board values-based educational ideas enthusiastically around 10 years ago. Most primary schools now teach some aspect of values-based education and Ofsted judgements for behaviour have been much more positive in recent years partly as a result.

The Family Values initiative was introduced to Herefordshire schools a year ago when one of the school improvement officers contacted us after hearing how successful the scheme had been in another authority. At the time, the authority had access to a school improvement grant and was keen to use the grant to help schools to create more effective partnerships with parents. Schools were identified for inclusion in the scheme based on two criteria. The first was that the schools involved had to be either in the local authority category three or four. Schools in these two categories include the most vulnerable schools within the LA in terms of poor pupil performance and socio-economic status (e.g. they have a high percentage of pupils on free school meals).

The second criteria were those schools who had identified in their own self-evaluation reports that they needed to improve their partnerships with their parents. A total of ten primary schools and one children's centre met the criteria and signed up for the scheme.

The training

The next step was for each nominated school to identify a key person who would lead the scheme in school, and this person was then invited to a training session delivered by one of the trainers. The appointment of a key person within each school who acted as the FVS champion was crucial for the scheme to be successful. This person's primary role was to inform all stakeholders and to monitor the introduction and progress of the scheme within his or her school. The person taking on the role of key person varied within each school from a teaching assistant to a deputy head teacher. Every key person received an initial 2 days of training that covered the following.

Course objectives

- To understand the importance of early intervention and brain development;
- to recognise 'good enough' interaction and engagement;
- to discuss the different types of parenting;
- to gain knowledge on the theoretical aspect of the Family Values Scheme;
- to introduce the scheme's four key areas;
- to provide practical and realistic ways to implement the scheme; and
- to give effective ways to use the scheme (e.g. with hard-to-reach families).

A half-day evaluation session was planned 3 months after the training was carried out with all the schools. This was necessary to find out exactly how the scheme had made an impact in individual schools and also to share good practice.

Half-day workshop objectives

- To share good practice and discuss issues arisen;
- to update on current research;
- to discuss new ways to engage families, including the 'hard to reach';
- to discuss other effective ways the Family Values Scheme can be used; and
- to update on new packs and resources.

Delegate testimonials

We will now include a few testimonials provided by a range of delegates from different parts of the UK who attended this or similar Family Values Scheme training events.

> *An extremely useful resource, presented in a highly motivating and empowering way, many thanks.*
> (Dr Helen Flanagan, Associate Director, SHARES, Lancashire Ltd)

> *Fantastic training event. All information and resources were truly inspirational. Family unit is the way forward! Thank you, Nic.*
> (Elizabeth Brown, Ridgewood Community High School)

> *I feel that I have been given a good background to the theory, as well as plenty of practical ideas and resources to take the Family Values Scheme back into school.*
>
> (Paul Gabriel, Head Teacher, Lancaster Road Primary)

> *I feel the training today has left me fully prepared to launch the scheme to impact positively on the school community as a whole – an excellent day and very worthwhile. I would fully recommend.*
>
> (Sarah Coldbeck, Deputy Head, Mereside Primary, Blackpool)

> *A really worthwhile scheme to become involved in. The strength of the programme is that the 'ownership' is with the pupil and his or her family. The approach is respectful to parents and allows family-centred improvement.*
>
> (Mrs Pat Jones, ESIS Adviser, south Wales)

What is interesting is that each school in Herefordshire and around the country tends to implement the scheme differently according to their school's setting and needs. This is, in fact, one of the key strengths of the scheme, as it can be used to target different audiences and yet still make a similar impact.

The following list provides an insight into the different ways in which the scheme was introduced into the eleven schools in Herefordshire to illustrate this point succinctly:

- by inviting parents to a weekly coffee afternoon;
- by sending out a monthly newsletter to all parents informing them of the scheme;
- by linking the monthly values to school curriculum topics and home work activities;
- by targeting nursery and reception class parents in the foundation stage;
- by targeting a specific year group;
- by targeting classes with a high percentage of families on the child protection register;
- by targeting families who are on child in need registers;
- by targeting single parent families who have involvement in CAFCASS (children and family court advisory and support services) – this organisation looks after the interests of children involved in family proceedings; they work with children and their families, and then advise the courts on what they consider to be in the best interests of individual children; and
- by targeting parents of looked after children by the local authority.

One primary head teacher said, '*We chose families who we thought would benefit from being part of the Family Values Scheme because of known problems such as: poor relationships, poor communication at home and challenging behaviour.*'

Impact of the FVS

When the school champions and head teachers were asked if the FVS had made a difference to improving the quality of their relationships with their parents, their responses included the reinforcement of the following positive outcomes:

- lots more focused family events in school than they had before;
- improved home–school relations by more parents coming into school;
- raised the profile of values-based education in school;
- reinforced the values used in school at home;
- whole-family involvement, not just the main carer;
- increase in the enjoyment of reading by families reading at home;
- families a lot more confident, and now lots to celebrate;
- supporting common assessment framework adult programmes;
- fun for every family member;
- better relationships with extended family members;
- families now build family time into busy lifestyles;
- improved behaviour of children;
- improved communication with families and the local community;
- enriched existing personal and social education programmes, including circle time sessions;
- meets the criteria for healthy schools initiatives;
- improved community links by teachers, parents and members of the community, and facilitates governors, staff and parents working better together;
- improves the hidden curriculum for the under fives, the golden stuff; and
- improved attendance and reduced lateness by making the children actually want to attend school.

The next step!

The school improvement officer for Herefordshire, when asked about the future of the FVS in the county, responded by stating that:

> Even in this short time the introduction of *Family Values* has had a significant impact in our schools and communities that have taken it on board. It will be exciting to see how these impacts grow as *Family Values* gets embedded more into the local communities.

All eleven schools were keen for the scheme to be sustainable to achieve the best possible results. They all said that they would be prepared to fund it themselves in the future. This funding would come from a range of sources, including the school budget. One head teacher said she would approach their parent–teacher association for assistance through fund-raising activities to raise money to deliver the scheme to the children's families in the future. There is a strong sense of unity among all the schools in Herefordshire using the scheme that it is an initiative worth continuing with and developing in the future.

Other comments made by the school representatives included:

> '*This has been a really positive step for our families. If possible I would like regular time/funding for the learning mentor to become fully involved and spend time with individual families to guide them through the activities.*'
>
> '*The intention is to target classes for more focused events to strengthen home-school links.*'
>
> '*I have improved the recording system to make it more accessible and user friendly – this was in response to a parent comment.*'
>
> '*I hope to introduce a "coffee and chat" session for families before the Family Value assembly. This will be a good opportunity for the families to discuss the scheme and answer any questions and guide, etc.*'
>
> '*We plan to introduce some kind of review sheet for parents.*'
>
> '*The scheme is excellent and is working well so far although it is early days.*'
>
> '*It would be useful to have a termly forum with other schools in Herefordshire who are using Family Values.*'
>
> '*The training for Family Values was fantastic – very inspiring and thought provoking. I am sure that this is going to have an extremely positive impact on some of our families here, and I would hopefully like to broaden who we can offer it to later in the year. The packs look fun and the activities appeal to children of all ages.*'
>
> '*The activities have proved to be popular, but the evaluation forms are very elusive! Feedback has been that the families have enjoyed the activities and like the ideas but some don't want to send paperwork back.*'

However, one school originally ear-marked for the start of the scheme did not fare quite so well:

> Regarding Family Values, despite all the best intentions, we did not manage to launch it last year. However, the school is very committed to the programme as we can see the benefits that it will bring to our school, parents and children. Someone now has responsibility for Family Values and has included it in our school improvement plan. We intend trialling it in a Year 4 and Year 2 class during the autumn and spring terms, and then extend to the whole of Year 2 and Year 4 in the summer term. At the end of the summer term, we will then evaluate and plan the next steps.

But for those who were included in the start of the scheme, they are starting to see some wider possibilities:

> '*I would be keen to deliver this across all children's centres, especially with transitions to school and the new school Ofsted inspections and dual inspections, as many children's centres are on school sites.*'

> '*Harder-to-reach families will be encouraged to join the scheme through meetings with the housing association as part of their "dream scheme". School, church, police and housing associations meet regularly to plan for greater community cohesion. There are plans to start both a youth club and a "parent and toddler" group in the village as a result.*'

We will now take one of the eleven schools chosen by the authority to take part in the scheme and to provide a more detailed study of the strengths and pitfalls of the implementation of the scheme. It also provides a contrast from the earlier case study school: Coed Eva Primary.

A short case study of Clehonger Primary School in Herefordshire

Clehonger Primary is a small rural primary school about 5 miles outside Hereford. The children attending the school come from a very wide variety of socio-economic backgrounds, with over half choosing to travel to the school from the city of Hereford. The school has had a difficult journey over recent years after coming out of special measures in 2009 after an unfavourable Ofsted inspection. The school has since focused on improving pupil attainment in the core subjects. Last year, the school was inspected again and came out with an overall 'satisfactory'. However, on the positive front, the report highlighted the fact that the school had a very caring and supporting ethos and extremely good links with parents and recognised this aspect as 'outstanding'.

The school has 116 pupils enrolled, with 15 pupils receiving free school meals and 23 pupils on the special educational needs code of practice. There are five classes, mostly mixed year groups with pupils of different ages and abilities in each class. There are eight teachers, including two teachers who job-share, and a part-time special educational needs coordinator.

The school has a high percentage of boys, around 65 per cent. Perhaps this unusually high distribution has had an impact on the behaviour of the pupils in the school, as some children have often displayed challenging behaviour. However, new strategies for these pupils are in place and proving to be effective.

The school was introduced to the FVS in February 2011 as part of the local authority's initiative to help schools who needed to improve their partnerships with their parents. The scheme was initially funded by the local authority, and a coordinator attended the 2-day training session. Upon her return to the school, the scheme was introduced and implemented in the whole school in March 2011.

The reason why the school felt that it would benefit from introducing the scheme was that it had identified a significant number of hard-to-reach families who still needed support from them. Children of these families were finding it difficult to access and learn across the curriculum, often because of their emotional and social difficulties. The school has carried out extensive work analysing individual pupil data and identified that the majority of pupils in these families were poor attainers. The school wanted to use the scheme to improve relationships within the home and as a tool to bridge the gap between home and school.

The scheme was initially introduced to the whole school and, out of a total of 95 families in the school, 13 families signed up on the first night to participate in the scheme. This might not sound many, but it was far more than ever previously attended the school's parent–teacher association meetings.

We will now include a few testimonials from these families on different perspectives on the FVS from some of these stakeholders.

Testimonials from parents/grandparents on the FVS

> '*Family Values strengthens family foundations and gives great ideas to make family time more fun and special.*'

> '*The value of tolerance made us think that we can all be more tolerant at times, which makes all family members feel more valued.*'

> '*Being part of the Family Values Scheme, we try to do more as a whole family as opposed to individuals.*'

> '*We have learnt about the things we tolerate on a daily/weekly basis and how it affects us.*'

> '*Since taking part in Family Values, we are all very happy!*'

> '*Since taking part in the Family Values Scheme, we use lots of the values that we have learnt about.*'

> '*Since taking part in the Family Values Scheme, we are closer as a family and we make the most of our free time together.*'

Testimonials from governors who are members of the FVS

Two governors are part of the FVS team at the school and they are our most ardent supporters, giving this positive message to all of the parents and members of the children's families. Their involvement is a most fundamental aspect of our school's use of the scheme.

Testimonials from pupils whose families are members of the scheme:

> '*I love doing my values-based activities with my mum and dad.*'
>
> '*The Family Values Scheme is fun. It is about learning and enjoyment.*'

The staff feel the same way:

> *The children speak confidently about values. In a lesson today, I witnessed some of the children discussing the elements of our school and putting them in order of importance. These Year 2 children very quickly, and firmly, stated that values came top of the list 'because family life is important to everybody'.*

The next step!

Our next step will take place later in 2012. This is to invite more families (selected by the head teacher and learning mentor for their level of need) to join the group. Current members have planted a sunflower seed and made an invitation note, which will be sent to all the potential new families. We hope that at least some will come along to our picnic in June and will enjoy what they find.

The key to our successful usage of the FVS is in the flexibility. Families are clearly informed that they are not required to do everything – just as much as they are comfortable with. The children love the mega challenges and get very excited at the prospect of coming along. It is tradition that the activity is usually a surprise, although the pancake race plan had to be shared so that families could provide the frying pans!

Family Values is a scheme that is unique in the way it allows those barriers between the school 'authority' and the family unit, particularly those of families with low self-esteem, to be crossed.

Other local schools have expressed an interest in the scheme, and the local authority hold us up now as an example of good practice in our work with parents. We have also been selected to be part of a pilot for another scheme engaging with parents, simply because of the success of Family Values. This has raised staff's self-esteem and improved confidence.

Summary

In this chapter, we have considered in some detail how Herefordshire and, in particular, one of its schools has introduced and implemented the FVS into selected schools. As so much of the earlier evidence in the book was drawn from schools in Wales, we decided to show how the scheme is already operating in parts of England by using Herefordshire as a case example. In the next and final chapter, we present our conclusions.

Chapter 14

Conclusion

This book has been about the development of the emerging Family Values Scheme. Prior to considering and presenting the FVS, we placed our work with the scheme into its context in terms of the previously published literature and research in relevant fields. In particular, we noticed the changes that have taken place within the family unit and its role over the last 40 to 50 years and the significant rise in the number of one-parent families, as well as the relationship between deprivation and underachievement in our schools. We then considered the evidence on how best to engage with families. Hornby and Lafaele (2011) have recently examined the barriers to parent involvement in education and considered some exploratory models. We believe that our own model of using the Family Values Scheme is worthy of further consideration in its own right because of its potential for working with all kinds of families, including those in deprived and disadvantaged areas, and helping them to achieve successfully.

In recent years, a number of major reports (e.g. NBAR, 2008) have called for much earlier intervention with low-achieving, difficult and disadvantaged pupils. Often, in the past, this has not happened. Consequently, interventions with pupils who have, for example, behaviour or attendance problems have occurred much too late and especially after many of these pupils have developed literacy and numeracy deficits that have impeded their educational progress (Reid, 2011). Therefore, the FVS was developed with this at the forefront of our minds as an appropriate early intervention strategy that can be used in infant, junior, primary and secondary schools. At a time when governments in the UK and from around the world are looking forward for better home–school relationships and combating the perceived decline in parenting values and skills, we believe the use, introduction and implementation of the FVS can help to fill this void.

From Chapter 6 onwards, we focused upon the FVS itself. First, in Chapter 6, we considered how the FVS works and its key principles. Then, in Chapter 7, we examined how the scheme operates in practice. Following on from this, we decided to tell the FVS story. Therefore, in Chapter 8, we recounted how the FVS had been devised, utilised and implemented at its founding school, Coed Eva Primary in south Wales. In the next two chapters, we considered some family case studies and looked at the scheme from the head teacher's perspective.

In Chapter 11, we presented evidence from the use of the log files – a crucial part of the scheme. This was followed in Chapter 12 by a presentation of one of the 22 values-based packs used in the scheme. This focused upon the value of 'courage'. As you will have seen, these are very practically focused materials and they are presented in an attractive format for the children, staff, their parents and families to use. All the materials utilised in the scheme are similarly presented in this attractive and easy-to-use way. Further details on their usage and how schools can join the scheme can be found at www.behaviourstop.co.uk.

In Chapter 13, we looked at how the scheme has started to spread and so we presented some further case study evidence based on primary schools in Herefordshire. However, the number of FVS schools is beginning to grow. Explicitly, Gurnos Nursery School is a good example of the scheme in use with younger-age children.

We believe there are some real advantages in using the FVS. First, it is a practical, fun-based scheme that can be easily adapted and applied to every school's situation, irrespective of location. It does, however, provide a particular opportunity for schools that are located in deprived and disadvantaged backgrounds.

Second, it can be used with all types of parents, children and families, and not just those with learning, economic or geographical difficulties or disadvantages. The scheme provides participating families with an agenda, timetable and method to provide better communication within the home and between the family home and its extended family members and the school and within the local community. It provides a structure for the children's learning and moral development, while, at the same time, providing a range of home-based and outdoor activities where families can spend some quality time together. All of these are undertaken in a fun and often friendly and competitive way!

In our opinion, the major advantage of the scheme is that it has made and is making a real and very positive impact upon improving relationships within the home and between family members, as well as between families and schools involved in the scheme. There are five major reasons for this:

1 the quality of the training provided and the materials used;
2 the adaptability and flexibility of the scheme's parameters;
3 the fact that the FVS is a unique concept and is adopted and implemented in a slightly different and specific way by every school engaged with the scheme;
4 the scheme is both sustainable and flexible; and
5 it can be used with selected pupils in schools and their families, such as those pupils with literacy, numeracy, behavioural or attendance needs, or alternatively, it can be used with all the children in the school and their parents and families; you can just imagine its potential for children attending small schools.

Part of the reason why the FVS is so unique is that it is not a parent programme. Nor, like some other schemes, is it time lagged or controlled. For example, some schemes offer short programmes that may last for only 6, 8, 10 or 12 weeks in total or at a time. The FVS is flexible. It is a whole-school or selected or targeted scheme for adoption and use, depending upon each school's needs.

We believe that the FVS provides major school improvement opportunities for schools and local authorities alike (irrespective of foundation or country of origin) to improve the quality of their home–school relationships. It also provides an opportunity for head teachers, staff, parents, families and children to work together in an exciting and innovative way.

In this book, we have focused upon the FVS and its inception, usage and potential. In our follow-up book, we are specifically looking at its use and the evidence of the gains made by pupils and schools in which literacy, attendance and behaviour are problematic. We very much hope you have enjoyed reading this book and may wish to read our follow-up text. Alternatively, you can visit www.behaviourstop.co.uk and contact us directly.

References

Adelman, C. (1980) *The Self-Evaluating Institutes: Practice and Principles in the Management of Educational Change*, London: Methuen.
Allen, G. M. P. (2010) *Early Intervention: The Next Steps*, London: Department for Education and Skills (DfES).
Allen, S. M. and Daly, K. (2002) 'The effects of father involvement: a summary of the research evidence', *The F11-ONEWS*, 1: 1–11.
American Association of Single Parents (2012) Various Publications, AASP.
American College of Sports Science (2011) 'Sedentary behaviours in youth predict inactivity levels and risk of obesity in later life', *Technique*, 23: 8.
Aronson, J. Z. (1996) 'How schools can recruit hard-to-reach parents', *Educational Leadership*, 53 (7): 58–60.
Astone, N. M. and McLanahan, S. S. (1991) 'Family structure, parental practices, and high school completion', *American Sociological Review*, 56: 309–20.
Ball, C. (1994) *Start Right: The Importance of Early Learning*, London: Royal Society for the Encouragement of Arts.
Balli, S. J., Demo, D. H. and Wedman, J. F. (1998) 'Family involvement with children's homework: an intervention in the middle grades', *Family Relations*, 47 (2): 149–57.
Barlow, J. (1998) 'Parent-training programmes and behaviour problems: findings from a systematic review', in A. Buchanan and B. L. Hudson (eds) *Parenting, Schooling and Children's Behaviour*, Aldershot: Ashgate, pp. 89–109.
Basic Skills Agency (2001) *Adult Numeracy Core Curriculum*, London: Basic Skills Agency.
Bassey, M. (2000) *Case Study Research in Educational Settings*, Buckingham: Open University Press.
Bastiani, J. (2003) *Materials for Schools: Involving Parents, Raising Achievement*, London: DfES.
Bernbaum, G., Patrick, H. and Reid, K. (1982) *The Structure and Process of Initial Teacher Education in Universities in England and Wales*, Sponsored Research Report for the DfES, Leicester: University of Leicester.
Bernbaum, G., Patrick, H. and Reid, K. (1983) *The Probationary Year*, Sponsored Research Report for the DfES, Leicester: University of Leicester.
Blanden, J. (2006) *Bucking the Trend: What Enables Those Who Are Disadvantaged in Childhood to Succeed Later in Life?* Working Paper No. 21, London: Department for Work and Pensions.

Bogenschneider, K. and Johnson, C. (2004) 'Family involvement in education: how important is it? What can legislators do?', in K. Bogenschneider and E. Gross (eds) *A Policymaker's Guide to School Finance: Approaches to Use and Questions to Ask*, Wisconsin Family Impact Seminar Briefing Report No. 20, Madison, WI: University of Wisconsin Center for Excellence in Family Studies, pp. 19–29.

Bone, M. and Meltzer, H. (1989) *OPCS Report 3: The Prevalence of Disability Among Children*, London: HMSO.

Bowshill, D. (1980) *Single Parents*, London: Fontana.

Bray, J. H. and Hetherington, E. M. (1993) 'Families in transition: introduction and overview', *Journal of Family Psychology*, 7: 3–8.

Brazelton, T., Koslowski, B. and Main, M. (1974) 'The origins of reciprocity: the early mother-infant interaction', in B. Lewis and L. Rosenblum (eds) *The Effect of the Infant on its Caregiver*, London: Wiley.

Bronfenbrenner, U. (1979) *The Ecology of Human Development: Experiments by Nature and Design*. Cambridge, MA: Harvard University Press.

Browne, C. S. and Rife, J. C. (1991) 'Social, personality and gender differences in at-risk and not-at-risk sixth grade students', *Journal of Early Adolescence*, 11: 482–95.

Buchanan, A. et al. (2008) *Involved Grand Parenting and Child Well-Being: Full Research Report ESRC End of Award Report*, RES-000-22-2283, Swindon: Economic and Social Research Council (ESRC).

Bus, A. G., van Lizendoorm, M. H. and Pellegrini, A. D. (1995) 'Joint book reading makes for success in learning to read: a meta-analysis of inter-generational transmission of literacy', *Review of Educational Research*, 65: 1–21.

Bywater, T. and Utting, D. (2012) 'Support from the start: effective programmes for 9–13 year-olds', *Journal of Children's Services*, 7 (1): 41–53.

Carspecken, P. F. (1996) *Critical Ethnography in Education Research: A Theoretical and Practical Guidance*, New York and London: Routledge.

Cashmore, E. E. (1985) *Having to: The World of One Parent Families*, London: Allen & Unwin.

Centre for Social Justice (2011) *Strengthening the Family and Tackling Family Breakdown*, London: Centre for Social Justice.

Centre for Social Justice (2012) *Is it Time to Back Marriage?* London: Centre for Social Justice.

Chamberlain, T., Lewis, K., Teeman, D. and Kendall, L. (2006) *Schools' Concerns and their Implications for Local Authorities: Annual Survey of Trends in Education, 2006*, LGA Research Report, 5/06, Slough: NFER.

Coed Eva (2009) *Self Evaluation Report*, Coed Eva: Coed Eva Primary School.

Cohen, L. and Manion, L. (2011) *Research Methods in Education*, 3rd edn, London: Routledge.

Common Assessment Framework (2009) *A Guide for Practitioners: Early Identification, Assessment of Needs and Intervention*, IW91/0709.

Covey, S. (1989) *The Seven Habits Of Highly Effective People*, New York: Free Press.

Covey, S., Merrill, A. R. and Merrill, R. R. (1994) *First Things First: To Live, To Love, To Learn, To Leave a Legacy*, New York: Simon & Schuster.

Cowan, P. and Cowan, C. P. (2008) 'Diverging family policies to promote children's well-being in the UK and US: some relevant data from family research and intervention studies', *Journal of Children's Services*, 3 (4): 4–16.

Crozier, G., Reay, D. and Vincent, C. (2005) *Activating Participation: Parents and Teachers Working Towards Partnership*, Stoke-on-Trent: Trentham Books.
Daly, M. (2011) 'What adult worker model? A critical look at recent social policy reform in Europe from a gender and family perspective', *Social Politics*, 18 (1): 1–23.
Dalziel, D. and Henthorne, K. (2005) *Parents'/Carers' Attitudes Towards School Attendance*, London: DfES.
Desforges, C. and Abouchaar, A. (2003) *The Impact of Parental Involvement, Parental Support and Family Education on Pupil Achievement and Adjustment: A Literature Review*, Research Report 433, London: DfEE.
Desforges, C., Crozier, G., Reay, D. and Vincent, C. (2005) *Activating Participation: Parents and Teachers Working Towards Partnership*, Stoke-on-Trent: Trentham Books.
Disability Rights Commission (2002) *Code of Practice for Schools: Disability Discrimination Act 1995, Part 4 (July 2002)*, London: Disability Rights Commission.
Douglas, H. (2004) *Solihull Approach Resource Pack, The School Years, For Care Professionals Who Work with School-Aged Children, Young People and Their Parents*, Solihull: National Health Service Care Trust.
Dutch, H. (2005) 'Redefining parental involvement in Head Start: a two-generation approach', *Early Childhood Development and Care*, 175 (1): 23–35.
Ebbutt, D. and Elliott, J. (1985) *Issues in Teaching for Understanding*, York: Longman.
Ellis, G. and Morgan, N. S. (2009) *The Family Values Scheme*, Monmouth: Behaviour Stop.
Epstein, J. (1992) 'School and family partnerships', in M. Aitken (ed.) *Encyclopedia of Educational Research*, New York: Macmillan.
Epstein, J. (1996) Perspectives and previews on research and policy for school, family and community partnership', in A. Booth and F. Dunn (eds) *Family-School Links: How Do they Affect Educational Outcomes*, Hillsdale, NJ: Lawrence Erlbaum Associates, pp. 209–46.
Epstein, J. L. (2001) *School, Family, and Community Partnerships: Preparing Educators and Improving Standards*, Boulder, CO: Westview Press.
Epstein, N. B., Bishop, D., Ryan, C., Miller, I. and Keitner, G. (1993) 'The McMaster Model view of healthy family functioning', in F. Walsh (ed.) *Normal Family Processes*, New York/London: The Guilford Press, pp. 138–60.
ESTYN (2010) *Coed Eva Primary School Inspection Under Section 28 of the Education Act 2005*, School No. 6782324, Estyn No. 1128009, Cardiff: ESTYN..
ESTYN (2011) *An Evaluation of the Implementation of the Foundation Phase for Five to Six Year Olds in Primary Schools with Specific Reference to Literacy*, Cardiff: Her Majesty's Inspectorate for Education and Training in Wales.
Evans, J. (2000) 'Parental participation: what's it all about?', *Early Childhood Matters*, 95: 7–17.
Fan, X. and Chen, M. (2001) 'Parental involvement and student's academic achievement: a meta-analysis', *Educational Psychology Review*, 13 (1): 1–22.
Farrington, D. P. (1995) 'The development of offending and antisocial behaviour from childhood: key findings from the Cambridge Study in Delinquent Development', *Journal of Clinical Child and Adolescent Psychology*, 360 (6): 929–64.
Feinstein, L. (2003) 'Inequality in early cognitive development of British children in the 1970 cohort', *Economica*, 70 (227): 73–97.
Feinstein, L. and Symons, J. (1999) 'Attainment in secondary school', *Oxford Economics Papers*, 51: 300–21.

Ferber, R. (1985) *Solve Your Child's Sleep Problems: The Complete Practical Guide for Parents*, London: Dorling Kingsley.
Flouri, E. (2005) *Fathering and Child Outcomes*, Chichester: Wiley.
Flouri, E. and Buchanan, A. (2004) 'Early father's and mother's involvement and child's later educational outcomes', *British Journal of Educational Psychology*, 74: 141–53.
Fruchter, N., Galetta, A. and White, J. L. (1992) *New Directions in Parent Involvement*, Washington, DC: Academy for Educational Development.
Fulkerson, J. A., Neumark-Sztainer, D. and Story, M. (2006) 'Adolescent and parent views of family needs', *Journal of American Dietetic Association*, 106 (4): 526–32.
Gershuny, J. (2003) *Changing Times: Work and Leisure in Post Industrial Society*, new edn, Oxford: Oxford University Press.
Gest, S. D., Freeman, N. R., Domitrovich, C. E. and Welsh, J. A. (2004) 'Shared book reading and children's language comprehension skills: the moderating role of parental discipline practice', *Early Childhood Research Quarterly*, 19: 319–36.
Gingerbread (2012) *Single Parents, Equal Families*, London: Gingerbread.
Green, H., McGinnity, A., Meltzer, H., Ford, T. and Goodman, R. (2005) *Mental Health of Children and Young People in Great Britain (2004)*, Basingstoke: Palgrave Macmillan.
Gross, J. (2011) *Two Years On: Final Report of the Communication Champion for Children*, London: Office of the Communication Champion.
Haralambos, M. and Holborn, M. (1995) *Sociology Themes and Perspectives*, 4th edn, London: HarperCollins.
Harris, A. and Goodall, J. (2007) *Engaging Parents in Raising Achievement: Do Parents Know They Matter?* London: Department for Children, Schools and Families.
Harris, A. and Goodall, J. (2008) 'Do parents know they matter? Engaging all parents in learning', *Educational Research*, 50 (3): 277–89.
Harvard Family Research Project (2006) *Family Involvement in Early Childhood Education. Family Involvement Makes a Difference: Evidence that Family Promotes School Success for Every Child of Every Age*, Cambridge, MA: Harvard FRP.
Hawkes, N. (2005) *Does Teaching Values Improve the Quality of Education in Primary Schools?* Oxford University, D.Phil thesis, published by VDM (2010).
Hawkes, N. (2009) 'Values and quality teaching at West Kidlington Primary School', in T. Lovat and R. Toomey (eds) *Values Education and Quality Teaching: The Double Helix Effect*. Dordrecht, Netherlands: Springer.
Heck, A. Collins, J. and Peterson, L. (2001) 'Decreasing children's risk taking on the playground', *Journal of Applied Behavior Analysis*, 34: 349–52.
Hitchcock, G. and Hughes, D. (1985) *Research and the Teacher: A Qualitative Introduction to School Based Research*, London: Routledge.
HMSO (2004) *The Children Act, 2004*, London: HMSO.
Hooper, D. and Clulow, C. (2008) 'Postmodern parenting: pointers for supporting contemporary parents', *Journal of Children's Services*, 3 (4): 30–1.
Hoover-Dempsey, K. V. and Sandler, H. M. (1997) 'Why do parents become involved in their children's education?', *Review of Educational Research*, 67 (1): 3–42.
Hoover-Dempsey, K. V., Battiato, A. C., Walker, J. M., Reed, R. P., Dejong, J. M. and Jones, K. P. (2001) 'Parental involvement in homework', *Educational Psychologist*, 36 (3): 195–209.
Hopkins, D. and Reid, K. (1985) *Rethinking Teacher Education*, London: Croom Helm.
Hopkins, D. and Reid, K. (2012) *Rethinking Teacher Education*, 2nd edn, London: Routledge.

Hornby, G. and Lafaele, R. (2011) 'Barriers to parental involvement in education: an exploratory model', *Educational Review*, 63 (1): 37–52.

Humphrey, N., Kalambuka, A., Bolton, J., Lendrum, A., Wigelsworth, M., Lennie, C. and Farrell, P. (2008) *Primary Social and Emotional Aspects of Learning (SEAL) Research Report No. DCSF RR064*, London: DfCSF.

Hutchins, J. and Gardner, F. (2012) 'Support from the start: effective programmes for 3 to 8 year olds', *Journal of Children's Services*, 7 (1): 29–41.

Jenkins, J. and Keating, D. (1998) *Risk and Resilience in 6 and 10 Year Old Children*, Applied Research Branch, Human Resources Development Canada, Strategic Policy.

Jordan, B. (2008) 'A good childhood: searching for values in a competitive age', *Journal of Children's Services*, 3 (4): 59–60.

Jordan, G. E., Snow, C. E. and Porsche, M. V. (2000) 'Project EASE: the effect of a family literacy project on kindergarten students' early literacy skills', *Reading Research Quarterly*, 35: 524–46.

Katz, I., La Placa, V. and Hunter, S. (2007) *Barriers to Inclusion and Successful Engagement of Parents in Mainstream Services*, York: Joseph Rowntree Foundation.

Lally, P., van Jaarsveld, C. H. M., Potts, H. W. and Wardle, J. (2009) 'How are habits formed: modeling habit formation in the real world', *European Journal of Social Psychology*, 40 (6): 998–1009.

Layard, R. and Dunn, J. (2009) *A Good Childhood: Searching for Values in a Competitive Age*, London: Penguin.

Lewis, K., Chamberlain, T., Riggall, T., Gagg, A. and Rudd, P. (2007) *How is the Every Child Matters Agenda Affecting Schools? Annual Survey of Trends in Education, 2007: Schools' Concerns and their Implications for Local Authorities*, LGA Research Report 4/07, Slough: NFER.

Lewis, M. and Wray, D. (1997) *Writing Frames: Scaffolding Children's Non-Fiction Writing in a Range of Genres*, Reading: University of Reading.

Lifelong Learning UK (2005) *Final Report: National Occupational Standards – Work with Parents' and Family Learning*, London: Lifelong Learning UK.

Lovat, T., Smith, R., Dally, K., Clement, N. (2009) *Final Report for Australian Government Department of Education, Employment and Workplace Relations Project to Test and Measure the Impact of Values Education on Student Effects and School Ambience*, Newcastle, Australia: The University of Newcastle.

Marjoribanks, K. (1979) *Families and Their Learning Environments: An Empirical Analysis*, London: Routledge and Kegan Paul.

Marjoribanks, K. (2002) *Family and School Capital: Towards a Context Theory of Students' School Outcomes*, Dordrecht, Netherlands: Kluwer Academic Publisher.

Massey, M. (1976) *What You Are is Where You Were When . . . Again?* Boulder, CO: University Press of Colorado.

Masters, G. (2004) 'Beyond political rhetoric: what makes a school good', *On Line Opinion – eJournal of Social and Political Debate*.

Meiselman, H. L. (2000) *Dimensions of the Meal: The Science, Culture, Business and Art of Eating*, Gaithersburg, MD: Aspen.

Melhuish, E., Sylva, C., Sammons, P., Siraj-Blatchford, I. and Taggart, B. (2001) *Social, Behavioural and Cognitive Development at 3 to 4 years in Relation to Family Background. The Effective Provision of Pre-school Education*, EPPE Project, DfEE, London: The Institute of Education.

Melhuish, E., Quinn, L., Hanna, K., Sylva, K., Sammons, P., Siraj-Blatchford, I. and Taggart, B. (2006) *Effective Pre-School Provision in Northern Ireland (EPPNI)*, Research Report No. 41, Bangor: DENI.
Moran, P., Ghate, D. and van der Merwe, A. (2004) *What Works in Parenting Support? A Review of the international Evidence*, DfES Research Report 574, Policy Research Bureau, London: DfES.
Morgan, N. S. (2009) *Behaviour Management Ideas for the Classroom*, London: Jessica Kingsley.
Morgan, N. S. and Ellis, G. (2009) *The 5-Step Behaviour Programme: A Whole-School Approach to Behaviour Management*, Cardiff: Behaviour Stop.
Morgan, N. S. and Ellis, G. (2011) *A Kit Bag for Promoting Positive Behaviour in the Classroom*, London: Jessica Kingsley.
Morgan, N. S. and Ellis, G. (2012) *Good Choice Teddy Approach*, Monmouth: Good Choice Teddy.
Mosley, J. and Thompson, E. (1995) 'Fathering behaviour and child outcomes: the role of race and poverty', in W. Marsiglio (ed.) *Fatherhood: Contemporary Theory, Research and Social Policy*, Thousand Oaks, CA: Sage, pp. 148–65.
Mullis, R. L., Mullis, A. K., Comille, T. A., Ritchson, A. D. and Sullender, M. S. (2004) *Early Literacy Outcomes and Parental Involvement*, Tallahassee, FL: Florida State University.
National Center for Education Statistics (1997) *Father's Involvement in Their Child's Schools*, Washington, DC: US Government Printing Office.
National Center for Fathering (2009) *Survey of Fathers' Involvement in Their Children's Learning*, Kansas City, MO: National Center for Fathering.
National College for School Leadership (2010) *Leadership for Parental Engagement*, London: NCSL.
National Society for Children and Family Contact (2012) Various Publications, NSCFC.
NBAR (2008) *National Behaviour and Attendance Review*, Professor K. Reid (chair), a report of a review group for the Welsh Assembly Government, Cardiff: DfES.
Nisbet, J. and Watt, C. (1984) *Educational Research Methods*, London: University of London Press.
OECD (2012) *The Family Database*, Paris: OECD.
Office for National Statistics (2006) *Lifestyles and Social Participation: Social Trends 41*, info@statistics.gsi.gov.uk.
Ofsted (2010) *The Effectiveness of the School's Engagement with Parents and Carers: Briefing for Section 5 of Inspectors Guide for Inspections*, London: Ofsted.
Page, J., Whitting, G., and McLean, C. (2008) *Engaging Effectively with Black and Minority Ethnic Parents in Children's and Parental Services*, DCSF Research Report 013, London: DCSF.
Patterson, G. R., Dishion, T. J. and Chamberlain, P. (1993) 'Outcomes and methodological issues relating to treatment of antisocial children', in T. R. Giles (ed.) *Handbook of Effective Psychotherapy*, New York: Plenum Press.
Penn, H., Barreau, S., Butterworth, L., Lloyd, E., Moyles, J., Potter, S. and Sayeed, R. (2004) *What is the Impact of Out-of-Home Integrated and Education Settings on Children Aged 0–6 and Their Parents?* Research Evidence in Education Library, EPPI-Centre, Social Science Research Unit, London: Institute of Education.
Pleck, J. H. and Masciadrelli, B. P. (2004) 'Paternal involvement by U.S. residential fathers: levels, sources and consequences', in M. E. Lamb (ed.) *The Role of the Father in Child Development*, 4th edn, Hoboken, NJ: Wiley.

Plowden Report (1967) *Children and their Primary Schools, Central Advisory Council for Education (CACE)*, London: HMSO.
Pugh, G. (2010) *Principles for Engaging with Families: A Framework for Local Authorities and National Organisations to Evaluate and Improve Engagement with Families*, Dame Gillian Pugh (chair), National Quality Improvement Network, London: National Children's Bureau.
Quinton, D. (2004) *Supporting Parents: Messages from Research*, London: Jessica Kingsley.
Rawkins, S. (2010) 'Family routines show an increase in health and well being', *Best Health Magazine*, January/February: 7.
Reid, K. (1980) *Whose Children?* Maesteg: Gibbs.
Reid, K. (1985) *Truancy and School Absenteeism*, London: Hodder & Stoughton.
Reid, K. (1986) *Disaffection from School*, London: Methuen.
Reid, K. (1987) *Combating School Absenteeism*, London: Hodder & Stoughton.
Reid, K. (1989a) *Helping Troubled Pupils in Secondary Schools*, vol. 1, Oxford: Basil Blackwell.
Reid, K. (1989b) *Helping Troubled Pupils in Secondary Schools*, vol. 2, Oxford: Basil Blackwell.
Reid, K. (1989c) 'One parent families, pupils and schools', in K. Reid *Helping Troubled Pupils in Secondary Schools*, vol. 1, Oxford: Basil Blackwell, ch. 6.
Reid, K. (1999) *Truancy and Schools*, London: Routledge.
Reid, K. (2000) *Tackling Truancy in the Secondary School*, London: Routledge.
Reid, K. (2002a) *Truancy: Short and Long-Term Solutions*, London: Routledge.
Reid, K. (2002b) 'An evaluation of an out-of-school learning project in south Wales', *Mentoring and Tutoring*, 11 (3): 331–48.
Reid, K. (2011) *Update on National Behaviour and Attendance Report (NBAR): Improving School Attendance In Wales*, Special Report for the Minister for Education and Skills in Wales, Swansea: Swansea Metropolitan University.
Reid, K. (2012a) 'Reflections of being "a man of truancy": forty years on', *Educational Studies*, 38 (3): 327–40.
Reid, K. (2012b) 'The strategic management of truancy and school absenteeism: Finding solutions from a national perspective', *Educational Review*, 64 (2): 196–211.
Reid, K. (2012c) *Disaffection from School*, London: Routledge.
Reid, K. and Morgan, N. S. (2012) *Tackling Behaviour in Your Primary School*, London: Routledge.
Reid, K., Hopkins, D. and Holly, P. (1987) *Towards the Effective School*, Oxford: Basil Blackwell.
Reid, K., Challoner, A., Lancett, G., Jones, G., Rhydiart, A. and Challoner, S. (2010a) 'The views of primary pupils on school attendance at Key Stage 2 in Wales', *Educational Studies*, 36 (5): 465–79.
Reid, K., Challoner, A., Lancett, G., Jones, G., Rhydiart, A. and Challoner, S. (2010b) 'The views of primary pupils at Key Stage 2 on school behaviour in Wales', *Educational Review*, 62 (1): 97–115.
Richardson, J. and Joughin, C. (2002) *Parent-Training Programmes for the Management of Young Children with Conduct Disorders: Findings from Research*, London: Gaskell.
Rowe, K. (1991) 'The influence of reading activity at home on students' attitudes towards reading, classroom attentiveness and reading achievement: an application of structural equation modelling', *British Journal of Educational Psychology*, 61: 19–36.

Rutter, M., Maughan, B., Mortimore, P. and Ouston, J. (1979) *Fifteen Thousand Hours: Secondary Schools and Their Effects on Children*, Cambridge, MA: Harvard University Press.

Sammons, P., Hillman, J. and Mortimer, P. (1995) *Key Characteristics of Effective Schools*, London: Office for Standards in Education.

Sarkadi, A., Kristiansson, R., Oberklaid, F. and Bremberg, S. (2008) 'Fathers' involvement and children's developmental outcomes: a systematic review of longitudinal studies', *Acta Paediatrica*, 97 (2): 153–58.

Schaeffer, E. (1975) *What is a Family?* London: Hodder & Stoughton.

Scott, S., Knapp, M., Henderson, J. and Maughan, B. (2001) 'Financial costs of social exclusion: follow up study of antisocial children into adulthood', *BMJ*, 323: 1–5.

Scottish Government (2008a) *Building Parenting and Family Capacity Pre and Post-Birth*, Edinburgh: Scottish Government.

Scottish Government (2008b) *Early Years Framework: Evidence Briefing*, Edinburgh: Scottish Government.

SEAL (2005) *Excellence and Enjoyment: Social and Emotional Aspects of Learning (Guidance)*, Nottingham: DfES.

SEAL (2006) *Excellence and Enjoyment: Social and Emotional Aspects of Learning – Key Stage 2 Small Group Activities*, Nottingham: DfES.

SEAL (2007) *Social and Emotional Aspects of Learning (SEAL) for Secondary Schools, Guidance Booklet*, Nottingham: DfES.

Senechal, M. and LeFevre, J. (2002) 'Parental involvement in the development of children's reading skill: a five-year longitudinal study', *Child Development*, 73 (2): 445–60.

Sharp, P. (2001) *Nurturing Emotional Literacy: A Practical Guide for Teachers, Parents and Those in the Caring Professions*, London: David Fulton.

Sheridan, S. M. and Kratochwill, T. R. (2007) *Conjoint Behavioural Consultation: Promoting Family-School Connections and Interventions*, New York: Springer.

Shonkoff, J. P. and Phillips, D. A. (eds) (2000) *From Neurons to Neighborhoods: The Science of Early Childhood Development*, Washington, DC: National Academy Press.

Silverman, D. (1993) *Interpreting Qualitative Data*, London: Sage.

Simon, H. (1982) *Conversation Piece: The Practice of Interviewing in Case Study Research*, R. McCormick Colling (ed.), London: Heinemann.

Single Parent Action Network (2012) Various Publications, SPAN.

Sleep Council (2012) *Teachers Say a Lack of Sleep Devastates the School Day*, Skipton: Sleep Council.

Smit, F. and Driessen, G. (2007) 'Parents and Schools as partners in a multicultural, multi-religious society', *Journal of Empirical Theology*, 20: 1–20.

Sunderland, M. (2006) *The Science of Parenting*, London: Dorling Kindersley.

Sylva, K., Melhuish, E., Sammons, P., Siraj-Blatchford, I. and Taggart, B. (2004) *The Effective Provision of Pre-School Education (EPPE) Project: Final Report, A Longitudinal Study Funded by the DfES, 1997–2004*, London: DfES.

Sylva, K., Evangelou, M., Edward, A., Smith, T. and Good, J. (2008) *National Evaluation of the Early Learning Partnership Project*, London: NEELPP.

Wade, B. and Moore, M. (2000) 'A sure start with books', *Early Years*, 20: 39–46.

Walberg, H. J. (1984) 'Families as partners in educational productivity', *Phi Delta Kappan*, 65: 397–400.

Waldfogel, J. and Washbrook, E. (2010) *Low Income and Early Cognitive Development in the UK: A Report for the Sutton Trust*, London: The Sutton Trust.

Waldman, J., Bergeron, C., Morris, M., O'Donnell, L., Benefield, P., Harper, A. and Sharp, C. (2008) *Improving Children's Attainment through a Better Quality of Family-Based Support for Early Learning*, London, Centre for Excellence and Learning Outcome in Children and Young People's Services (C4EO), London: NFER.

Walker, J. (2008) 'Family life in the 21st Century: the implications for parenting policy in the UK', *Journal of Children's Services*, 3 (4): 17–30.

Webster-Stratton, C. (1999) 'Researching the impact of parent training programmes on child conduct problems', in E. Lloyd (ed.) *Parenting Matters*. London: Barnardos.

White-Clark, R. and Decker, L. E. (1996) *The 'Hard-to-Reach' Parent: Old Challenges, New Insights*, Fairfax, VA: National Community Education Association.

Williams, B., Williams, J. and Ullman, A. (2002) *Parental Involvement in Education*, London: Department for Education and Skills.

Williams, M. V. (1997) *Reconceptualizing Father Involvement*, unpublished master's thesis, Georgetown University, Washington, DC.

Index

22 values 84, 85–102

Abouchaar, A. 4, 7–9, 31, 39, 40
adult learning 49, 51
appreciation 59, 120
assemblies 47, 121
attendance levels 105–106

barriers: to engagement 23–24, 86; to learning 86
basic skills 77
behavioural theory, the 71
benefits of involving families in school life 34–35

campfire singalong 117
caring 59
case studies 124–134, 135–142, 177–196, 197–205; and family perspective 125–126, 127; and head teacher's perspective 125–142; and personal views 141–142; positives and pitfalls 139–141
celebration and achievement time 117
changes to family life 5–6, 14–17
children 18–20
Clehonger Primary School 203–205
Coed Eva story 103–123
communication 74–75, 90
cooperation 60, 120
courage 59
courage pack 167–175
crèche facilities 50
Cup, Family Values 94

delegate testimonials 199–201
Desforges, C. 4, 7–9, 31, 39, 40
developing confidence in number 78–79

ecological theory 70–71
effective home-school communication 44–45
emotional literacy 80–81
engaging: families 36–37, 38–51; fathers 37–38; grandparents 38; with parents 30–51; parents in raising achievement 26
ethics 52–67

face painting 116
family: bush craft 116; drop-in service 49; forest walk 116; initiatives 40; meals 75; meal times 118; learning 76; life 1–13, 14–29; perspectives 125–126, 127; reading time 75–78; testimonials, 204–205
Family Values Scheme (FVS) 68–207; aims 73; assemblies 121; attendance and participation 90; behavioural theory 71; champion 86–87; Coed Eva story, the 103–123; commencing the scheme 111; communication 90; conclusions 207–208; cup 94; displays 121; ecological theory 70–71; establishing the scheme 103–123; evaluation 87, 124–207; family-centred approach 71; genesis of scheme 109–110; head teacher's perspective 135–142; impact of scheme 120–131; inviting families 90; involving external agencies 121; key principles 68–83; links to SEAL 72; log files 92,120,143–176, 177–196; practice 84–102; providing evidence 92; rewarding families 92; role of adult helper 111–113; scheme packs 94–9; STAR evaluation 92; start and end date 90; submitting the pack 92; theoretical concepts 69–72; timings 90; values 71–72

Index

fathers 20–37; in one parent families 21–22; who no longer live with their children 22
feedback 51
freedom 60, 119, 162–167
friendship 60, 120, 152–162

get creative for parents' evening 48
getting involved 49–50
grandparents 38

happiness 60
hard to-reach families 39
head teacher's perspective 135–142
Herefordshire 195–205; Clehonger Primary school 203–205; delegate testimonials 199–201; education 198; and training 198–199; and values-based education 198
home time 46
home-school communication 44–45
honesty 60, 120
hope 61
humility 61

identified children 88
identified families 88
impact of parental involvement 7–9
imprint period 53
information evening 49
internal system 16
involving external agencies 121
involving parents in school life 32–34, 35–41

listening game 117
literacy and numeracy 77–78
log files 92, 120, 143–176, 177–196
love 61

mega challenge evening 48
modelling period 53–54

next step 119
not following direction 113–115
numeracy 77–78
nurture groups 106

one-parent families 14–38
open days 47
outcomes of weekend 118

parental testimonials 204
parent involvement policy 40–44
parenting programmes 88–90
parents 1–208; and literacy 26–28; and numeracy 77–78; and raising achievement 26; and reading 26–28; and schools 23, 68–208
parents' evening 48
partnerships between home and school 36–51
pastoral support worker 106–107
patience 61
peace 61
personal values 54–55
personal views 141–142
play and interaction 76
portfolio 48
practical ways to engage families 44
practice 84–102
providing evidence 92
providing services to parents 12

quality 63

raft building for parents 116
raising achievement 14–28
reading 77–78
reflection times 117
relationships 73–74
respect 63
responsibility 62
role of adult helper 111–113

scheme packs 94–95
school: assemblies 47; and one parent families 24–25; perspective 121–123; welcome pack 45; year group 88
simplicity 62
sleep 81–82
social and emotional aspects of learning (SEAL) 72, 80, 107–108
socialisation period 54
start and end date 90
STAR evaluation 92
stigma 17
submitting the FVS pack 92
support for parents 51

target audience 85
team building 117
tell them about yourself 46

Index

tell us about your family 46
ten truths about parental involvement 40
testimonials 204–205; from families 118–119; from governors 204–205; from grandparents 204; from parents 204
theoretical model partnerships 69–72
thoughtful 62
thoughtfulness 149–152
tips for parents 28
tolerance 62, 127–130
traditional family values 56, 73–74
training 198–199
trust 62, 119

understanding 63, 145–149

understanding behaviour 79–80
unity 63

values 52–67, 71–72; application process 66; discovering 54–55; and education 56–58; meaning of 53; and SEAL 107–108
values-based education 52–67, 107; quality mark 65–67; in schools 63–65

welcome back to school 45
welcoming new parents 45
what works in parenting support? 10–12
where did values come from? 53

your child is a star 49

Taylor & Francis
eBooks
FOR LIBRARIES

ORDER YOUR FREE 30 DAY INSTITUTIONAL TRIAL TODAY!

Over 23,000 eBook titles in the Humanities, Social Sciences, STM and Law from some of the world's leading imprints.

Choose from a range of subject packages or create your own!

Benefits for you
- Free MARC records
- COUNTER-compliant usage statistics
- Flexible purchase and pricing options

Benefits for your user
- Off-site, anytime access via Athens or referring URL
- Print or copy pages or chapters
- Full content search
- Bookmark, highlight and annotate text
- Access to thousands of pages of quality research at the click of a button

For more information, pricing enquiries or to order a free trial, contact your local online sales team.

UK and Rest of World: **online.sales@tandf.co.uk**
US, Canada and Latin America:
e-reference@taylorandfrancis.com

www.ebooksubscriptions.com

ALPSP Award for BEST eBOOK PUBLISHER 2009 Finalist

Taylor & Francis eBooks
Taylor & Francis Group

A flexible and dynamic resource for teaching, learning and research.